BASIC WORD LIST

Samuel C. Brownstein
Formerly Chairman Science Department
George W. Wingate High School, Brooklyn, N.Y.

Mitchel Weiner
Formerly Member, Department of English
James Madison High School, Brooklyn, New York

Barron's Educational Series, Inc. / Woodbury, New York

All inquiries should be addressed to:
Barron's Educational Series, Inc.
113 Crossways Park Drive
Woodbury, New York 11797

Library of Congress Catalog Card No. 76-54226

International Standard Book No. 0-8120-709-3

Library of Congress Cataloging in Publication Data
Brownstein, Samuel C   1909-
  Barron's basic word list.
  Abbreviated version of Barron's vocabulary builder.
  1. Vocabulary.   2. English language — Examinations,
questions, etc.   I. Weiner, Mitchell, 1907-   joint
author.   II. Title.
PE1449.B76 1977   428'.1   76-54226
ISBN 0-8120-0709-3

PRINTED IN THE UNITED STATES OF AMERICA

5 6 7 8 9

Contents

Preface

Barron's Basic Word List, a convenient pocket-size vocabulary builder, presents a systematic plan for building a more powerful vocabulary. In the current age of testing, where the ability to handle words is part of most testing programs, this publication will prove valuable to those planning to take college entrance examinations, various achievement tests, competitive scholarship tests, teacher examinations, and various qualifying tests.

Basically, Barron's Basic Word List is an abbreviated version of Vocabulary Builder, which has already established itself as a useful study guide. Both teachers and students have found the list of selected words, each of which is illustrated with an explanatory sentence, clearly defined and explained. They have found the review of prefixes, roots, and suffixes useful. And they have acknowledged the fact that the practice exercises simulate the types of questions commonly encountered on examinations.

This convenient pocket-size edition will be most valuable if it is kept in your purse or pocket. You may then be able to put it to work for you during some precious moments that might otherwise go to waste. If, after using this book, you feel you need more review, you should immediately begin work with the most widely used college entrance examination review book, Barron's How to Prepare for College Entrance Examinations. This comprehensive test preparation guide (with over 650 pages) reviews, drills, and tests the verbal and mathematical phases of the SAT and the PSAT/NMSQT; and can serve as a firm foundation for these and other standardized examinations.

1 How and What to Study

Since most students who study the material in this book are preparing for an important test involving knowledge of vocabulary, it becomes advisable that they have a plan of the methods they will enjoy in trying to master as much of the material as possible in the time they have available. Two plans are presented for the efficient study of our Basic Word List.

Plan 1

(For those who have approximately one month or less to prepare for the SAT or another examination.) You must recognize that in so short a period of time it is foolish to try to master all the words in the Word List. We recommend that you concentrate on the words which appear in the Tests which follow each of the 30 Word Lists. Take one or two of these tests each day (depending on how much time you have before the day of the test).

Plan 2

(For those who begin their studying for the examination at least four months before the actual test.) Use the following procedure:

Step 1: Beginning with Junior Word List 1, read through the forty-two words listed there. As you read, try to suggest a synonymous word or phrase for each word in the list. If a synonym comes to your mind, even though it is inexact, you probably know the word. When a word stimulates no association in your mind, note the unknown word by underlining it.

Step 2: On a separate sheet of paper write down the underlined words in a vertical list on the left hand side of your paper. The very process of copying these words will add to your sense of familiarity with them.

Step 3:   Look up the definitions of these words in the Word List. Jot down brief definitions or meaningful synonyms beside each of the words. Also, if an antonym of the word comes to mind, jot that down also.

Step 4:   After an interval of time — preferably the next day — repeat step 1 for the underlined words only. Recheck the definitions of any word or words which do not stir any meaningful associations in your mind.

Repeat this process until you have completed the Junior Word List. Then move ahead to the Senior Word List on p. 9.

Step 5:   (the last two or three weeks). Take each of the 30 Tests that follow the Word Lists as outlined in Plan 1 (above). Conclude your studying by taking the Synonym Test, Antonym Test, and Vocabulary Test in Chapter 3.

If you do the work suggested in Plan 1 or 2, you should be able to obtain a score on the Verbal Part of the test you are taking which will reflect your effort and improved ability.

The Basic Word List (30 lists) is here divided into three categories:

1.   Junior Words
2.   Senior Words
3.   Honor Senior Words

It is advisable that you see how many of the words in each category you know.

Junior Word List

FROM WORD LIST 1 (page 21)

abash, abdicate, abominate, aboriginal, abrogate, abscond, abstemious, accelerate, accessory, accolade, accomplice, accord, accost, acoustics, acquittal, acrimonious, actuate, acumen, adamant, adapt, addiction, adhere, admonish, adroit, adulation, adulterate, adverse, adversity, advocate, aesthetic, affected, affiliation, affirmation, affluence, aggregate, aghast, agility, agitate, alacrity, alias, alienate, allege

FROM WORD LIST 2 (page 27)

allude, allusion, aloof, altercation, altruism, ambiguous, amble, ambulatory, ameliorate, amenable, amphitheatre, ample, amputate, anaesthetic, analogous, analogy, anarchy, andirons, animated, animosity, annals, annihilate, annul, anomalous, antagonism, anticlimax, antiseptic, apathetic, aphorism, aplomb, apocryphal, apostate, apotheosis, appellation, append, apprehensive, apprise, appurtenances

FROM WORD LIST 3 (page 34)

arbiter, arbitrary, arcade, archipelago, arduous, aromatic, arraign, arrant, arrogance, ascetic, ascribe, ashen, askew, aspirant, aspiration, assail, assay, astral, astringent, atheistic, athwart, attenuate, attribute, attrition, augment, augury, auspicious, austerity, authenticate, autocrat, autonomous, autopsy, averse, avid, avow, awe, babble, badger, baffle, balk

FROM WORD LIST 4 (page 40)

barb, barrage, batten, bedraggle, beguile, behoove, belated, benediction, benefactor, beneficiary, benevolent, benighted, berate, bestow, bête noir, bicameral, bizarre, blandishment, blasphemous, blatant, bleak, bloated, bludgeon, bolster, bountiful, bourgeois, bravado, breach, brevity, broach, brocade, brochure, brooch, brusque, bullion, bulwark, bungle, buttress, cabal, cadaverous

FROM WORD LIST 5 (page 46)

cajole, callous, calumniate, calumny, canny, cant, capitulate, caprice, caption, caricature, carping, carrion, cascade, castigate, casualty, catapult, catastrophe, cathartic, cauterize, cavalcade, cede, celestial, censor, cerebral, cerebration, cession, chafe, chagrin, chalice, chameleon, chaotic, charlatan, chary, chasm, chassis, chastise, chauvinist, checkered, chicanery, chronic

FROM WORD LIST 6 (page 52)

circlet, circumscribe, circumspect, circumvent, citadel, clairvoyant, clamber, clarion, clavicle, cleave, clemency, cliché, climactic, clique, cloister, coalesce, cog, cogitate, collaborate, collateral, collusion, colossal, comely, comity, commensurate, commiserate, compact, compatible, compilation, complacent, complaisant, complement, comport, compunction, compute, concatenate, concentric, conception, concise

FROM WORD LIST 7 (page 57)

concoct, concurrent, condescend, condign, condiments, condole, congeal, congruence, conjugal, connivance, connotation, consecrate, consort, constraint, consummate, context, contiguous, contingent, contortions, contumacious, contusion, convene, conveyance, convivial, convoke, coquette, corporeal, corroborate, cortege, cosmic, covenant, covert, covetous, cower, crass, credulity, creed, crevice, criterion, crone

FROM WORD LIST 8 (page 63)

culinary, cull, culmination, culpable, cursory, dally, dearth, debase, debutante, decadence, deciduous, decorous, decoy, deducible, defamation, defeatist, deference, difinitive, deflect, defunct, deign, delete, delineation, delirium, delusion, demean, demeanor, demise, demolition, demur, demure, depict, deplete, deprecate, deprecatory, depreciate, depredation, derelict, derision, desiccate

FROM WORD LIST 9 (page 69)

despotism, desultory, detergent, detonation, detraction, detriment, deviate, devious, dexterous, diadem, diaphanous, dictum, diffusion, digressive, dilapidation, dilemma, dilettante, dint, dire, dirge, disavowal, discernible, discerning, disclaim, disconcert, discordant, discursive, disdain, disparage, dispersion, disputatious, dissemble, disseminate, dissertation, dissimulate, dissolute, dissuade, distortion, diverge, diverse

FROM WORD LIST 10 (page 75)

diversity, divest, dolorous, dolt, dregs, dross, drudgery, duplicity, earthy, ebullient, eccentricity, ectasy, eerie, effectual, effervesce, effete, efficacy, effrontery, effulgent, effusive, egoism, egotism, egregious, ejaculation, elegiacal, elicit, elucidate, elusory, emanate, emancipate, embroil, emolument, emulate, encompass, encumber, endearment, energize, engender, engross, enigma

FROM WORD LIST 11 (page 81)

enormity, enrapture, enthrall, entree, entrepreneur, epicurean, epigram, epilogue, epitaph, epithet, epitome, epoch, equestrian, equinox, equity, equivocate, erode, errant, escapade, esoteric, espionage, esprit de corps, estranged, ethereal, eulogy, evanescent, evince, evoke, exemplary, exhort, exigency, exotic, expatiate, expediency, expeditiously, expiate, expunge, expurgate, extant, extirpate, extort

FROM WORD LIST 12 (page 87)

extrude, exuberant, fabricate, facetious, facile, facilitate, faction, fallacious, fallible, fallow, fanaticism, fancied, fantastic, fastidious, faux pas, fawning, feint, felicitous, fervent, fester, fetid, fetter, fictitious, filial, finale, finesse, finicky, fissure, fitful, flaccid, flagging, flagrant, flay, flick, flippancy, flotilla, flout, fluctuation, fluency, fluster

FROM WORD LIST 13 (page 93)

foible, forbearance, foreboding, forte, fortitude, fractious, frantic, fraudulent, fraught, fray, frenzied, friction, frigid, frolicsome, froward, frowzy, fruition, frustrate, fulminate, fulsome, funereal, fusion, gainsay, gamut, gape, gauntlet, gazette, generality, geniality, genteel, gentry, gesticulation, ghastly, gibber, gibbet, gibe, glaze, glean, gloaming, gloat

FROM WORD LIST 14 (page 98)

glut, gluttonous, gnarled, goad, gory, gossamer, granary, grandiloquent, graphic, gratis, grueling, gruesome, gruff, guffaw, guile, guileless, gustatory, gutteral, haggle, hallowed, hallucination, hamper, harangue, harass, harbinger, harping, harry, haughtiness, hazardous, hazy, hedonism, heedless, heinous, heresy, hiatus, hibernate, hierarchy, hindmost, histrionic, holocaust, homespun

FROM WORD LIST 15 (page 104)

homogenous, humane, humdrum, humid, humility, hypochondriac, hypocritical, ideology, idiom, idiosyncrasy, igneous, ignoble, ignominious, illimitable, imbecility, imbibe, imminent, immobility, immune, impasse, impending, impenitent, imperious, impermeable, impertinent, imperturbability, impiety, impious, implacable, implication, implicit, imprecate, impregnable, impropriety, improvident, impugn, inanimate, inadvertence, inarticulate, incapacitate

FROM WORD LIST 16 (page 109)

incessant, incipient, incisive, incite, inclusive, incommodious, incongruity, incredulity, increment, incumbent, incursion, indefatigable, indict, indigenous, indisputable, indomitable, indulgent, inept, inexorable, infamous, inference, infinitesimal, inflated, influx, infraction, infringe, inherent, inhibit, iniquitous, inkling, innate, innocuous, innovation, innuendo, inordinate, inscrutable, insomnia, instigate, insuperable, insurgent, integrity

FROM WORD LIST 17 (page 115)

interment, interminable, intimate, intimidation, intrude, intuition, invective, invidious, invulnerable, iota, irascible, ironical, irreconcilable, irreparable, irrevocable, iterate, itinerant, jargon, jeopardy, jocose, jocular, jocund, jubilation, judicious, knavery, knell, labyrinth, lacerate, laconic, laggard, laity, languid, languish, lassitude, latent, latitude, lave, lavish, lesion, lethal

FROM WORD LIST 18 (page 121)

libelous, licentious, linguistic, liquidate, loathe, longevity, loquacious, lout, lucent, lucid, lucrative, luminous, lunar, luscious, lustrous, luxuriant, macerate, machinations, maelstrom, magnanimous, magnate, maim, malicious, malignant, mammoth, mandatory, manipulate, marauder, maritime, masticate, maudlin, maxim, meander, meddlesome, mediate, meditation, medley, melee, mendacious, mendicant

FROM WORD LIST 19 (page 127)

mercenary, mercurial, mete, metropolis, mettle, mien, migratory, militate, mincing, misadventure, misapprehension, miscreant, misgivings, mishap, missile, mite, mitigate, mobile, mode, modicum, molten, momentous, monotheism, moodiness, morbid, morose, mortician, mortify, mote, mountebank, muddle, multiform, multiplicity, murkiness, muse, musky, mutable, mutilate, mutinous, nadir

FROM WORD LIST 20 (page 132)

naiveté, natal, nauseous, nemesis, nepotism, nettle, nib, nicety, nomadic, nonchalance, noncommittal, nonentity, non sequitur, nostalgia, novice, noxious, nugatory, numismatist, nutrient, oaf, obfuscate, obliterate, oblivion, obnoxious, obtrude, obtrusive, obviate, occult, odoriferous, odorous, officious, olfactory, oligarch, ominous, omniverous, onerous, onomatopoeia, onslaught, opaque, opprobrious

FROM WORD LIST 21 (page 138)

ordinance, ornate, ornithologist, oscillate, ostensible, ostracize, overt, pacifist, palatable, palatial, pallid, palpable, paltry, panacea, pandemonium, panegyric, panorama, pantomime, paragon, paregoric, parley, parody, paroxysm, parricide, partiality, passive, pastoral, pathetic, pathos, patriarch, peccadillo, pedulate, pecuniary, pedagogue, pedantic, pediatrician, pell-mell, penance, pensive, penury, perdition, perfidious

FROM WORD LIST 22 (page 144)

perjury, perpetrate, perusal, pervade, perverse, perversity, pessimism, pestilential, philanthropist, philology, pied, piquant, pithy, pittance, placid, plagiarism, platitude, plebeian, plethora, podiatrist, podium, poignant, politic, polygamist, polyglot, portend, portent, portentous, portly, posthumous, postulate, potentate, potential, potion, potpourri, practical, pragmatic, prate, prattle, precarious

FROM WORD LIST 23 (page 150)

precipitate, precipitous, preclude, precocious, precursor, predatory, preeminent, premonition, preposterous, prevaricate, procrastinate, profligate, profusion, progenitor, progeny, prognosticate, prolific, promiscuous, prone, propagate, propensity, propitiate, propound, propriety, propulsive, prostrate, protégé, protrude, provident, provocation, proximity, proxy, pseudonym, pugnacious, pulmonary, pulsate, pungent, puny, purge, purloin

FROM WORD LIST 24 (page 156)

pyromaniac, quack, qualms, quell, querulous, quibble, quip, quirk, quizzical, rabid, ramp, rancid, rancor, rant, rapacious, rationalize, ravenous, recalcitrant, recant, recapitulate, recession, recipient, reciprocal, reciprocate, recluse, reconcile, recourse, recrimination, rectitude, recumbent, recurrent, redolent, redoubtable, redress, redundant, reek, refutation, regale, regeneration, regime

FROM WORD LIST 25 (page 161)

relegate, relevancy, relinquish, remedial, reminiscence, remnant, remunerative, rend, render, renegade, renounce, renovate, renunciation, reparable, replete, reprehensible, reprieve, reprimand, requisite, rescind, resonant, respite, restitution, resuscitate, retaliate, retraction, retribution, retrieve, retroactive, revelry, reverberate, revile, revulsion, ribald, rift, rigor, risible, risqué, rococo, roseate

FROM WORD LIST 26 (page 167)

rote, ruminate, rummage, ruse, sacrilegious, sacrosanct, salient, saline, sallow, salutary, sangfroid, sanguinary, sapid, sapient, sardonic, sate, satiate, satiety, saturnine, saunter, savant, savoir faire, scavenger, schism, scintilla, scourge, scrupulous, scuttle, sedate, sedulous, seethe, seine, semblance, sensual, serenity, serrated, severance, shackle, shimmer

FROM WORD LIST 27 (page 173)

simian, simile, simulate, sinuous, skimp, skulk, solicitous, soliloquy, solstice, somnambulist, spasmodic, specious, spectral, spurious, squalid, staid, stamina, stentorian, stigmatize, stint, stipend, stoic, stolid, strident, subjugate, sub rosa, subsequent, subservient, subsistence, substantiate, subterfuge, subtlety, subversive, succinct, succulent, suffuse, sully, sultry, sumptuous, sunder

FROM WORD LIST 28 (page 179)

supersede, supine, supplicate, surcease, surly, surmise, surveillance, sustenance, swelter, sylvan, synthesis, taciturn, tactile, taint, tantalize, tautological, temporize, tenet, tenuous, terrestrial, terse, testy, tether, therapeutic, thermal, throes, throttle, thwart, timidity, tirade, titanic, toady, topography, torpid, tortuous, touchy, toxic, tractable, tranquillity, transcend

FROM WORD LIST 29 (page 185)

transition, translucent, transparent, tremor, tremulous, trenchant, trepidation, tribulation, trite, truculent, tumid, turbid, turbulence, turgid, turpitude, tyro, ubiquitous, ulterior, ultimate, ultimatum, unassuming, unbridled, uncanny, unconscionable, uncouth, unctuous, unearthly, unequivocal, unfaltering, unfeigned, unique, unmitigated, unwonted, upbraid, urbane, vacuous, vagary, validate, vapid, variegated

FROM WORD LIST 30 (page 190)

veneer, venerable, vent, verbose, vernal, versatile, vicissitude, vie, vilify, vindicate, vindictive, virile, virtuoso, virus, viscous, vituper-ative, vivacious, vociferous, volatile, voluble, voracious, vulnerable, vying, waggish, waive, wan, wane, wanton, wary, wheedle, whet, wily, winsome, witless, witticism, wizened, wont, worldly, wrest, zenith

Senior Word List

FROM WORD LIST 1 (page 21)

abase, abhor, abjure, ablution, absolve, abstinence, accrue, acetic, acknowledge, acme, acquiescent, acrid, adage, addle, adept, adipose, affinity, agape, aggrandize, agnostic, albeit, alimentary, alimony

FROM WORD LIST 2 (page 27)

allocate, alloy, amalgamate, ambrosia, amiable, amicable, amnesia, amphibian, amuck, anemia, annuity, anonymous, anthropologist, antipathy, apex, apothecary, apparition, appraise, apprehend, aptitude

FROM WORD LIST 3 (page 34)

aquiline, arable, ardor, artifice, ascertain, asinine, aspersion, asteroid, atrocity, attest, audacity, audit, austere, auxiliary, awry, axiom, azure, balmy, banal, bandanna, bantering

FROM WORD LIST 4 (page 40)

barrister, barterer, bauble, belabor, benign, bereft, besmirch, betroth, biennial, bigotry, bilious, bland, blighted, blithe, bogus, boisterous, bouillon, brazen, buffoonery, burlesque, buxom, cadaver

FROM WORD LIST 5 (page 46)

caliber, cameo, canard, candor, canter, canvass, capacious, carat, carnal, carniverous, catechism, caustic, celibate, censure, centaur, centigrade, centrifugal, charisma, chassis, chattel, chide, chiropodist, churlish

FROM WORD LIST 6 (page 52)

cite, claustrophobia, cleft, coerce, cognomen, coincident, collier, combustible, commandeer, commodious, conciliate

FROM WORD LIST 7 (page 57)

condone, confiscate, conformity, congenital, connoisseur, connubial, consensus, contaminate, contentious, contraband, contrite, conversant, copious, cornice, corpulent, countermand, counterpart, coy, craven, crestfallen

FROM WORD LIST 8 (page 63)

cryptic, cuisine, curtail, cynic, dais, dauntless, dawdle, debonair, decrepit, default, defection, defile, deleterious, delude, depilate, deploy, depravity, deranged, deride, dermatologist, derogatory, desecrate, despicable, despise

FROM WORD LIST 9 (page 69)

devoid, devout, diabolical, diffidence, dilate, diminution, disconsolate, disgruntle, disheveled, disinterested, dismember, disparate, dispirited, dissection, dissipate, distend, distraught, diva

FROM WORD LIST 10 (page 75)

divulge, docile, doff, doggerel, domicile, dormant, droll, dubious, duress, efface, effeminate, effigy, elation, emaciated, embezzlement, eminent

FROM WORD LIST 11 (page 81)

ennui, ephemeral, epicure, escutcheon, ethnic, eulogistic, evasive, exasperate, exhume, exodus, exonerate, exorbitant, expatriate, extant, extemporaneous, extenuate, extol, extraneous, extricate, extrovert

FROM WORD LIST 12 (page 87)

facade, fanciful, fatalism, fatuous, fauna, feasible, feign, ferment, fervid, fervor, fete, fiasco, fickle, fidelity, filch, flail, flair, flamboyant, flora, fleck, florid

FROM WORD LIST 13 (page 93)

flux, foist, foment, foolhardy, foppish, forensic, formidable, foster, frailty, frenetic, frugality, furor, furtive, galleon, galvanize, gamester, garbled, garish, gist, glib

FROM WORD LIST 14 (page 98)

glossy, gnome, gouge, grandiose, gregarious, grisly, grotto, gruel, guise, gullible, gusty, hackneyed, haggard, haphazard, harridan, hawser, heterogeneous, hilarity, holster

FROM WORD LIST 15 (page 104)

homonym, hubbub, hybrid, hypothetical, idolatry, imbue, immaculate, impair, impassive, impeach, impetuous, impetus, import, impromptu, improvise, inalienable, inane

FROM WORD LIST 16 (page 109)

incentive, inclement, incognito, incorrigible, incriminate, inculcate, indigent, indolence, infallible, infirmity, ingrate, insinuate, insipid, insolent, insolvency, integrate, intellect

FROM WORD LIST 17 (page 115)

interim, intermittent, intrepid, introvert, inverse, irrelevant, irreverent, jaundiced, kismet, kleptomaniac, lackadaisical, lagoon, languish, lateral, laudatory, lethargic, levity

FROM WORD LIST 18 (page 121)

lewd, lexicon, libertine, libretto, litigation, livid, lucre, luster, malediction, malefactor, mall, maniacal, marital, martial, maternal, matricide, mausoleum, mediocre, memento

FROM WORD LIST 19 (page 127)

menial, mentor, mercantile, meringue, meticulous, migrant, mirage, misdemeanor, misogynist, modish, millify, molt, motif, muggy, mulct, munificent, musty

FROM WORD LIST 20 (page 132)

nave, nebulous, nefarious, negation, nocturnal, obelisk, obese, obituary, oblique, obsession, obsolete, obtuse, oculist, odious, ogle, omnipotent, opiate, opportune, optician, optometrist

FROM WORD LIST 21 (page 138)

ostentatious, palette, pallet, palpitate, papyrus, parable, paradox, parallelism, paranoia, paraphernalia, parasite, parlance, parry, parvenu, patent, patricide, pendant, pendent, perennial, perfidy, perfunctory

FROM WORD LIST 22 (page 144)

perimeter, periphery, permeate, pernicious, perpetual, pert, pertinent, perturb, petrify, petulant, phial, pillage, pinnacle, pious, pique, placate, plaintive, posterity, practicable, preamble, precedent (n.)

FROM WORD LIST 23 (page 150)

precept, prefatory, prelude, presentiment, presumption, prim, probity, prodigal, profane, promontory, protract, prurient, psychiatrist, puerile, pulchritude, punitive, purgatory, purveyor

FROM WORD LIST 24 (page 156)

putrid, quaff, quandary, quixotic, ragamuffin, raucous, ravage, raze, realm, rebate, reconnaisance, rectify, recuperate, refectory, regatta, rehabilitate, reimburse, reiterate

FROM WORD LIST 25 (page 161)

rejuvenate, relish, remediable, remonstrate, rendezvous, reparation, repartee, repellent, repertoire, replenish, replica, requiem, retentive, reverie, rhetoric, rife, roan, robust, rostrum

FROM WORD LIST 26 (page 167)

rotundity, rubble, ruddy, rueful, ruthless, sadistic, saga, sagacious, salvage, saturate, savor, secession, sedentary, senility, serendipity, servile, shambles, sherbert, shoddy, silt

FROM WORD LIST 27 (page 173)

sinister, skittish, sleazy, slovenly, sojourn, solvent, spangle, spatial, spawn, sporadic, stagnant, stanch, statute, stein, stellar, stupor, stymie, suavity, sublime, subsidiary, summation, sundry

FROM WORD LIST 28 (page 179)

superficial, superfluity, surfeit, swathe, synthetic, tacit, tantrum, tedium, tempo, tentative, tenure, tepid, tipple, toga, tome, torso, tract, transcribe

FROM WORD LIST 29 (page 185)

transgression, transient, traverse, treatise, trek, tribunal, tribute, trilogy, tumbrel, turnkey, unearth, unguent, unkempt, unruly, usury, vanguard, vantage, vaunted, veer

FROM WORD LIST 30 (page 190)

vegetate, venal, venial, vent, veracious, verdant, verity, vertigo, vestige, viand, vicarious, victuals, vigilance, viper, virulent, visage, visionary, vogue, whit, wizardry, zephyr

Honor Senior Word List

FROM WORD LIST 1 (page 21)

abettor, abeyance, abortive, abrade, abstruse, acclivity, accoutre, accretion, acidulous, actuarial, adduce, adjuration, adumbration, adventitious, affray, agglomeration, alchemy, allay, allegory

FROM WORD LIST 2 (page 27)

alleviate, alluvial, amass, amenities, amnesty, amorphous, amplify, amulet, anathema, ancillary, animosity, anomaly, antediluvian, anthropod, antipodes, antithesis, aperture, apogee, apothegm, appease, apposite

FROM WORD LIST 3 (page 34)

argot, artifacts, artisan, asceticism, asseverate, assiduous, assuage, astute, atrophy, atypical, automaton, avarice, aver, avouch, avuncular, baneful

FROM WORD LIST 4 (page 40)

baroque, bate, beatific, bedizen, beleaguer, bellicose, berserk, bivouac, blazon, bode, bombastic, bootless, braggadocio, brazier, bucolic, bumptious, burgeon, burnish, cache, cacophony

FROM WORD LIST 5 (page 46)

calorific, canker, cantata, canto, comparison, capricious, captious, carmine, carnage, carousal, carte blanche, cataclysm, catholic, cavil, censer, centurion, cessation, chaffing, champ, chimerical, choleric

FROM WORD LIST 6 (page 52)

ciliated, circuitous, clandestine, coadjutor, cockade, cogent, cognate, cognizance, cohere, cohesion, cohorts, collate, collation, colloquy, comestible, compliant

FROM WORD LIST 7 (page 57)

conclave, concomitant, conglomeration, conifer, consanguinity, construe, contemn, continence, contravene, controvert, contumely, corrosive, corsair, coterie, crabbed, credence, crux

FROM WORD LIST 8 (page 63)

cupidity, curry, dank, dastard, daunt, debauch, debilitate, decant, declivity, decry, defalcate, delusive, demagogue, demoniac, denizen, deposition, descant, descry, despoil

FROM WORD LIST 9 (page 69)

destitute, desuetude, devolve, dialectic, dichotomy, dilatory, dipso-maniac, discomfit, discretion, discrete, disingenuous, disjointed, disparity, disport, disquisition, dissonance, dissuasion, distrait, diurnal, divers

FROM WORD LIST 10 (page 75)

divination, dogmatic, dorsal, dotage, doughty, dour, ecclesiastic, edify, educe, efflorescent, effusion, egress, elusive, embellish, emblazon, emend, emetic, enamored, enclave, encomiastic, en-croachment, endive, endue, enervate, enhance

FROM WORD LIST 11 (page 81)

ensconce, entity, environ, equable, equanimity, equipage, equivo-cal, erudite, eschew, euphemism, euphonious, ewer, exaction, exchequer, exculpate, execrable, exiguous, expostulation, extra-dition, extrinsic

FROM WORD LIST 12 (page 87)

exude, facet, factitious, factious, factotum, fain, fancier, fealty, fecundity, fell, ferret, fetish, fiat, figment, flagellate, flaunt, fledgling, flotsam

FROM WORD LIST 13 (page 93)

foray, fortuitous, franchise, freebooter, fresco, freshet, frieze, fructify, functionary, fustian, gadfly, gaff, gambol, garner, garrulity, genre, gentility, germane, gig

FROM WORD LIST 14 (page 98)

gorge, gourmand, gourmet, gratuitous, gusto, habiliments, halcyon, hap, hapless, harrow, hauteur, heretic, hermitage, hibernal, hieroglyphic, hireling, hirsute, hoary, hogshead

FROM WORD LIST 15 (page 104)

horticultural, hostelry, humus, hypercritical, iconoclastic, illusion, imbroglio, immolate, immutable, impale, impeccable, impecunious, impervious, impolitic, importune, imprecate, impunity, imputation, incarcerate, incarnate

FROM WORD LIST 16 (page 109)

incendiary, inchoate, incompatible, inconsequential, incontrovertible, incorporeal, incubate, indemnify, indenture, indignity, indite, indubitably, ineffable, ingenuous, ingratiate, inimical, insatiable, insensate, insidious, insular

FROM WORD LIST 17 (page 115)

intelligentsia, inter, intransigent, intrinsic, inundate, inured, inveigle, inveterate, inviolability, iridescent, irremediable, jaded, jettison, jingoism, junket, junto, ken, kiosk, kith, knoll, lagniappe, lambent, laminated, lampoon, lapidary, largess, lascivious, lecherous

FROM WORD LIST 18 (page 121)

liaison, libidinous, lieu, limn, limpid, lithe, loath, lode, lope, lugubrious, macabre, Machiavellian, madrigal, magniloquent, magnitude, malevolent, malign, malingerer, malleable, manifest, manifesto, marrow, martinet, matrix, mauve, mellifluous, memorialize

FROM WORD LIST 19 (page 127)

meretricious, mesa, metallurgical, metamorphosis, metaphysical, mews, misanthrope, miscegenation, miscellany, misnomer, modulation, moiety, monetary, moot, mordant, mores, moribund, motley, multilingual, mundane

FROM WORD LIST 20 (page 132)

natation, necrology, necromancy, neophyte, nexus, niggardly, noisome, nosegay, nurture, obdurate, obeisance, objugate, obliquity, obloquy, obsequious, omniscient, opalescent

FROM WORD LIST 21 (page 138)

opulence, oratorio, orifice, osteopath, paean, palaver, palliate, pander, paraphrase, pariah, parsimonious, patrimony, paucity, pelf, pellucid, penchant, penitent, penumbra, penurious, percussion, peremptory, perforce

FROM WORD LIST 22 (page 144)

peripatetic, permeable, persiflage, perspicacious, pertinacious, perturbation, perversion, pervious, philander, philistine, pillory, pinion, piscatorial, plauditory, plenary, plenipotentiary, plumb, poltroon, pommel, poultice

FROM WORD LIST 23 (page 150)

precedent (adj.), predilection, preponderate, presage, pretentious, primordial, pristine, privy, proboscis, prodigious, prognosis, prolix, promulgate, propitious, prorogue, proscribe, prosody, protocol, provender, proviso, psyche, puissant, punctilious, purport, purview

FROM WORD LIST 24 (page 156)

pusillanimous, quail, quay, quiescent, quietude, quintessence, qui vive, ramification, rampant, rapprocchement, rarefied, ratiocination, ravening, recondite, recreant, refection, refraction, refractory, refulgent, regimen

FROM WORD LIST 25 (page 161)

remiss, repercussion, repository, reprisal, reprobation, repudiate, repugnance, requite, rescission, resplendent, restive, retinue, retrograde, retrospective, rheumy

FROM WORD LIST 26 (page 167)

rubicund, rudimentary, rusticate, sacerdotal, saffron, salubrious, sanguine, scintillate, scion, scullion, scurrillous, sebaceous, secular, sententious, sepulcher, sequester, sheaf, sheathe, shibboleth, shoal, sidereal

FROM WORD LIST 27 (page 173)

sinecure, slake, sloth, slough, sluggard, sobriety, solecism, somnolent, sonorous, soupcon, splenetic, sportive, squander, stratagem, striated, stricture, stringent, subaltern, sublimate

FROM WORD LIST 28 (page 179)

superannuated, supercilious, suppliant, supposititious, surreptitious, sycophantic, synchronous, tawdry, temerity, temporal, tenacious, terminus, tertiary, theocracy, thrall, threnody, tithe, titular, traduce

FROM WORD LIST 29 (page 185)

transmute, transpire, travail, travesty, trident, troth, trumpery, tryst, tutelage, umbrage, unanimity, unassuaged, unction, undulate, unimpeachable, unison, unseemly, unsullied, untenable, unwitting, uxorious, vacillation, vainglorious

FROM WORD LIST 30 (page 190)

vehement, vellum, venerate, ventral, verbiage, verdigris, vertex, virago, vitiate, vitriolic, volition, voluptuous, votary, vouchsafe, whimsical, wraith, wreak, zealot

2 Basic Word List

The approximately 2,100 words in this list have been compiled from various sources. They have been taken from the standard literature read by high school students throughout the country and from the many tests taken by high school and college students. Ever since this book first appeared in 1954, countless students have reported that mastering this list has been of immense value in the taking of all kinds of college entrance and scholarship tests. It has been used with profit by people preparing for civil service examinations, placement tests, and promotion examinations in many industrial fields.

For each word, the following is provided:

1. The word is printed in heavy type (words are arranged in strict alphabetical order for ease in locating).
2. Its part of speech is given.
3. Where needed, the pronunciation of a difficult syllable or sound is indicated. For this, a simplified key is used:

KEY

ā — ale	ə — event, allow	ou — out
ă — add	ī — ice	th — thin
ä — arm	ĭ — ill	ū — use
a — ask	ō — old	ŭ — up
ē — eve	ŏ — odd	zh — pleasure
ĕ — end	ô — orb	
ê — err, her	oo — food	

4. A brief definition of the word.
5. A sentence illustrating the use of the word.
6. Whenever useful, related words are provided.
7. Following each list of words will be a group of common prefixes, suffixes, and stems. Studying these

can be of help to many students in reinforcing the impression the word has made. It will help the student interpret other words he or she encounters. However, it must be remembered that many words have lost their original meanings and have taken on more specific and limited meanings. These prefixes, suffixes, and roots should be used as a guide when in doubt about the meaning of a strange word. There is no substitute for learning the exact meaning of each word as it is used today.

Basic Word List

Word List 1   abase-allegory

* **abase** v. lower; humiliate. His refusal to *abase* himself in the eyes of his followers irritated the king who wanted to humiliate the proud leader. abasement, N.

abash v. embarrass. He was not at all *abashed* by her open admiration.

abdicate v. renounce; give up. When Edward VIII *abdicated* the British throne, he surprised the entire world.

* **abettor** N. encourager. He was accused of being an aider and *abettor* of the criminal. abet, v.

abeyance (-*bā'*-) N. suspended action. The deal was held in *abeyance* until his arrival.

abhor v. detest; hate. He *abhorred* all forms of bigotry. abhorrence, N.

abjure v. renounce upon oath. He *abjured* his allegiance to the king. abjuration, N.

ablution N. washing. His daily *ablutions* were accompanied by loud noises which he humorously labeled "Opera in the Bath."

abominate v. loathe; hate. Moses *abominated* idol worship.

aboriginal ADJ. being the first of its kind in a region; primitive; native. His studies of the primitive art forms of the *aboriginal* Indians were widely reported in the scientific journals. aborigine, N.

abortive ADJ. unsuccessful; fruitless. We had to abandon our *abortive* attempts.

* **abrade** v. wear away by friction; erode. The skin of his leg was *abraded* by the sharp rocks. abrasion, N.

* **abrogate** v. abolish. He intended to *abrogate* the decree issued by his predecessor.

abscond v. depart secretly and hide. The teller *absconded* with the bonds and was not found.

absolve v. pardon (an offense). The father confessor *absolved* him of his sins. absolution, N.

abstemious (-*stēm'*-) ADJ. temperate; sparing in drink, etc. The drunkards mocked him because of his *abstemious* habits.

abstinence N. restraint from eating or drinking. The doctor recommended

---

ā — ale; ă — add; ä — arm; å — ask; ē — eve; ĕ — end; ê — err, her; ə — event, allow,
ī — ice; ĭ — ill; ō — old; ŏ — odd; ô — orb; oo — food; ou — out; th — thin; ū — use;
ŭ — up; zh — pleasure

total *abstinence* from alcoholic beverages. abstain, v.

abstruse ADJ. obscure; profound; difficult to understand. He read *abstruse* works in philosophy.

accelerate v. move faster. In our science class, we learn how falling bodies *accelerate*. acceleration, N.

accessory N. additional object; useful but not essential thing. The *accessories* she bought cost more than the dress. also ADJ.

✳ **acclivity** (-*klĭv'*-) N. sharp upslope of a hill. The car could not go up the *acclivity* in high gear.

accolade (-*lād'*) N. award of merit. In Hollywood, an "Oscar" is the highest *accolade*.

accomplice N. partner in crime. She was his *accomplice* in the murder.

accord N. agreement. He was in complete *accord* with the verdict.

✳ **accost** v. approach and speak first to a person. The salesman *accosted* the young lady.

accoutre (-*cōōt'*-) v. equip. The fisherman was *accoutred* with the best that the sporting goods store could supply. accoutrements, N.

accretion (-*krē'*-) N. growth; increase. The *accretion* of wealth marked the family's rise in power.

accrue v. come about by addition. You must pay the interest which has *accrued* on your debt as well as the principal sum. accrual, N.

acetic (-*sĕt'*-) ADJ. vinegary. The salad had an exceedingly *acetic* flavor.

acidulous (-*sĭd'*-) ADJ. slightly sour; sharp; caustic. The spinster spurned him with an *acidulous* retort.

acknowledge v. recognize; admit. When pressed for an answer, he *acknowledged* the existence of another motive for the crime.

acme (*ăk'-mē*) N. top; pinnacle. His success in this role marked his *acme* as an actor.

acoustics (-*kōōs'*-) N. science of sound; quality that makes a room easy or hard to hear in. Carnegie Hall is liked by music lovers because of its fine *acoustics*.

acquiescent (-*kwē- ĕs'*-) ADJ. accepting passively. His *acquiescent* manner did not indicate the extent of his reluctance to join the group. acquiesce, v.

acquittal N. deliverance from a charge. His *acquittal* by the jury surprised those who had thought him guilty. acquit, v.

acrid ADJ. sharp; bitterly pungent. The *acrid* odor of burnt gunpowder filled the room after the pistol had been fired.

acrimonious ADJ. stinging; caustic. His tendency to utter *acrimonious* remarks alienated his audience. acrimony, N.

ā — ale; ă — add; ä — arm; à — ask; ē — eve; ĕ — end; ê — err, her; ə — event, allow,
ī — ice; ĭ — ill; ō — old; ŏ — odd; ô — orb; ōō — food; ou — out; th — thin; ū — use;
ŭ — up; zh — pleasure

actuarial ADJ. calculating; pertaining to insurance statistics. According to recent *actuarial* tables, life expectancy is greater today than it was a century ago.

actuate V. motivate. I fail to understand what *actuated* you to reply to this letter so nastily.

acumen (-*kū'*-) N. mental keenness. His business *acumen* helped him to succeed where others had failed.

adage (*ăd'*-) N. wise saying; proverb. There is much truth in the old *adage* about fools and their money.

adamant (*ăd'*-) ADJ. hard; inflexible. He was *adamant* in his determination to punish the wrongdoer.   adamantine, ADJ.

adapt V. alter; modify. This play was *adapted* from the French novel.

addiction N. compulsive, habitual need. His *addiction* to drugs caused his friends much grief.

addle ADJ. rotten; muddled; crazy. This *addle*-headed plan is so preposterous that it does not deserve any consideration.   also V.

adduce V. offer as example or reason. When you *adduce* evidence of this nature, you must be sure of your sources.

adept (-*dĕpt'*) ADJ. expert at. He was *adept* at the fine art of irritating people.

adhere V. stick fast. I will *adhere* to this opinion until proof that I am wrong is presented.   adhesion, N.

adipose (*ăd'*-) ADJ. fatty. Excess *adipose* tissue should be avoided by middle-aged people.

adjuration (*ă-jŏŏ-rā'*-) N. solemn urging. His *adjuration* to tell the truth did not change the witness's testimony.   adjure, V.

admonish V. warn; reprove. He *admonished* his listeners to change their wicked ways.   admonition, N.

adroit ADJ. skillful. His *adroit* handling of the delicate situation pleased his employers.

adulation N. flattery; admiration. He thrived on the *adulation* of his henchmen.

adulterate V. make impure by mixing with baser substances. It is a crime to *adulterate* food without informing the buyer.

adumbration (-*brā'*-) N. foreshadowing; outlining. The *adumbration* of the future in science fiction is often astonishing.   adumbrate, V.

adventitious (-*tĭ'*-) ADJ. accidental; casual. He found this *adventitious* meeting with his friend extremely fortunate.

adverse (-*vĕrse'*) ADJ. unfavorable; hostile. *Adverse* circumstances compelled him to close his business.

adversity N. poverty; misfortune. We must learn to meet *adversity* gracefully.

advocate V. urge; plead for. The abolitionists *advocated* freedom for the

ā — ale; ă — add; ä — arm; å — ask; ē — eve; ĕ — end; ê — err, her; ə — event, allow,
ī — ice; ĭ — ill; ō — old; ŏ — odd; ô — orb; ōō — food; ou — out; th — thin; ū — use;
ŭ — up; zh — pleasure

slaves.   advocate, N.

aesthetic (*ĕs-thĕt'-*) ADJ. artistic; dealing with or capable of appreciation of the beautiful. Because of his *aesthetic* nature, he was frequently disturbed by ugly things.   aesthete, N.

affected ADJ. artificial; pretended. His *affected* mannerisms irritated many of us who had known him before his promotion.   affectation, N.

affiliation N. joining; associating with. His *affiliation* with the political party was of short duration for he soon disagreed with his colleagues.

affinity N. kinship. He felt an *affinity* with all who suffered; their pains were his pains.

affirmation N. solemn pledge by one who refuses to take an oath. The Constitution of this country provides for oath or *affirmation* by officeholders.

affluence (*ăff'-*) N. abundance; wealth. Foreigners are amazed by the *affluence* and luxury of the American way of life.

affray N. public brawl. He was badly mauled by the fighters in the *affray*.

agape (*a-gāp'*) ADJ. open-mouthed. He stared, *agape* at the many strange animals in the zoo.

agglomeration N. collection; heap. It took weeks to assort the *agglomeration* of miscellaneous items he had collected on his trip.

aggrandize (*ăg'-*) V. increase or intensify. The history of the past quarter century illustrates how a president may *aggrandize* his power to act aggressively in international affairs without considering the wishes of Congress.

aggregate ADJ. sum; total. The *aggregate* wealth of this country is staggering to the imagination.   aggregate, V.

aghast ADJ. horrified. He was *aghast* at the nerve of the speaker who had insulted his host.

agility N. nimbleness. The *agility* of the acrobat amazed and thrilled the audience.

agitate V. stir up; disturb. His fiery remarks *agitated* the already angry mob.

agnostic N. one who is skeptical of the existence of a god. The *agnostic* demanded proof before he would accept the statement of the minister.   also ADJ.

alacrity N. cheerful promptness. He demonstrated his eagerness to serve by his *alacrity* in executing the orders of his master.

albeit (*ôl-bē-ít*) CONJ. although. *Albeit* fair, she was not sought after.

alchemy N. medieval chemistry. The changing of baser metals into gold was the goal of the students of *alchemy*.   alchemist, N.

alias (*ā'-lē-əs*) N. an assumed name. John Smith's *alias* was Bob Jones.

ā — ale; ă — add; ä — arm; á — ask; ē — eve; ĕ — end; ê — err, her; ə — event, allow, ī — ice; ĭ — ill; ō — old; ŏ — odd; ô — orb; ōō — food; ou — out; th — thin; ū — use; ŭ — up; zh — pleasure

alienate v. make hostile; separate. His offensive manner *alienated* many of his neighbors.

alimentary ADJ. supplying nourishment. The *alimentary* canal in our bodies is so named because digestion of foods occurs there.

alimony N. payment by a husband to his divorced wife. Mrs. Jones was awarded $200.00 monthly *alimony* by the court when she was divorced from her husband.

allay v. calm; pacify. The crew tried to *allay* the fears of the passengers by announcing that the fire had been controlled.

allege v. state without proof. It is *alleged* that he had worked for the enemy. allegation, N.

allegory N. story in which characters are used as symbols; fable. *Pilgrim's Progress* is an *allegory* of the temptations and victories of man's soul. allegorical, ADJ.

ETYMOLOGY 1.

AB, ABS (from, away from) prefix

> **abduct** lead away, kidnap
>
> **abjure** renounce (swear away from)
>
> **abject** degraded (thrown away from)

ABLE, IBLE (capable of) adjective suffix

> **portable** able to be carried
>
> **legible** able to be read
>
> **interminable** unable to be ended

AC, IC (like, pertaining to) adjective suffix

> **cardiac** pertaining to the heart
>
> **aquatic** pertaining to water
>
> **dramatic** pertaining to drama

AC, ACR (sharp)

> **acrimonious** bitter
>
> **acerbity** bitterness of temper
>
> **acidulate** to make somewhat acidic or sour

AD (to, forward) prefix

> **adjure** request earnestly
>
> **admit** allow entrance
>
> **Note:** by assimilation, the AD prefix is changed to

AC in accord

AF in affliction

ā — ale; ǎ — add; ä — arm; à — ask; ē — eve; ě — end; ê — err, her; ə — event, allow,
ī — ice; ǐ — ill; ō — old; ǒ — odd; ô — orb; ōō — food; ou — out; th — thin; ū — use;
ǔ — up; zh — pleasure

AG in aggregation
AN in annexation
AP in apparition
AR in arraignment
AS in assumption
AT in attendance
AEV (age, era)

> **primeval (primaeval)** of the first age
> **coeval (coaeval)** of the same age or era
> **medieval (mediaeval)** of the middle ages

AG, ACT (to do)

> **act** deed
> **agent** doer
> **retroactive** having a backward or reversed action

AGOG (leader)

> **demagogue** false leader of people
> **pedagogue** teacher (leader of children)
> **synagogue** house of worship (leading together of people)

AGRI, AGRARI (field)

> **agrarian** one who works in the fields; farmer
> **agriculture** cultivation of fields
> **peregrination** wandering; going through fields

ALI (another)

> **alias** assumed (another) name
> **alienate** estrange (divert from another)
> **inalienable** unable to be diverted from another

TEST — Word List 1 — Synonyms

Each of the questions below consists of a word printed in bold,
followed by five words or phrases numbered 1 to 5. Choose the
numbered word or phrase which is most nearly similar in meaning
to the word in bold and write the number of your choice on your
answer paper.

1. **aborigines** 1. first designs 2. absolutions 3. finales 4. concepts
   5. primitive inhabitants
2. **abeyance** 1. obedience 2. discussion 3. excitement 4. suspended action 5. editorial

---

ā — ale; ă — add; ä — arm; à — ask; ē — eve; ĕ — end; ê — err, her; a — event, allow,
ī — ice; ĭ — ill; ō — old; ŏ — odd; ô — orb; ōō — food; ou — out; th — thin; ū — use;
ŭ — up; zh — pleasure

3. abjure 1. discuss 2. renounce 3. run off secretly 4. perjure 5. project

4. ablution 1. censure 2. forgiveness 3. mutiny 4. survival 5. washing

5. abortive 1. unsuccessful 2. consuming 3. financing 4. familiar 5. fruitful

6. abasement 1. incurrence 2. taxation 3. ground floor 4. humility 5. humiliation

7. abettor 1. conception 2. one who wagers 3. encourager 4. evidence 5. protection

8. abstruse 1. profound 2. irrespective 3. suspended 4. protesting 5. not thorough

9. acclivity 1. index 2. report 3. upslope of a hill 4. character 5. negotiator

10. accoutre 1. compromise 2. equp 3. revise 4. encounter 5. visit

11. accrue 1. come about by addition 2. reach summit 3. create a crisis 4. process 5. educate

12. accretion 1. mayonnaise 2. ban 3. increase 4. protection 5. ceremony

13. acme 1. pinnace 2. skin disease 3. basement 4. congestion 5. pinnacle

14. acidulous 1. recommended 2. witty 3. realistic 4. slightly sour 5. very generous

15. abstinence 1. restrained eating or drinking 2. vulgar display 3. deportment 4. reluctance 5. population

16. acrid 1. soft 2. bitterly pungent 3. sweet 4. salty 5. very hard

17. adipose 1. sandy 2. round 3. fatty 4. alkali 5. soft

18. adventitious 1. incidental 2. happy 3. courageous 4. accidental 5. foretelling

19. affluence 1. wealth 2. fear 3. persuasion 4. consideration 5. neglect

20. allegory 1. fable 2. poem 3. essay 4. anecdote 5. novel

Word List 2   alleviate-aptitude

alleviate (-*lē'-vē-*) v. relieve. This should *alleviate* the pain; if it does not, we shall have to use stronger drugs. **alleviation**, N.

ā — ale; ă — add; ä — arm; à — ask; ē — eve; ĕ — end; ê — err, her; ə — event, allow, ī — ice; ĭ — ill; ō — old; ŏ — odd; ô — orb; ōō — food; ou — out; th — thin; ū — use; ŭ — up; zh — pleasure

allocate v. assign. Even though the Red Cross had *allocated* a large sum for the relief of the disaster victims, many people perished.

alloy N. a mixture as of metals. *Alloys* of gold are used more frequently than the pure metal.

allude v. refer indirectly. Try not to *allude* to this matter in his presence because it annoys him to hear of it.

allusion N. indirect reference. The *allusions* to mythological characters in Milton's poems may bewilder the reader who has not studied Latin.

alluvial ADJ. pertaining to soil deposits left by rivers, etc. The farmers found the *alluvial* deposits at the mouth of the river very fertile.

aloof ADJ. apart; reserved. He remained *aloof* while all the rest conversed.

altercation N. quarrel. Throughout the entire *altercation*, not one sensible word was uttered.

altruism (ăl'-trōō-) N. unselfish aid to others; generosity. The philanthropist was noted for his *altruism*.   altruistic, ADJ.

amalgamate (-măl'-) N. combine; unite in one body. The unions will attempt to *amalgamate* their groups into one national body.

amass (-măs') v. collect. The miser's aim is to *amass* and hoard as much gold as possible.

ambiguous (-bǐg'-) ADJ. doubtful in meaning. His *ambiguous* directions misled us; we did not know which road to take.   ambiguity, N.

amble v. move at an easy pace. When she first mounted the horse, she was afraid to urge the animal to go faster than a gentle *amble*.

ambrosia (-brō'-zhə) N. food of the gods. *Ambrosia* was supposed to give immortality to any human who ate it.

ambulatory (ăm'-) ADJ. able to walk. He was described as an *ambulatory* patient because he was not confined to his bed.

ameliorate (-mēl'-) v. improve. Many social workers have attempted to *ameliorate* the conditions of people living in the slums.

amenable (-mēn'-) ADJ. readily managed; willing to be led. He was *amenable* to any suggestions which came from those he looked up to; he resented advice from his inferiors.

amenities (-měn'-) N. agreeable manners; courtesies. He observed the social *amenities*.

amiable (ām'-) ADJ. agreeable; lovable. His *amiable* disposition pleased all who had dealings with him.

amicable (ăm'-) ADJ. friendly. The dispute was settled in an *amicable* manner with no harsh words.

amnesia N. loss of memory. Because she was suffering from *amnesia*, the

ā — ale; ă — add; ä — arm; å — ask; ē — eve; ĕ — end; ê — err, her; ə — event, allow, ī — ice; ĭ — ill; ō — old; ŏ — odd; ô — orb; ōō — food; ou — out; th — thin; ū — use; ŭ — up; zh — pleasure

police could not get the young lady to identify herself.

amnesty N. pardon. When his first child was born, the king granted *amnesty* to all in prison.

amorphous ADJ. shapeless. He was frightened by the *amorphous* mass which had floated in from the sea.

amphibian ADJ. able to live both on land and in water. Frogs are classified as *amphibian*. amphibian, N.

amphitheater N. oval building with tiers of seats. The spectators in the *amphitheater* cheered the gladiators.

ample ADJ. generous, more than sufficient. He had *ample* opportunity to dispose of his loot before the police caught up with him.

amplify V. enlarge. His attempts to *amplify* upon his remarks were drowned out by the jeers of the audience.

amputate V. cut off part of body. He cried when the doctors said they decided to *amputate* his leg to prevent the spread of gangrene. amputation, N.

amuck ADV. in a state of rage. The police had to be called in to restrain him after he ran *amuck* in the department store.

amulet (ăm'-) N. charm; talisman. Around his neck he wore the *amulet* which the witch doctor had given him.

anaesthetic (-thĕt'-) N. substance that removes sensation with or without loss of consciousness. His monotonous voice acted like an *anaesthetic;* his audience was soon asleep. anaesthesia, N.

analogous (-năl'-) ADJ. comparable. He called our attention to the things that had been done in an *analogous* situation and recommended that we do the same.

analogy N. similarity; parallelism. Your *analogy* is not a good one because the two situations are not similar.

anarchy (ăn'-) N. absence of governing body; state of disorder. The assassination of the leaders led to a period of *anarchy*.

anathema (-năth'-) N. solemn curse. He heaped *anathema* upon his foe.

ancillary (ăn'-sĭl'-) ADJ. serving as an aid or accessory; auxiliary. In an *ancillary* capacity he was helpful; however, he could not be entrusted with leadership.

andirons N. metal supports in a fireplace for logs. She spent many hours in the department stores looking for a pair of ornamental *andirons*.

anemia (-nēm'-) N. condition in which blood lacks red corpuscles. The doctor ascribed his fatigue to *anemia*. anemic, ADJ.

animadversion (-vĕr'-) N. critical remark. He resented the *animadversions* of his critics, particularly because he realized they were true.

ā — ale; ă — add; ä — arm; å — ask; ē — eve; ĕ — end; ê — err, her; ə — event, allow,
ī — ice; ĭ — ill; ō — old; ŏ — odd; ô — orb; ōō — food; ou — out; th — thin; ū — use;
ŭ — up; zh — pleasure

animated ADJ. lively. Her *animated* expression indicated a keenness of intellect. animation, N.

animosity N. active enmity. He incurred the *animosity* of the ruling class because he advocated limitations of their power.

annals N. records; history. In the *annals* of this period, we find no mention of democratic movements.

annihilate (-nī'-i-) V. destroy. The enemy in its revenge tried to *annihilate* the entire population.

annuity N. yearly allowance. The *annuity* he set up with the insurance company supplements his social security benefits so that he can live very comfortably without working.

annul (-nŭl') V. make void. The parents of the eloped couple tried to *annul* the marriage. annulment, N.

anomalous (-nŏm'-) ADJ. abnormal; irregular. He was placed in the *anomalous* position of seeming to approve procedures which he despised.

anomaly N. irregularity. A bird that cannot fly is an *anomaly*.

anonymous (-nŏn'-) ADJ. having or giving no name. He tried to ascertain the identity of the writer of the *anonymous* letter.

antagonism (-tăg'-) N. active resistance. We shall have to overcome the *antagonism* of the natives before our plans for settling this area can succeed.

antediluvian (-lōō'-) ADJ. antiquated; ancient. The *antediluvian* instincts had apparently not changed for thousands of years.

anthropoid (ăn'-) ADJ. manlike. The gorilla is the strongest of the *anthropoid* animals.

anthropologist (-pŏl'-) N. a student of the history and science of mankind. *Anthropologists* have discovered several relics of prehistoric man in this area.

anticlimax (-clīm'-) N. let-down in thought or emotion. After the fine performance in the first act, the rest of the play was an *anticlimax*. anticlimactic, ADJ.

antipathy (-tĭp'-) N. aversion; dislike. His extreme *antipathy* to dispute caused him to avoid argumentative discussions with his friends.

antiseptic N. substance that prevents infection. It is advisable to apply an *antiseptic* to any wound, no matter how slight or insignificant.

antithesis (-tĭ'-thē-) N. contrast; direct opposite of. This tyranny was the *antithesis* of all that he had hoped for and he fought it with all his strength.

apathetic ADJ. indifferent. He felt *apathetic* about the conditions he had

ā — ale; ă — add; ä — arm; à — ask; ē — eve; ĕ — end; ê — err, her; a — event, allow, ī — ice; ĭ — ill; ō — old; ŏ — odd; ô — orb; ōō — food; ou — out; th — thin; ū — use; ŭ — up; zh — pleasure

observed and did not care to fight against them.

aperture (ăp'-) N. opening; hole. He discovered a small *aperture* in the wall, through which the insects had entered the room.

apex N. tip; summit; climax. He was at the *apex* of his career.

aphorism (ăf'-ər-ĭzm) N. pithy maxim. An *aphorism* differs from an adage in that it is more philosophical or scientific. aphoristic, ADJ.

aplomb N. poise. His nonchalance and *aplomb* in times of trouble always encouraged his followers.

apocryphal (-pŏk'-) ADJ. not genuine; sham. His *apocryphal* tears misled no one.

apogee (ăp'-ə-jē) N. highest point. When the moon in its orbit is farthest away from the earth, it is at its *apogee*.

apostate (-pŏs'-) N. one who abandons his religious faith or political beliefs. Because he switched from one party to another, his former friends shunned him as an *apostate*.

apothecary (-pŏth'-) N. druggist. In the *apothecaries'* weight, twelve ounces equal one pound.

apothegm (ăp'-ə-thĕm) N. pithy, compact saying. Proverbs are *apothegms* that have become familiar sayings.

apotheosis (-thē-ō'-) N. deification; glorification. The *apotheosis* of a Roman emperor was designed to insure his eternal greatness.

apparition N. ghost; phantom. Hamlet was uncertain about the identity of the *apparition* that had appeared and spoken to him.

appease V. pacify; soothe. We have discovered that, when we try to *appease* our enemies, they make additional demands. appeasement, N.

appellation N. name; title. He was amazed when the witches hailed him with his correct *appellation*.

append V. attach. I shall *append* this chart to my report.

apposite (ăp'-) ADJ. appropriate; fitting. He was always able to find the *apposite* phrase, the correct expression for every occasion.

appraise V. estimate value of. It is difficult to *appraise* the value of old paintings; it is easier to call them priceless. appraisal, N.

apprehend (-hĕnd') V. arrest (a criminal); perceive. The police will *apprehend* the culprit before long.

apprehensive ADJ. fearful; discerning. His *apprehensive* glances at the people who were walking in the street revealed his nervousness. apprehension, N.

apprise (-prīz') V. inform. When he was *apprised* of the dangerous weather conditions, he decided to postpone his trip.

appurtenance N. subordinate possession. He bought the estate and all its

ā — ale; ă — add; ä — arm; à — ask; ē — eve; ĕ — end; ê — err, her; ə — event, allow.
ī — ice; ĭ — ill; ō — old; ŏ — odd; ô — orb; ōō — food; ou — out; th — thin; ū — use;
ŭ — up; zh — pleasure

appurtenances.

aptitude N. fitness; talent. The counselor gave him an *aptitude* test before advising him about the career he should follow.

ETYMOLOGY 2.

AMBI (both) prefix
    ambidextrous skilled with both hands (both right hands)
    ambiguous of double meaning
    ambivalent possessing conflicting (both) emotions

AN (without) prefix
    anarchy lack of government
    anemia lack of blood
    anaesthetize deprive of feeling

ANTE (before) prefix
    antecedent preceding event or word
    antediluvian ancient (before the flood)
    ante-nuptial before the wedding

ANIM (mind, soul)
    animadvert cast criticism upon (turn one's mind)
    unanimous of one mind
    magnanimity greatness of mind or spirit

ANN, ENN (year)
    annuity yearly remittance
    biennial every two years
    perennial flowering yearly; a yearly flowering plant

ANTHROP (man)
    anthropology study of man
    misanthrope recluse (hater of mankind)
    philanthropy love of mankind; charity

TEST — Word List 2 — Antonyms

Each of the following questions consists of a word printed in bold, followed by five words or phrases numbered 1 to 5. Choose the numbered word or phrase which is most nearly the same as or the opposite of the word in bold and write the number of your choice on your answer paper.

ā — ale; ă — add; ä — arm; à — ask; ē — eve; ĕ — end; ê — err, her; ə — event, allow,
ī — ice; ĭ — ill; ō — old; ŏ — odd; ô — orb; o͞o — food; ou — out; th — thin; ū — use;
ŭ — up; zh — pleasure

21. **alleviate** 1. endure 2. worsen 3. enlighten 4. maneuver 5. humiliate

22. **amalgamate** 1. equip 2. separate 3. generate 4. materialize 5. repress

23. **amass** 1. concentrate 2. rotate 3. concern 4. separate 5. recollect

24. **antediluvian** 1. transported 2. subtle 3. isolated 4. celebrated 5. modern

25. **antipathy** 1. profundity 2. objection 3. willingness 4. abstention 5. fondness

26. **appease** 1. agitate 2. qualify 3. display 4. predestine 5. interrupt

27. **apposite** 1. inappropriate 2. diagonal 3. exponential 4. unobtrusive 5. discouraging

28. **apprehend** 1. obviate 2. set free 3. shiver 4. understand 5. contrast

29. **aloof** 1. triangular 2. gregarious 3. comparable 4. honorable 5. savory

30. **amicable** 1. penetrating 2. compensating 3. unfriendly 4. zig-zag 5. inescapable

31. **amorphous** 1. nauseous 2. obscene 3. providential 4. definite 5. happy

32. **amplify** 1. distract 2. infer 3. publicize 4. decrease 5. pioneer

33. **antithesis** 1. velocity 2. maxim 3. similarity 4. acceleration 5. reaction

34. **anomaly** 1. desperation 2. requisition 3. registry 4. regularity 5. radiation

35. **aptitude** 1. sarcasm 2. inversion 3. adulation 4. lack of talent 5. gluttony

36. **anathema** 1. location 2. deception 3. regulation 4. radiation 5. blessing

37. **altruism** 1. good nature 2. height 3. descent 4. modernity 5. miserliness

38. **ambiguous** 1. salvageable 2. corresponding 3. responsible 4. clear 5. auxiliary

39. **anemic** 1. pallid 2. cruel 3. red-blooded 4. ventilating 5. hazardous

40. **anonymous** 1. desperate 2. signed 3. defined 4. expert 5. written

---

ā — ale; ă — add; ä — arm; â — ask; ē — eve; ĕ — end; ê — err, her; ə — event, allow,
ī — ice; ĭ — ill; ō — old; ŏ — odd; ô — orb; ōō — food; ou — out; th — thin; ū — use;
ŭ — up; zh — pleasure

Word List 3   aquiline-bantering

aquiline (ăk'-wə-) ADJ. curved; hooked. He can be recognized by his *aquiline* nose, curved like the beak of the eagle.

arable ADJ. fit for plowing. The land was no longer *arable;* erosion had removed the valuable top soil.

arbiter (är-bi-) N. a person with power to decide a dispute; judge. As an *arbiter* in labor disputes, he has won the confidence of the workers and the employers alike.

arbitrary ADJ. fixed or decided; despotic. Any *arbitrary* action on your part will be resented by the members of the board whom you do not consult.

arcade N. a covered passageway, usually lined with shops. The *arcade* was popular with shoppers because it gave them protection from the summer sun and the winter rain.

archaeology (-kē-ŏl'-) N. study of artifacts and relics of early mankind. The professor of *archaeology* headed an expedition to the Gobi Desert in search of ancient ruins.

archaic (-kā'-ĭk) ADJ. antiquated. "Proven" is the *archaic* form of the past participle of "prove" and should not be used.

archipelago (är-kə-pĕ'-) N. group of islands. When he looked at the map and saw the *archipelagoes* in the South Seas, he longed to visit them.

ardor N. heat; passion; zeal. His *ardor* was contagious; soon everyone was eagerly working.

arduous ADJ. hard; strenuous. His *arduous* efforts had sapped his energy.

argot (är'-gō) N. slang. In the *argot* of the underworld, he "was taken for a ride."

aromatic ADJ. fragrant. Medieval sailing vessels brought *aromatic* herbs from China to Europe.

arraign (-ān') V. charge in court; indict. After his indictment by the grand jury, the accused man was *arraigned* in the County Criminal Court.   arraignment, N.

arrant (ăr'-) ADJ. thorough; complete; unmitigated. "*Arrant* knave," an epithet found in books dealing with the age of chivalry, is a term of condemnation.

arrogance N. haughtiness. The *arrogance* of the nobility was resented by the middle class.

artifacts N. products of primitive culture. Archaeologists debated the signifi-

---

ā — ale; ă — add; ä — arm; à — ask; ē — eve; ĕ — end; ê — err, her; ə — event, allow,
i — ice; ĭ — ill; ō — old; ŏ — odd; ô — orb; ōō — food; ou — out; th — thin; ū — use;
ŭ — up; zh — pleasure

cance of the *artifacts* discovered in the ruins of Asia Minor and came to no conclusion.

artifice N. deception; trickery. The Trojan War proved to the Greeks that cunning and *artifice* were often more effective than military might.

artisan N. a manually skilled worker. Artists and *artisans* alike are necessary to the development of a culture.

ascertain (-*tān'*) v. find out for certain. Please *ascertain* his present address.

ascetic (*ə-sĕt'*-) ADJ. practicing self-denial; austere. The cavalier could not understand the *ascetic* life led by the monks.

asceticism N. doctrine of self-denial. His *asceticism* set him apart from his self-indulgent colleagues.

ascribe (-*krīb'*) v. refer; attribute; assign. I can *ascribe* no motive to his acts.

ashen ADJ. ash-colored; gray. His face was *ashen* with fear.

asinine ADJ. stupid. Your *asinine* remarks prove that you have not given this problem any serious consideration.

askance (-*kăns'*) ADV. with a sideways or indirect look. Looking *askance* at her questioner, she displayed her scorn.

askew (-*kū'*) ADV. crookedly; slanted; at an angle. When he placed his hat *askew* upon his head, his observers laughed.

asperity N. sharpness (of temper). These remarks, spoken with *asperity*, stung the boys to whom they had been directed.

aspersion N. slanderous remark. Do not cast *aspersions* on his character.

aspirant N. seeker after position or status. Although I am an *aspirant* for public office, I am not willing to accept the dictates of the party bosses.

aspiration N. noble ambition. Man's *aspirations* should be as lofty as the stars.

assail v. assault. He was *assailed* with questions after his lecture.

assay (-*sā'*) v. analyze; evaluate. When they *assayed* the ore, they found that they had discovered a very rich vein. assay, N.

asseverate (-*sĕv'*-) v. make a positive statement or solemn declaration. I will *asseverate* my conviction that he is guilty.

assiduous (-*sĭd'*-) ADJ. done with diligence. He worked *assiduously* at this task for weeks before he felt satisfied with his results. assiduity, N.

assuage (-*swāj'*) v. ease; lessen (pain). Your messages of cheer should *assuage* his suffering. assuagement, N.

asteroid N. small planet. *Asteroids* have become commonplace to the readers of interstellar travel stories in science fiction magazines.

astral ADJ. relating to the stars. He was amazed at the number of *astral* bodies the new telescope revealed.

astringent ADJ. binding; causing contraction. The *astringent* quality of un-

ā — ale; ă — add; ä — arm; à — ask; ē — eve; ĕ — end; ê — err, her; a — event, allow,
ī — ice; ĭ — ill; ō — old; ŏ — odd; ô — orb; oo — food; ou — out; th — thin; ū — use;
ŭ — up; zh — pleasure

sweetened lemon juice made swallowing difficult.

astute ADJ. wise; shrewd. That was a very *astute* observation. I shall heed it.

atheistic ADJ. denying the existence of God. His *atheistic* remarks shocked the religious worshippers.

athwart (-*thwôrt'*) ADV. across; in opposition to. His tendency toward violence was *athwart* the philosophy of the peace movement.

atrocity N. brutal deed. In time of war, many *atrocities* are committed by invading armies.

atrophy (*ă'-trə-fē*) N. cause to waste away. Infantile paralysis victims need physiotherapy to prevent the *atrophy* of affected limbs.

attenuate V. made thin; weaken. By withdrawing their forces, the generals hoped to *attenuate* their losses.

attest V. testify; bear witness. Having served as a member of the Grand Jury, I can *attest* that our system of indicting individuals is in need of improvement.

attribute (*ăt'-*) N. essential quality. His outstanding *attribute* was his kindness.

attrition N. gradual wearing down. They decided to wage a war of *attrition* rather than to rely on an all-out attack.

atypical ADJ. not normal. You have taken an *atypical* case that does not prove anything.

audacity N. boldness. His *audacity* at this critical moment encouraged us.

audit N. examination of accounts. When the bank examiners arrived to hold their annual *audit,* they discovered the embezzlements of the chief cashier.   also, V.

augment V. increase. How can we hope to *augment* our forces when our allies are deserting us?

augury N. omen; prophecy. He interpreted the departure of the birds as an *augury* of evil.   augur, V.

auspicious ADJ. favoring success. With favorable weather conditions, it was an *auspicious* moment to set sail.

austere ADJ. strict, stern. His *austere* demeanor prevented us from engaging in our usual frivolous activities.

austerity N. sternness; severity. The *austerity* and dignity of the court was maintained by the new justices.

authenticate V. prove genuine. An expert was needed to *authenticate* the original Van Gogh painting.

autocrat N. monarch with supreme power. The nobles tried in vain to limit the powers of the *autocrat*.   autocracy, N.

automaton (-*tŏm'-*) N. mechanism which imitates actions of humans. Long before science fiction readers became aware of robots, writers

ā — ale; ă — add; ä — arm; â — ask; ē — eve; ĕ — end; ê — err, her; ə — event, allow, ī — ice; ĭ — ill; ō — old; ŏ — odd; ô — orb; ōō — food; ou — out; th — thin; ū — use; ŭ — up; zh — pleasure

were presenting stories of *automatons* who excelled at many human tasks.

autonomous ADJ. self-governing. This island is a colony; however, in most matters it is *autonomous* and receives no orders from the mother country. autonomy, N.

autopsy (ō'-tŏp-sē)N. examination of a dead body; post-mortem. The medical examiner ordered an *autopsy* to determine the cause of death.

auxiliary ADJ. additional; subsidiary. To prepare for the emergency, they built an *auxiliary* power station. also N.

avarice N. greediness for wealth. King Midas' *avarice* has been fabled for centuries. avaricious, ADJ.

aver (ə vĕr) v. state confidently. I wish to *aver* that I am certain of success.

averse ADJ. reluctant. He was *averse* to revealing the sources of his information.

avid ADJ. greedy; eager for. He was *avid* for learning and read everything he could get. avidity, N.

avouch v. affirm; proclaim. I am willing to employ your friend if you will *avouch* for his integrity.

avow v. declare openly. I must *avow* that I am innocent.

avuncular (-vŭnk'-) ADJ. like an uncle. *Avuncular* pride did not prevent him from noticing his nephew's shortcomings.

awe N. solemn wonder. The tourists gazed with *awe* at the tremendous expanse of the Grand Canyon.

awry (-rī') ADV. distorted; crooked. He held his head *awry*, giving the impression that he had caught cold in his neck during the night.

axiom N. self-evident truth requiring no proof. Before a student can begin to think along the lines of Euclidean geometry, he must accept certain principles or *axioms*.

azure ADJ. sky blue. *Azure* sweaters pick up the blue in her eyes.

babble v. chatter idly. The little girl *babbled* about her doll.

bacchanalian (băk-à-nā'-) ADJ. drunken. Emperor Nero attended the *bacchanalian* orgy.

badger v. pester; annoy. The drunkard began to *badger* the bartender.

baffle v. frustrate; perplex. The new code *baffled* the enemy agents.

baleful ADJ. deadly; destructive. The drought was a *baleful* omen.

balk (băk)v. foil. He tried to *balk* the escape.

balmy ADJ. mild; fragrant. A *balmy* breeze refreshed us after the listless, humid days.

banal (bān'-) ADJ. hackneyed; commonplace; trite. His frequent use of clichés made his essay seem *banal*. banality, N.

ā — ale; ă — add; ä — arm; à — ask; ē — eve; ĕ — end; ê — err, her; ə — event, allow,
ī — ice; ĭ — ill; ō — old; ŏ — odd; ô — orb; ōō — food; ou — out; th — thin; ū — use;
ŭ — up; zh — pleasure

bandanna N. large, bright-colored handkerchief. She could be identified by the gaudy *bandanna* she wore on her head.

baneful ADJ. ruinous; poisonous. His *baneful* influence was feared by all.

bantering ADJ. good-natured ridiculing. They resented his *bantering* remarks because they thought he was being sarcastic.

ETYMOLOGY 3.

AQUA, AQUE (water)

    aqueduct   a passageway for conducting water; a conduit

    aquatic   living in water

    aqua fortis   nitric acid (strong water)

ARCH (chief, first) prefix

    archetype   original model

    archbishop   chief bishop

    archeology   study of antiquities (study of first things)

ARCH (government, ruler, first)

    monarch   sole ruler

    anarchy   lack of government

    archaeology   study of first or ancient times

ASTER, ASTR (star)

    astronomy   study of the stars

    asterisk   star-like type character (*)

    disaster   catastrophe (contrary star)

AUD, AUDIT (hear)

    audible   able to be heard

    auditorium   place where people may be heard

    audience   hearers

AUTO (self)

    autocracy   rule by self (one person)

    automobile   vehicle that moves by itself

    autobiography   story of a person's life written by himself

---

TEST — Word List 3 — Synonyms and Antonyms

Each of the following questions consists of a word printed in bold, followed by five words or phrases numbered 1 to 5. Choose the numbered word or phrase which is most nearly the same as or the

---

ā — ale; ă — add; ä — arm; å — ask; ē — eve; ĕ — end; ê — err, her; ə — event, allow.
ī — ice; ĭ — ill; ō — old; ŏ — odd; ô — orb; ōō — food; ou — out; th — thin; ū — use;
ŭ — up; zh — pleasure

opposite of the word in bold and write the number of your choice on your answer paper.

41. aquiline 1. watery 2. hooked 3. refined 4. antique 5. rodent-like

42. archaic 1. youthful 2. cautious 3. antiquated 4. placated 5. buttressed

43. ardor 1. zeal 2. paint 3. portal 4. group 5. excitement

44. artifice 1. spite 2. exception 3. anger 4. candor 5. loyalty

45. artisan 1. educator 2. decider 3. sculptor 4. discourser 5. unskilled laborer

46. ascertain 1. amplify 2. master 3. discover 4. retain 5. explode

47. asteroid 1. Milky Way 2. radiance 3. large planet 4. rising moon 5. setting moon

48. asperity 1. anguish 2. absence 3. innuendo 4. good temper 5. snake

49. assuage 1. stuff 2. describe 3. wince 4. worsen 5. introduce

50. astute 1. sheer 2. noisy 3. astral 4. unusual 5. foolish

51. atrocity 1. endurance 2. fortitude 3. session 4. heinous act 5. hatred

52. atypical 1. superfluous 2. booming 3. normal 4. clashing 5. lovely

53. audacity 1. boldness 2. asperity 3. strength 4. stature 5. anchorage

54. avarice 1. anxiety 2. generosity 3. statement 4. invoice 5. power

55. balmy 1. venturesome 2. dedicated 3. mild 4. fanatic 5. memorable

56. awry 1. recommended 2. commiserating 3. startled 4. straight 5. psychological

57. banal 1. philosophical 2. original 3. dramatic 4. heedless 5. discussed

58. baleful 1. doubtful 2. virtual 3. deadly 4. conventional 5. virtuous

59. auxiliary 1. righteous 2. prospective 3. assistant 4. archaic 5. mandatory

60. baneful 1. intellectual 2. thankful 3. decisive 4. nonpoisonous 5. remorseful

---

ā — ale; ă — add; ä — arm; å — ask; ē — eve; ĕ — end; ê — err, her; ə — event, allow, ī — ice; ĭ — ill; ō — old; ŏ — odd; ô — orb; ōō — food; ou — out; th — thin; ū — use; ŭ — up; zh — pleasure

---

Word List 4   barb-cadaverous

barb N. sharp projection from fishhook, etc. The *barb* from the fishhook caught in his finger as he grabbed the fish.   barbed, ADJ.

baroque (-rōk') ADJ. highly ornate. They found the *baroque* architecture amusing.

barrage (-äzh) N. barrier laid down by artillery fire. The company was forced to retreat through the *barrage* of heavy cannons.

barrister (bă-rəs) N. counselor-at-law. Galsworthy started as a *barrister* but, when he found the practice of law boring, turned to writing.

barterer N. trader. The *barterer* exchanged trinkets for the natives' furs.

bate (bāt) v. let down; restrain. Until it was time to open the presents, the children had to *bate* their curiosity.   bated, ADJ.

batten v. grow fat; thrive upon others. We cannot accept a system where a favored few can *batten* in extreme comfort while others toil.

bauble (bô-) N. trinket; trifle. The child was delighted with the *bauble* she had won in the grab-bag.

beatific (bē-ə-tĭf'-) ADJ. giving bliss; blissful. The *beatific* smile on the child's face made us very happy.

bedizen (bĕ-dĭz'-) v. dress with vulgar finery. The witch doctors were *bedizened* in all their gaudiest costumes.

bedraggle v. wet thoroughly. The little ducklings were *bedraggled* after the hurricane.   bedraggled, ADJ.

beguile (-gīl') v. delude; cheat; amuse. He *beguiled* himself during the long hours by playing solitaire.

behoove v. be suited to; be incumbent upon. In this time of crisis, it *behooves* all of us to remain calm and await the instructions of our superiors.

belabor v. beat soundly; assail verbally. He was *belaboring* his opponent.

belated ADJ. delayed. He sent *belated* greetings.

beleaguer v. besiege. Once the city was *beleaguered*, life became more subdued as the citizens began their long wait for outside assistance.   beleaguered, ADJ.

bellicose ADJ. warlike. His *bellicose* disposition alienated his friends.

benediction N. blessing. The appearance of the sun after the many rainy days was like a *benediction*.

benefactor N. gift giver; patron. Scrooge later became Tiny Tim's *benefactor*.

beneficiary N. person entitled to benefits or proceeds of an insurance policy or will. You may change your *beneficiary* as often as you wish.

ā — ale; ă — add; ä — arm; à — ask; ē — eve; ĕ — end; ê — err, her; ə — event, allow.
ī — ice; ĭ — ill; ō — old; ŏ — odd; ô — orb; ōō — food; ou — out; th — thin; ū — use;
ŭ — up; zh — pleasure

benevolent (-něv'-) ADJ. generous; charitable. His *benevolent* nature prevented him from refusing any beggar who accosted him.

benighted ADJ. overcome by darkness. In the *benighted* Middle Ages, intellectual curiosity was widely discouraged.

benign(-nīn') ADJ. kindly; favorable; not malignant. The old man was well-liked because of his *benign* attitude toward friend and stranger alike.

berate v. scold strongly. He feared she would *berate* him for his forgetfulness.

bereft ADJ. deprived of; lacking. The foolish gambler soon found himself *bereft* of funds.

berserk (bêr-sêrk') ADV. frenzied. Angered, he went *berserk* and began to wreck the room.

besmirch v. soil; defile. The scandalous remarks in the newspaper *besmirch* the reputations of every member of the society.

bestow v. confer. He wished to *bestow* great honors upon the hero.

bete noire (nwär') N. aversion; person or thing strongly disliked or avoided. Going to the opera was his personal *bete noire* because high-pitched sounds irritated him.

betroth (-trōth') v. become engaged to marry. The announcement that they had become *betrothed* surprised their friends who had not suspected any romance.   betrothal, N.

bicameral (bī-) ADJ. two-chambered, as a legislative body. The United States Congress is a *bicameral* body.

biennial (bī-) ADJ. every two years. The plant bore flowers *biennially*.

bigotry N. stubborn intolerance. Brought up in a democratic atmosphere, the student was shocked by the *bigotry* and narrow views expressed by several of his classmates.

billious ADJ. suffering from indigestion; irritable. His *billious* temperament was apparent to all who heard him rant about his difficulties.

bivouac (biv'-ōō-ăk) N. temporary encampment. While in *bivouac*, we spent the night in our sleeping bags under the stars.

bizarre (bĭ-zar') ADJ. fantastic; violently contrasting. The plot of the novel was too *bizarre* to be believed.

bland ADJ. soothing; mild. She used a *bland* ointment for her sunburn.

blandishment N. flattery. Despite his *blandishments*, the young lady rejected his companionship.

blasphemous (blăs'-fěm-) ADJ. profane; impious. The people in the room were shocked by his *blasphemous* language.

blatant (blā'-) ADJ. loudly offensive. I regard your remarks as *blatant* and ill-mannered.   blatancy, N.

ā — ale; ă — add; ä — arm; à — ask; ē — eve; ě — end; ê — err, her; ə — event, allow,
ī — ice; ĭ — ill; ō — old; ŏ — odd; ô — orb; ōō — food; ou — out; th — thin; ū — use;
ŭ — up; zh — pleasure

blazon (blāz'-) v. decorate with an heraldic coat of arms. *Blazoned* on his shield were the two lambs and the lion, the traditional coat of arms of his family.

bleak ADJ. cold; cheerless. The Aleutian Islands are *bleak* military outposts.

blighted ADJ. suffering from a disease; destroyed. The extent of the *blighted* areas could be seen only when viewed from the air.

blithe ADJ. gay; joyous. Shelley called the skylark a "*blithe* spirit" because of its happy song.

bloated ADJ. swollen or puffed as with water or air. The *bloated* corpse was taken from the river.

bludgeon (blŭj'-ən) N. club; heavy-headed weapon. His walking stick served him as a *bludgeon* on many occasions.

bode v. foreshadow; portend. The gloomy skies and the sulphurous odors from the mineral springs seemed to *bode* ill to those who settled in the area.

bogus ADJ. counterfeit; not authentic. The police quickly found the distributors of the *bogus* twenty-dollar bills.

boisterous ADJ. violent; rough; noisy. The unruly crowd became even more *boisterous* when he tried to quiet them.

bolster v. support; prop up. I do not intend to *bolster* your hopes with false reports of outside assistance. also N.

bombastic ADJ. pompous; using inflated language. The orator spoke in a *bombastic* manner. bombast, N.

bootless ADJ. useless. I "trouble deaf heaven with my *bootless* cries."

bouillon (bool'-yún) N. clear beef soup. The cup of *bouillon* served by the stewards was welcomed by those who had been chilled by the cold ocean breezes.

bountiful ADJ. generous; showing bounty. She distributed gifts in a *bountiful* and gracious manner.

bourgeois (boorzh'-wa) N. middle class person. The French Revolution was inspired by the *bourgeois*. also ADJ.

braggadocio (-dō'-shē-ō) N. boasting. He was disliked because his manner was always full of *braggadocio*.

bravado (-vàh'-dō) N. swagger; assumed air of defiance. The *bravado* of the young criminal disappeared when he was confronted by the victims of his brutal attack.

brazen (brā'-) ADJ. insolent. Her *brazen* contempt for authority angered the officials.

brazier (brā'-zhĕr) N. open pan in which live coals are burned. On chilly nights, the room was warmed by coals burning in *braziers*.

ā — ale; ă — add; ä — arm; à — ask; ē — eve; ĕ — end; ê — err, her; ə — event, allow, ī — ice; ĭ — ill; ō — old; ŏ — odd; ô — orb; ōō — food; ou — out; th — thin; ū — use; ŭ — up; zh — pleasure

breach N. breaking of contract or duty; fissure; gap. They found a *breach* in the enemy's fortifications and penetrated the lines.

brevity N. conciseness. "*Brevity* is the soul of wit."

bristling ADJ. rising like bristles; showing irritation. The dog stood there, *bristling* with anger.

broach V. open up. He did not even try to *broach* the subject of poetry.

brocade N. rich, textured fabric. The sofa was covered with expensive *brocade*.

brochure (brō-shôr') N. pamphlet. This *brochure* on farming was issued by the Department of Agriculture.

brooch (brōch-) N. ornamental clasp. She treasured the *brooch* because it was an heirloom.

brusque (brŭsk') ADJ. blunt; abrupt. She was offended by his *brusque* reply.

bucolic (bū-cŏl'-) ADJ. rustic; pastoral. The meadow was the scene of *bucolic* gaiety.

buffoonery N. clowning. Jimmy Durante's *buffoonery* was hilarious.

bullion (bool'-yŭn) N. gold and silver in the form of bars. Much *bullion* is stored in the vaults at Fort Knox.

bulwark (bŭl'-) N. earthwork or other strong defense; person who defends. The navy is our principal *bulwark* against invasion.

bumptious ADJ. self-assertive. His classmates called him a "show-off" because of his *bumptious* airs.

bungle V. spoil by clumsy behavior. I was afraid you would *bungle* this assignment but I had no one else to send.

burgeon (bu'-jən) V. grow forth; send out buds. In the spring, the *burgeoning* plants are a promise of the beauty that is to come.

burlesque V. give an imitation that ridicules. In his caricature, he *burlesqued* the mannerisms of his adversary.   also N.

burnish V. make shiny by rubbing; polish. The *burnished* metal reflected the lamplight.

buttress N. support or prop. The huge cathedral walls were flanked by flying *buttresses*.   also V.

buxom (bŭx'-) ADJ. plump; vigorous; jolly. The soldiers remembered the *buxom* nurse who had always been so pleasant to them.

cabal (-bál') N. small group of persons secretly united to promote their own interests. The *cabal* was defeated when its scheme was discovered.

cache (kăsh) N. hiding place. The detectives followed the suspect until he led them to the *cache* where he had stored his loot.

cacophony (kə-kŏf'-) N. discordant sound. Some people seem to enjoy the

ā — ale; ă — add; ä — arm; á — ask; ē — eve; ĕ — end; ê — err, her; ə — event, allow.
ī — ice; ĭ — ill; ō — old; ŏ — odd; ô — orb; ōō — food; ou — out; th — thin; ū — use;
ŭ — up; zh — pleasure

cacophony of an orchestra that is tuning up.

cadaver (kə-dăv'-) N. corpse. In some states, it is illegal to dissect *cadavers*.

cadaverous ADJ. like a corpse; pale. By his *cadaverous* appearance, we could see how the disease had ravaged him.

ETYMOLOGY 4.

BELLI (war)
- **bellicose**   inclined to fighting
- **belligerent**   engaged in war
- **rebellious**   warring against authority

BEN, BON (well, good)
- **benefactor**   one who does good
- **benevolence**   charity (wishing good)
- **bonus**   something extra above regular pay

BI (two) prefix
- **bicameral**   legislature consisting of two houses
- **biennial**   every two years
- **bicycle**   two-wheeled vehicle

BIBL (book)
- **bibliography**   list of books
- **bibliophile**   lover of books
- **Bible**   The Book

BIO (life)
- **biology**   study of living things
- **biography**   writing about a person's life
- **biochemist**   a student of the chemistry of living things

BREV, BREVE (short)
- **brevity**   briefness
- **abbreviate**   shorten
- **breve**   mark placed over vowel to indicate that it is short (a, as in hat)

CAD, CAS (to fall)
- **decadent**   deteriorating
- **cadence**   intonation, terminal musical phrase
- **cascade**   waterfall

ā — ale; ă — add; ä — arm; å — ask; ē — eve; ĕ — end; ê — err, her; ə — event, allow.
ī — ice; ĭ — ill; ō — old; ŏ — odd; ô — orb; ōō — food; ou — out; th — thin; ū — use;
ŭ — up; zh — pleasure

TEST — Word List 4 — Synonyms

Each of the questions below consists of a word printed in bold, followed by five words or phrases numbered 1 to 5. Choose the numbered word or phrase which is most nearly similar in meaning to the word in bold and write the number of your choice on your answer paper.

61. **baroque** 1. polished 2. constant 3. transformed 4. highly ornate 5. aglow

62. **benign** 1. tenfold 2. peaceful 3. blessed 4. wavering 5. favorable

63. **boisterous** 1. conflicting 2. noisy 3. testimonial 4. grateful 5. adolescent

64. **brazen** 1. shameless 2. quick 3. modest 4. pleasant 5. melodramatic

65. **barrister** 1. specialist 2. teacher 3. attorney 4. conductor 5. professor

66. **biennial** 1. yearly 2. every two years 3. favorable 4. impressive 5. celebrated

67. **bombastic** 1. sensitive 2. pompous 3. rapid 4. sufficient 5. expensive

68. **bucolic** 1. diseased 2. repulsive 3. rustic 4. twinkling 5. cold

69. **bauble** 1. mainstay 2. gas 3. soap 4. trifling piece of jewelry 5. expense

70. **bigotry** 1. arrogance 2. approval 3. mourning 4. promptness 5. intolerance

71. **bouillon** 1. insight 2. chowder 3. gold 4. clear soup 5. stew

72. **buxom** 1. voluminous 2. indecisive 3. convincing 4. plump 5. bookish

73. **beatific** 1. glorious 2. blissful 3. theatrical 4. crooked 5. hand- some

74. **bland** 1. mild 2. meager 3. soft 4. uncooked 5. helpless

75. **braggadocio** 1. Cyrano 2. boastfulness 3. skirmish 4. encounter 5. position

76. **cache** 1. lock 2. hiding place 3. tide 4. automobile 5. grappling hook

77. **bellicose** 1. war-like 2. navel 3. amusing 4. piecemeal 5. errant

ā — ale; ă — add; ä — arm; à — ask; ē — eve; ĕ — end; ê — err, her; ə — event, allow, ī — ice; ĭ — ill; ō — old; ŏ — odd; ô — orb; ōō — food; ou — out; th — thin; ū — use; ŭ — up; zh — pleasure

78. blithe   1. spiritual   2. profuse   3. gay   4. hybrid   5. comfortable
79. brochure   1. opening   2. pamphlet   3. censor   4. bureau   5. pin
80. cacophony   1. dissonance   2. dance   3. applause   4. type of telephone   5. rooster

---

Word List 5   cajole-churlish

cajole (-jōl') v. coax; wheedle. I will not be *cajoled* into granting you your wish.

caliber N. ability; capacity. A man of such *caliber* should not be assigned such menial tasks.

callous ADJ. hardened; unfeeling. He had worked in the hospital for so many years that he was *callous* to the suffering in the wards.   callus, N.

calorific (kăl-ə-rĭf'-) ADJ. heat producing. Coal is much more *calorific* than green wood.

calumniate (-ŭm'-) v. slander. Shakespeare wrote that love and friendship were subject to envious and *calumniating* time.

calumny (kăl'-) N. malicious misrepresentation; slander. He could endure his financial failure, but he could not bear the *calumny* that his foes heaped upon him.

cameo N. shell or jewel carved in relief. Tourists are advised not to purchase *cameos* from the street peddlers of Rome who sell poor specimens of the carver's art.

canard (när'd) N. unfounded rumor; exaggerated report. It is almost impossible to protect oneself from such a base *canard*.

candor N. frankness. The *candor* and simplicity of his speech impressed all.   candid, ADJ.

canker N. any ulcerous sore; any evil. Poverty is a *canker* in the body politic; it must be cured.

canny ADJ. shrewd; thrifty. The *canny* tourist was more than a match for the swindlers.

cant N. jargon of thieves; pious phraseology. Many listeners were fooled by the *cant* and hypocrisy of his speech.

cantata (-tä'h) N. story set to music, to be sung by a chorus. The choral society sang the new *cantata* composed by its conductor.

canter N. slow gallop. Because the race horse had outdistanced its competition so easily, the reporter wrote that the race was won in a *canter*.

ā — ale; ă — add; ä — arm; á — ask; ē — eve; ĕ — end; ê — err, her; ə — event, allow,
ī — ice; ĭ — ill; ō — old; ŏ — odd; ô — orb; ōō — food; ou — out; th — thin; ū — use;
ŭ — up; zh — pleasure

canto N. division of a long poem. In *The Man Without a Country,* Philip Nolan is upset when he reads one of Sir Walter Scott's *cantos.*

canvass V. determine votes, etc. After *canvassing* the sentiments of his constituents, the congressman was confident that he represented the majority opinion of his district.

capacious ADJ. spacious. In the *capacious* areas of the railroad terminal, thousands of travelers lingered while waiting for their trains.

caparison N., V. showy harness or ornamentation for a horse; put showy ornamentation on a horse. The gaily *caparisoned* horses made their entrance into the circus ring to the accompaniment of a lively march played by the band.

capitulate V. surrender. The enemy was warned to *capitulate* or face annihilation.

caprice (*-prēs'*) N. whim. Do not act on *caprice.* Study your problem.

capricious (*-pri'-*) ADJ. fickle; incalculable. He found her *capricious;* she changed her mind constantly without reason.

caption N. title; chapter heading; text under illustration. I find the *captions* which accompany these cartoons very clever and humorous.

captious ADJ. fault-finding. His criticisms were always *captious* and frivolous, never offering constructive suggestions.

carat N. unit of weight for precious stones; measure of fineness of gold. He gave her a three-*carat* diamond mounted in an eighteen-*carat* gold band.

caricature N. distortion; burlesque. The *caricatures* he drew always emphasized personal weaknesses of the people he burlesqued.

carmine (*kâr'-min*) N. rich red color. Her *carmine*-painted lips appeared black in the photograph.

carnage N. slaughter; mass of carcasses. The medics gagged at the sight of the *carnage* strewn across the battlefield.

carnal ADJ. concerning the body. The public was more interested in *carnal* pleasures than in spiritual matters.

carnivorous ADJ. meat-eating. The lion is a *carnivorous* animal. carnivore, N.

carousal (*-rouz'-*) N. drunken revel. The party degenerated into an ugly *carousal.*

carping ADJ. finding fault. A *carping* critic disturbs sensitive people.

carrion N. rotting flesh of a dead body. The buzzards ate the *carrion.*

carte blanche (*kârt-blähnsh*) N. unlimited authority or freedom. Use your own discretion in this matter; I give you *carte blanche.*

cascade N. small waterfall. We could not appreciate the beauty of the many

---

ā — ale; ă — add; ä — arm; å — ask; ē — eve; ĕ — end; ê — err, her; ə — event, allow, ī — ice; ĭ — ill; ō — old; ŏ — odd; ô — orb; o͞o — food; ou — out; th — thin; ū — use; ŭ — up; zh — pleasure

cascades as we were forced to make detours around each of them.

castigate v. punish. He decided to *castigate* the culprit personally.

casualty N. serious or fatal accident. The number of *casualties* on this holiday weekend was high.

cataclysm N. violent; upheaval. A *cataclysm* such as the French Revolution affects all countries. cataclysmic, ADJ.

catapult N. slingshot; a hurling machine. Airplanes are sometimes launched from battleships by *catapults*.

catastrophe N. calamity. The Johnstown flood was a *catastrophe*.

catechism N. book for religious instruction; instruction by question and answer. He taught by engaging his pupils in a *catechism* until they gave him the correct answer.

cathartic N. purgative. Some drugs act as laxatives when taken in small doses, but act as *cathartics* when taken in much larger doses.

catholic ADJ. broadly sympathetic; liberal. He was extremely *catholic* in his reading tastes.

caustic ADJ. burning; sarcastically biting. The critic's *caustic* remarks angered the unlucky actors who were the subjects of his sarcasm.

cauterize (*kôt'*-) v. burn with hot iron or caustic. In order to prevent infection, the doctor *cauterized* the wound.

cavalcade N. procession; parade. As described by Chaucer, the *cavalcade* of Canterbury pilgrims was a motley group.

cavil (*kăv'*-) v. make frivolous objections. I respect your sensible criticisms, but I dislike the way you *cavil* about unimportant details. also N.

cede (*sēd*) v. transfer; yield title to. I intend to *cede* this property to the city.

celestial ADJ. heavenly. He wrote about the music of "*celestial* spheres."

celibate (*sĕl'-ə-bət*) ADJ. unmarried; abstaining from sexual intercourse. He vowed to remain *celibate*. celibacy, N.

censor N. overseer of morals; person who reads to eliminate inappropriate remarks. Soldiers dislike having their mail read by a *censor* but understand the need for this precaution.

censure v. blame; criticize. He was *censured* for his ill-advised act. also N.

centaur (*sĕn-tôr*) N. mythical figure, half man and half horse. I was particularly impressed by the statue of the *centaur* in the Roman Hall of the museum.

centrifugal (*-trif'*-) ADJ. radiating; departing from the center. Many automatic drying machines remove excess moisture from clothing by *centrifugal* force.

centurion N. Roman army officer. Because he was in command of a company of one hundred soldiers, he was called a *centurion*.

ā — ale; ă — add; ä — arm; á — ask; ē — eve; ĕ — end; ê — err, her; ə — event, allow. ī — ice; ĭ — ill; ō — old; ŏ — odd; ô — orb; ōō — food; ou — out; th — thin; ū — use; ŭ — up; zh — pleasure

cerebral (*sĕ'-*) ADJ. pertaining to the brain or intellect. The content of philosophical works is *cerebral* in nature and requires much thought.

cerebration N. thought. Mathematics problems sometimes require much *cerebration*. cerebrate, V.

cessation N. stopping. The workers threatened a *cessation* of all activities if their demands were not met.

cession N. yielding to another; ceding. The *cession* of Alaska to the United States is discussed in this chapter.

chafe V. warm by rubbing; make sore by rubbing. The collar *chafed* his neck.

chaffing ADJ. bantering; joking. Sometimes his flippant and *chaffing* remarks annoy us.

chagrin (*shə-grin'*) N. vexation; disappointment. His refusal to go with us filled us with *chagrin*.

chalice N. goblet; consecrated cup. In a small room adjoining the cathedral, many ornately decorated *chalices* were on display.

chameleon (*ke-mēl'-yən*) N. lizard that changes color in different situations. Like the *chameleon*, he assumed the political thinking of every group he met.

champ V. chew noisily. His dining companions were amused by the way he *champed* his food.

chaotic (*kā-*) ADJ. in utter disorder. He tried to bring order into the *chaotic* state of affairs. chaos, N.

charisma (*kə-riz'-*) N. divine gift; great popular charm or appeal of a political leader. Political commentators have explored the importance of a candidate's *charisma* in these days of television campaigning.

charlatan (*shär'-*) N. quack; pretender to knowledge. This advertisement is the work of a *charlatan*.

chary (*chăr'-ē*) ADJ. cautiously watchful. She was *chary* of her favors.

chasm (*kăzm*) N. abyss. They could not see the bottom of the *chasm*.

chassis (*chăs'-ē*) N. framework and working parts of an automobile. Examining the car after the accident, the owner discovered that the body had been ruined but that the *chassis* was unharmed.

chaste (*chāst*) ADJ. pure. Her *chaste* and decorous garb was appropriately selected for the solemnity of the occasion. chastity, N.

chastise V. punish. I must *chastise* you for this offense.

chattel N. personal property. When he bought his furniture on the installment plan, he signed a *chattel* mortgage.

chauvinist (*shōv'-*) N. blindly devoted patriot. A *chauvinist* cannot recognize any faults in his country, no matter how flagrant they may be.

ā—ale; ă—add; ä—arm; à—ask; ē—eve; ĕ—end; ê—err, her; ə—event, allow;
ī—ice; ĭ—ill; ō—old; ŏ—odd; ô—orb; oo—food; ou—out; th—thin; ū—use;
ŭ—up; zh—pleasure

50 Basic Word List

checkered ADJ. marked by changes in fortune. During his *checkered* career he had lived in palatial mansions and in dreary boarding houses.

chicanery (shĭ-kā'-) N. trickery. The lawyer was guilty of *chicanery* in freeing his client.

chide V. scold. Grandma began to *chide* Junior for his lying.

chimerical (kĭ-mĕr'-) ADJ. fantastic; highly imaginative. Poe's *chimerical* stories are sometimes too morbid for reading in bed. chimera, N.

chiropodist (kĭr-ŏp'-) N. one who treats disorders of the feet. The *chiropodist* treated the ingrown nail on the boy's foot.

choleric (kŏl'-) ADJ. hot-tempered. His flushed, angry face indicated a *choleric* nature.

chronic ADJ. long-established as a disease. His *chronic* headaches worried the doctors.

churlish ADJ. boorish; rude. Dismayed by his *churlish* manners at the party, the girls vowed never to invite him again.

ETYMOLOGY 5.

CAP, CAPT, CEP, CIP (to take)
    participate take part
    precept a wise saying (originally a command)
    capture seize
CAP (head)
    decapitate behead
    captain chief
    capital major city or site; first-rate
CATA (down) prefix
    catastrophe disaster (turning down)
    cataract waterfall
    catapult hurl (throw down)
CED (to yield, to go)
    recede go back, withdraw
    antecedent that which goes before
    concede yield, agree with
CENT (one hundred)
    century one hundred years
    centennial hundredth anniversary
CHRONOS (time)
    chronology time table of events

ā — ale; ă — add; ä — arm; à — ask; ē — eve; ĕ — end; ê — err, her; ə — event, allow; ī — ice; ĭ — ill; ō — old; ŏ — odd; ô — orb; ōō — food; ou — out; th — thin; ū — use; ŭ — up; zh — pleasure

anachronism a thing out of time sequence, as Shakespeare's reference to clocks in *Julius Caesar*
chronicle register events in order

TEST — Word List 5 — Antonyms

Each of the questions below consists of a word printed in bold, followed by five words or phrases numbered 1 to 5. Choose the numbered word or phrase which is most nearly opposite in meaning to the word in bold and write the number of your choice on your answer paper.

81. **candid** 1. vague 2. secretive 3. experienced 4. anxious 5. sallow
82. **carnivorous** 1. gloomy 2. tangential 3. productive 4. weak 5. vegetarian
83. **celibate** 1. investing 2. married 3. retired 4. commodious 5. dubious
84. **chimerical** 1. developing 2. wonderful 3. disappearing 4. economical 5. realistic
85. **capacious** 1. warlike 2. cordial 3. curious 4. not spacious 5. not capable
86. **carousal** 1. awakening 2. sobriety 3. acceleration 4. direction 5. production
87. **censure** 1. process 2. enclose 3. interest 4. praise 5. penetrate
88. **choleric** 1. irascible 2. episodic 3. cool-headed 4. global 5. seasonal
89. **capricious** 1. satisfied 2. insured 3. photographic 4. scattered 5. steadfast
90. **catholic** 1. religious 2. pacific 3. narrow 4. weighty 5. funny
91. **cessation** 1. premium 2. gravity 3. beginning 4. composition 5. stoppage
92. **churlish** 1. marine 2. economical 3. polite 4. compact 5. young
93. **captious** 1. tolerant 2. capable 3. frivolous 4. winning 5. recollected
94. **carte blanche** 1. capitalistic 2. investment 3. importance 4. restriction 5. current
95. **chaste** 1. clean 2. clear 3. curt 4. wanton 5. outspoken

---

ā — ale; ă — add; ä — arm; à — ask; ē — eve; ĕ — end; ê — err, her; ə — event, allow, ī — ice; ĭ — ill; ō — old; ŏ — odd; ô — orb; oō — food; ou — out; th — thin; ū — use; ŭ — up; zh — pleasure

96. **chaffing**   1. achieving   2. serious   3. capitalistic   4. sneering   5. expensive
97. **carnal**   1. impressive   2. minute   3. spiritual   4. actual   5. private
98. **centrifugal**   1. centripetal   2. ephemeral   3. lasting   4. barometric   5. algebraic
99. **chide**   1. unite   2. fear   3. record   4. skid   5. praise
100. **carping**   1. acquiescent   2. mean   3. limited   4. farming   5. racing

---

Word List 6   ciliated-concise

ciliated ADJ. having minute hairs. The paramecium is a *ciliated*, one-celled animal.

circlet N. small ring; band. This tiny *circlet* is very costly because it is set with precious stones.

circuitous (-kū'-) ADJ. roundabout. Because of the traffic congestion on the main highways, he took a *circuitous* route.

circumscribe V. limit; confine. Although I do not wish to *circumscribe* your activities, I must insist that you complete this assignment before you start anything else.

circumspect ADJ. prudent; cautious. Investigating before acting, he tried always to be *circumspect*.

circumvent V. outwit; baffle. In order to *circumvent* the enemy, we will make two preliminary attacks in other sections before starting our major campaign.

citadel N. fortress. The *citadel* overlooked the city like a protecting angel.

cite V. quote; commend. He could *cite* passages in the Bible from memory.

clairvoyant (klãr-vôy'-) ADJ., N. having foresight; fortuneteller. Cassandra's *clairvoyant* warning was not heeded by the Trojans. clairvoyance, N.

clamber V. climb by crawling. He *clambered* over the wall.

clandestine (-dĕs'-tĭn) ADJ. secret. After escaping their chaperone, the lovers had a *clandestine* meeting.

clarion ADJ. shrill; trumpet-like sound. We woke to the *clarion* of the bugle.

claustrophobia (klôs-) N. fear of being enclosed. His fellow classmates laughed at his *claustrophobia* and often threatened to lock him in his room.

clavicle N. collarbone. He broke his *clavicle* in the football game.

cleave V. split asunder. The lightening *cleaves* the tree in two.   cleavage, N.

ā — ale; ă — add; ä — arm; à — ask; ē — eve; ĕ — end; ê — err, her; ə — event, allow,
ī — ice; ĭ — ill; ō — old; ŏ — odd; ô — orb; ōō — food; ou — out; th — thin; ū — use;
ŭ — up; zh — pleasure

cleft N. split. There was a *cleft* in the huge boulder.

clemency N. disposition to be lenient; mildness, as of the weather. The judge was noted for his *clemency* toward first offenders.

cliché (*klē-shā'*) N. phrase dulled in meaning by repetition. High school compositions are often marred by such *clichés* as "strong as an ox."

climactic ADJ. relating to the highest point. When he reached the *climactic* portion of the book, he could not stop reading.

clique (*klic*) N. small exclusive group. He charged that a *clique* had assumed control of school affairs.

cloister N. monastery or convent. The nuns lived in the *cloister*.

coadjutor (*kō-ăj'-*) N. assistant; colleague. He was assigned as *coadjutor* to the bishop.

coalesce V. combine; fuse. The brooks *coalesce* into one large river.

cockade N. decoration worn on hat. Members of that brigade can be recognized by the green and white *cockade* on their helmets.

coerce (*kō-ùrs'*) V. force. Do not *coerce* me into doing this.

cog N. tooth projecting from a wheel. On steep slopes, *cog* railways are frequently used to prevent slipping.

cogent (*kō'-jĕnt*) ADJ. convincing. He presented *cogent* arguments to the jury.

cogitate (*cŏj'-*) V. think over. *Cogitate* on this problem; the solution will come.

cognizance (*kŏg'-*) N. knowledge. During the election campaign, the two candidates were kept in full *cognizance* of the international situation.

cognomen N. family name. He asked the court to change his *cognomen* to a shorter name.

cohere V. stick together. Solids have a greater tendency to *cohere* than liquids.

cohesion N. force which keeps parts together. In order to preserve our *cohesion*, we must not let minor differences interfere with our major purposes.

cohort N. armed band. Caesar and his Roman *cohorts* conquered almost all of the known world.

coincident ADJ. occurring at the same time. Some people find the *coincident* events in Hardy's novels annoying.

collaborate V. work together. Two writers *collaborated* in preparing this book.

collate V. examine or compare critically; arrange in order. They *collated* the newly found manuscripts to determine their age.

collateral N. security given for loan. The sum you wish to borrow is so large that it must be secured by *collateral*.

ā — ale; ă — add; ä — arm; â — ask; ē — eve; ĕ — end; ê — err, her; a — event, allow,
ī — ice; ĭ — ill; ō — old; ŏ — odd; ô — orb; ōō — food; ou — out; th — thin; ū — use;
ŭ — up; zh — pleasure

collation N. a light meal. The ladies were served canapés at the *collation*.

collier N. worker in coal mine; ship carrying coal. The extended strike has prevented the *colliers* from delivering the coal to the docks as scheduled.

colloquy (kŏl'-) N. informal discussion. I enjoy our *colloquies*, but I sometimes wish that they could be made more formal and more searching.

collusion N. conspiring in a fraudulent scheme. The swindlers were found guilty of *collusion*.

colossal ADJ. huge. Radio City Music Hall has a *colossal* stage.

combustible ADJ. easily burned. After the recent outbreak of fires in private homes, the fire commissioner ordered that all *combustible* materials be kept in safe containers.

comely (kŭm'-) ADJ. attractive; agreeable. He would rather have a *comely* wife than a rich one.

comestible (-mĕs'-) N. something fit to be eaten. The roast turkey and other *comestibles*, the wines, and the excellent service made this Thanksgiving dinner particularly memorable.

comity N. courtesy; civility. A spirit of *comity* should exist among nations.

commandeer V. to draft for military purposes; to take for public use. The policeman *commandeered* the first car that approached and ordered the driver to go to the nearest hospital.

commensurate ADJ. equal in extent. Your reward will be *commensurate* with your effort.

commiserate V. feel or express pity or sympathy for. Her friends *commiserated* with the widow.

commodious ADJ. spacious and comfortable. After sleeping in small roadside cabins, they found their hotel suite *commodious*.

compact N. agreement; contract. The signers of the Mayflower *Compact* were establishing a form of government.

compatible ADJ. harmonious; in harmony with. They were *compatible* neighbors, never quarreling over unimportant matters.

compilation N. listing of statistical information in tabular or book form. The *compilation* of available scholarships serves a very valuable purpose.

complacent (-plā'-) ADJ. self-satisfied. There was a *complacent* look on his face as he examined his paintings.   complacency, N.

complaisant (kŏm-) ADJ. trying to please; obliging. The courtier obeyed the king's orders in a *complaisant* manner.

complement N. that which completes. A predicate *complement* completes the

ā — ale; ă — add; ä — arm; à — ask; ē — eve; ĕ — end; ê — err, her; ə — event, allow,
ī — ice; ĭ — ill; ō — old; ŏ — odd; ô — orb; ōō — food; ou — out; th — thin; ū — use;
ŭ — up; zh — pleasure

meaning of the subject. also V.

compliant ADJ. yielding. He was *compliant* and ready to conform to the pattern set by his friends.

comport V. bear oneself; behave. He *comported* himself with great dignity.

compunction N. remorse. Have you no *compunction* when you see the results of your act?

compute V. reckon; calculate. He failed to *compute* the interest.

concatenate V. link as in chain. It is difficult to understand how these events could *concatenate* as they did without outside assistance.

concentric ADJ. having a common center. The target was made of *concentric* circles.

conception N. beginning; forming of an idea. At the *conception* of the work, he was consulted.

conciliate V. pacify; win over. She tried to *conciliate* me with a gift. conciliation, N. conciliatory, ADJ.

concise ADJ. brief and compact. The essay was *concise* and explicit.

ETYMOLOGY 6.

CID, CIS (to cut, to kill)
        incision   a cut (surgical)
        homicide   killing of a man
        fratricide   killing of a brother

CIRCUM (around) prefix
        circumnavigate   sail around world
        circumspect   cautious (looking around)
        circumscribe   place a circle around

CIT, CITAT (to call, to start)
        incite   stir up, start up
        excite   stir up
        recitation   a calling-back again

CIVI (citizen)
        civilization   society of citizens, culture
        civilian   member of a community
        civil   courteous

CLAM, CLAMAT (to cry out)
        clamorous   loud
        declamation   a speech
        acclamation   shouted approval

ā — ale; ă — add; ä — arm; ă — ask; ē — eve; ĕ — end; ê — err, her; ə — event, allow,
ī — ice; ĭ — ill; ō — old; ŏ — odd; ô — orb; ōō — food; ou — out; th — thin; ū — use;
ŭ — up; zh — pleasure

CLAUD, CLAUS, CLOS, CLUD (to close)
    claustrophobia   fear of close places
    enclose   close in
    conclude   finish

CLE, CULE (small) noun suffix
    molecule   small mass
    corpuscle   blood cell
    follicle   small sac

COGNOSC, COGNIT (to learn)
    agnostic   lacking knowledge, skeptical
    incognito   traveling under assumed identity (without knowledge)
    cognition   knowledge

COM (with, together) prefix
    combine   merge with
    commerce   trade with
    communicate   correspond with by assimilation

COMP (to fill)
    complete   filled out
    complement   that which completes something
    comply   fulfill

TEST — Word List 6 — Synonyms and Antonyms

Each of the questions below consists of a word printed in bold, followed by five words or phrases numbered 1 to 5. Choose the numbered word or phrase which is most nearly the same as or the opposite of the word in bold and write the number of your choice on your answer paper.

101. clandestine   1. abortive   2. secret   3. tangible   4. doomed   5. approved

102. cognomen   1. family name   2. dwarf   3. suspicion   4. kind of railway   5. pseudopod

103. combustible   1. flammable   2. industrious   3. waterproof   4. specific   5. plastic

104. compliant   1. numerous   2. veracious   3. soft   4. adamant   5. livid.

105. ciliated   1. foolish   2. swift   3. early   4. constructed   5. hairy

---

ā — ale; ă — add; ä — arm; å — ask; ē — eve; ĕ — end; ê — err, her; ə — event, allow,
ī — ice; ĭ — ill; ō — old; ŏ — odd; ô — orb; ōō — food; ou — out; th — thin; ū — use;
ŭ — up; zh — pleasure

106. cleft   1. split   2. waterfall   3. assembly   4. parfait   5. surplus
107. cohesion   1. independence   2. pedestrian   3. shift   4. pharmacy   5. climbing
108. comestible   1. vigorous   2. fit to be eaten   3. liquid   4. beautiful   5. circumvented
109. circuitous   1. direct   2. complete   3. obvious   4. aware   5. tortured
110. cliché   1. increase   2. vehicle   3. morale   4. original   5. pique
111. coincidental   1. simultaneous   2. changing   3. fortuitous   4. startling   5. trivial
112. collation   1. furor   2. emphasis   3. distillery   4. spree   5. lunch
113. claustrophobia   1. lack of confidence   2. fear of spiders   3. love of books   4. fear of grammar   5. fear of closed places
114. cite   1. galvanize   2. visualize   3. locate   4. quote   5. signal
115. coerce   1. recover   2. total   3. force   4. license   5. ignore
116. cognizance   1. policy   2. ignorance   3. advance   4. omission   5. examination
117. colloquy   1. dialect   2. diversion   3. announcement   4. discussion   5. expansion
118. conciliate   1. defend   2. activate   3. integrate   4. quarrel   5. react
119. commiserate   1. communicate   2. expand   3. repay   4. diminish   5. sympathize
120. commodious   1. numerous   2. accommodating   3. leisurely   4. limited   5. expensive

---

Word List 7   conclave-crux

conclave N. private meeting. He was present at all their *conclaves* as a sort of unofficial observer.

concoct V. prepare by combining; make up or devise. How did you ever *concoct* such a strange dish?   concoction, N.

concomitant N. that which accompanies. Culture is not always a *concomitant* of wealth.   also ADJ.

concurrent ADJ. happening at the same time. In America, the colonists were resisting the demands of the mother country; at the *concurrent* moment in France, the middle class was sowing the seeds of

---

ā — ale; ă — add; ä — arm; á — ask; ē — eve; ĕ — end; ê — err, her; a — event, allow,
ī — ice; ĭ — ill; ō — old; ŏ — odd; ô — orb; o͞o — food; ou — out; th — thin; ū — use;
ŭ — up; zh — pleasure

rebellion.

condescend v. bestow courtesies with a superior air. The king *condescended* to grant an audience to the friends of the condemned man. condescension, N.

condign (*-dīn'*) ADJ. adequate; deservedly severe. The public approved the *condign* punishment.

condiments N. seasonings; spices. Spanish food is full of *condiments*.

condole v. express sympathetic sorrow. His friends gathered to *condole* with him over his loss. condolence, N.

condone v. overlook; forgive. We cannot *condone* your recent criminal cooperation with the gamblers.

confiscate v. seize; commandeer. The army *confiscated* all available supplies of uranium.

conformity N. harmony; agreement. In *conformity* with our rules and rregulations, I am calling a meeting of our organization.

congeal (*-jēl'*) v. freeze; coagulate. His blood *congealed* in his veins as he saw the dread monster rush toward him.

congenital ADJ. existing at birth. His *congenital* deformity disturbed his parents.

conglomeration N. mass of material sticking together. In such a *conglomeration* of miscellaneous statistics, it was impossible to find a single area for analysis.

congruence N. correspondence of parts; harmonious relationship. The student demonstrated the *congruence* of the two triangles by using the hypotenuse-arm theorem.

conifer N. pine tree; cone-bearing tree. According to geologists, the *conifers* were the first plants to bear flowers.

conjugal ADJ. pertaining to marriage. Their dreams of *conjugal* bliss were shattered as soon as their temperaments clashed.

connivance (*-nī'-*) N. pretense of ignorance of something wrong; passive cooperation. With the *connivance* of his friends, he plotted to embarrass the teacher. connive, v.

connoisseur (*kŏn-ə-sûr'*) N. person competent to act as a judge of art, etc.; a lover of an art. He had developed into a *connoisseur* of fine china.

connotation N. suggested or implied meaning of an expression. Foreigners frequently are unaware of the *connotations* of the words they use.

connubial (*-nū'-*) ADJ. pertaining to marriage or the matrimonial state. In his telegram, he wished the newlyweds a lifetime of *connubial* bliss.

consanguinity N. kinship. The lawsuit was interrupted by a charge that

---

ā — ale; ă — add; ä — arm; à — ask; ē — eve; ĕ — end; ê — err, her; ə — event, allow,
ĭ — ice; ĭ — ill; ō — old; ŏ — odd; ô — orb; ōō — food; ou — out; th — thin; ū — use;
ŭ — up; zh — pleasure

consanguinity existed between the defendant and one of the jurors.

consecrate V. dedicate; sanctify. We shall *consecrate* our lives to this noble purpose.

consensus N. general agreement. The *consensus* indicates that we will not enter into this pact.

consort V. associate with. We frequently judge people by the company with whom they *consort*. also N.

constraint N. restraint; repression of feelings. There was a feeling of *constraint* in the room because no one dared to criticize the speaker.

construe V. explain; interpret. If I *construe* your remarks correctly, you disagree with the theory already advanced.

consummate (-sŭm'-) ADJ. complete. You are a *consummate* idiot. also V.

contaminate V. pollute. The sewage system of the city so *contaminated* the water that swimming was forbidden.

contemn V. regard with contempt; despise. I will not tolerate those who *contemn* the sincere efforts of this group.

contentious ADJ. quarrelsome. We heard loud and *contentious* noises in the next room.

context N. writings preceding and following passage quoted. Because these lines are taken out of *context*, they do not convey the message the author intended.

contiguous ADJ. adjacent to; touching upon. The two countries are *contiguous* for a few miles; then they are separated by the gulf.

continence N. self-restraint; sexual chastity. He vowed to lead a life of *continence*. continent, ADJ.

contingent ADJ. conditional. The continuation of this contract is *contingent* upon the quality of your first output. contingency, N.

contortion N. twisting; distortion. As the effects of the opiate wore away, the *contortions* of the patient became more violent.

contraband N., ADJ. illegal trade; smuggling. The Coast Guard tries to prevent traffic in *contraband* goods.

contravene V. contradict; infringe on. I will not attempt to *contravene* your argument for it does not affect the situation.

contrite ADJ. penitent. Her *contrite* tears did not influence the judge when he imposed sentence. contrition, N.

controvert V. oppose with arguments; contradict. To *controvert* your theory will require much time but it is essential that we refute it.

contumacious ADJ. disobedient; resisting authority. The *contumacious* mob

---

ā — ale; ă — add; ä — arm; à — ask; ē — eve; ĕ — end; ê — err, her; ə — event, allow, ī — ice; ĭ — ill; ō — old; ŏ — odd; ô — orb; ōō — food; ou — out; th — thin; ū — use; ŭ — up; zh — pleasure

shouted defiantly at the police.   contumacy, N.

contumely (*kŏn'-tūm-lē*) N. scornful insolence; insult. The "proud man's *contumely*" is distasteful to Hamlet.

contusion N. bruise. He was treated for *contusions* and abrasions.

convene V. assemble. The assembly will *convene* in January.

conversant (*kŏn'-*) ADJ. familiar with. The lawyer is *conversant* with all the evidence.

conveyance N. vehicle; transfer. During the transit strike, commuters used various kinds of *conveyances*.

convivial ADJ. festive; gay; characterized by joviality. The *convivial* celebrators of the victory sang their college songs.

convoke V. call together. Congress was *convoked* at the outbreak of the emergency.

copious ADJ. plentiful. He had *copious* reasons for rejecting the proposal.

coquette (*kō-kĕt'*) N. flirt. Because she refused to give him any answer to his proposal of marriage, he called her a *coquette*.

cornice N. projecting moulding on building (usually above columns). Because the *cornice* stones had been loosened by the storms, the police closed the building until repairs could be made.

corporeal (*-pôr'-ē-əl*) ADJ. bodily; material. He was not a churchgoer; he was interested only in *corporeal* matters.

corpulent ADJ. very fat. The *corpulent* man resolved to reduce.   corpulence, N.

corroborate V. confirm. Unless we find a witness to *corroborate* your evidence, it will not stand up in court.

corrosive ADJ. eating away by chemicals. Stainless steel is able to withstand the effects of *corrosive* chemicals.

corsair (*kôrs'-*) N. pirate; pirate ship. The *corsairs*, preying on shipping in the Mediterranean, were often inspired by racial and religious hatreds as well as by the desire for money and booty.

cortege (*kôr-tĕzh'*) N. procession. The funeral *cortege* proceeded slowly down the avenue.

cosmic ADJ. pertaining to the universe; vast. *Cosmic* rays derive their name from the fact that they bombard the earth's atmosphere from outer space.

coterie (*kōt'-*) N. group that meets socially; select circle. After his book had been published, he was invited to join the literary *coterie* that lunched daily at the hotel.

countermand V. cancel; revoke. The general *countermanded* the orders is-

ā — ale; ă — add; ä — arm; à — ask; ē — eve; ĕ — end; ê — err, her; ə — event, allow,
ī — ice; ĭ — ill; ō — old; ŏ — odd; ô — orb; ōō — food; ou — out; th — thin; ū — use;
ŭ — up; zh — pleasure

sued in his absence.

counterpart N. a thing that completes another; things very much alike. Night and day are *counterparts*.

covenant N. agreement. We must comply with the terms of the *covenant*.

covert (kŭ'-) ADJ. secret; hidden; implied. He could understand the *covert* threat in the letter.

covetous ADJ. avaricious; eagerly desirous of. He was *covetous* of fame. covet, V.

cower V. shrink quivering, as from fear. The frightened child *cowered* in the corner of the room.

coy ADJ. shy; modest; coquettish. She was *coy* in her answers to his offer.

crabbed (krăb'-ed) ADJ. sour; peevish. The *crabbed* old man was avoided by the children because he scolded them when they made noise.

crass ADJ. very unrefined; grossly insensible. The philosophers deplored the *crass* commercialism.

craven (crā'-) ADJ. cowardly. His *craven* behavior in this critical period was deplored.

credence (krē'-) N. belief. Do not place any *credence* in his promises.

credulity (krĭ-dū'-) N. readiness to believe. The witch doctor took advantage of the *credulity* of the superstitious natives.   credulous, ADJ.

creed N. system of religious or ethical belief. In any loyal American's *creed*, love of democracy must be emphasized.

crestfallen ADJ. dejected; dispirited. We were surprised at his reaction to the failure of his project; instead of being *crestfallen*, he was busily engaged in planning new activities.

crevice N. crack; fissure. The mountain climbers found footholds in the tiny *crevices* in the mountainside.

criterion N. standard used in judging. What *criterion* did you use when you selected this essay as the prize winner?   criteria, PL.

crone N. hag. The toothless *crone* frightened us when she smiled.

crux N. crucial point. This is the *crux* of the entire problem.

ETYMOLOGY 7.

CONTR (against)
        contradict   disagree
        controversy   dispute (turning against)
        contrary   opposed

ā — ale; ă — add; ä — arm; á — ask; ē — eve; ĕ — end; ê — err, her; ə — event, allow, ī — ice; ĭ — ill; ō — old; ŏ — odd; ô — orb; ōō — food; ou — out; th — thin; ū — use; ŭ — up; zh — pleasure

CORD (heart)
- **accord**   agreement (from the heart)
- **cordial**   friendly
- **discord**   lack of harmony

CORPOR (body)
- **incorporate**   organize into a body
- **corporeal**   pertaining to the body or physical mass
- **corpse**   a dead body

CRED (to believe)
- **incredulous**   not believing, skeptical
- **credulity**   gullibility
- **credence**   belief

TEST — Word List 7 — Synonyms

Each of the questions below consists of a word printed in bold, followed by five words or phrases numbered 1 to 5. Choose the numbered word or phrase which is most nearly similar in meaning to the word in bold and write the number of your answer on your answer paper.

121. **condone**   1. stop   2. evaluate   3. pierce   4. infuriate   5. overlook

122. **consanguinity**   1. kinship   2. friendship   3. blood-letting   4. relief   5. understanding

123. **continence**   1. humanity   2. research   3. embryology   4. bodies of land   5. self-restraint

124. **confiscate**   1. discuss   2. discover   3. seize   4. exist   5. convey

125. **consensus**   1. general agreement   2. project   3. insignificance   4. sheaf   5. crevice

126. **conformity**   1. agreement   2. ambition   3. confinement   4. pride   5. restraint

127. **construe**   1. explain   2. promote   3. reserve   4. erect   5. block

128. **congenital**   1. slight   2. obscure   3. thorough   4. existing at birth   5. classified

129. **contaminate**   1. arrest   2. prepare   3. pollute   4. beam   5. inform

130. **connoisseur**   1. gourmand   2. lover of art   3. humidor   4. delinquent   5. interpreter

131. **contentious**   1. squealing   2. surprising   3. quarrelsome   4.

ā — ale; ă — add; ä — arm; å — ask; ē — eve; ĕ — end; ê — err, her; ə — event, allow, ī — ice; ĭ — ill; ō — old; ŏ — odd; ô — orb; o͞o — food; ou — out; th — thin; ū — use; ŭ — up; zh — pleasure

smug   5. creative

132. contraband   1. purpose   2. rogue   3. rascality   4. difficulty   5. smuggled goods

133. copious   1. plentiful   2. cheating   3. dishonorable   4. adventurous   5. inspired

134. contrite   1. smart   2. penitent   3. restful   4. recognized   5. perspiring

135. corpulent   1. regenerate   2. obese   3. different   4. hungry   5. bloody

136. controvert   1. question   2. contradict   3. mind   4. explain   5. swing

137. craven   1. desirous   2. direct   3. cowardly   4. civilized   5. controlled

138. contumely   1. sensation   2. noise   3. silence   4. insult   5. classic

139. crux   1. acne   2. spark   3. events   4. crucial point   5. belief

140. conversant   1. ignorant   2. speaking   3. incorporated   4. familiar   5. pedantic

---

Word List 8   cryptic-despoil

cryptic ADJ. mysterious; hidden; secret. His *cryptic* remarks could not be interpreted.

cuisine (kwə-zēn′) N. style of cooking. French *cuisine* is noted for its use of sauces and wines.

culinary (kūl′-) ADJ. relating to cooking. Many chefs attribute their *culinary* skills to the wise use of spices.

cull V. pick out; reject. Every month the farmer *culls* the nonlaying hens from his flock and sells them to the local butcher.

culmination N. attainment of highest point. His inauguration as president of the United States marked the *culmination* of his political career. culminate, V.

culpable ADJ. deserving blame. Corrupt politicans who condone the activities of the gamblers are equally *culpable*.

cupidity N. greed. The defeated people could not satisfy the *cupidity* of the conquerors who demanded excessive tribute.

curry V. dress; treat leather; seek favor. The courtier *curried* the favors of the king.

ā — ale; ă — add; ä — arm; à — ask; ē — eve; ĕ — end; ê — err, her; ə — event, allow,
ī — ice; ĭ — ill; ō — old; ŏ — odd; ô — orb; ōō — food; ou — out; th — thin; ū — use;
ŭ — up; zh — pleasure

cursory ADJ. casual; hastily done. A *cursory* glance revealed no trace of the missing book.

curtail V. shorten; reduce. During the oil shortage, we had to *curtail* our use of this vital commodity.

cynic N. one who is skeptical or distrustful of human motives. A *cynic* at all times, he was suspicious of all altruistic actions of others. cynical, ADJ.

dais (dā'-əs) N. raised platform for guests of honor. When he approached the *dais*, he was greeted by cheers from the people who had come to honor him.

dally V. trifle with; procrastinate. Laertes told Ophelia that Hamlet could only *dally* with her affections.

dank ADJ. damp. The walls of the dungeon were *dank* and slimy.

dastard N. coward. This sneak attack is the work of a *dastard*. dastardly, ADJ.

daunt V. intimidate. Your threats cannot *daunt* me.

dauntless ADJ. bold. Despite the dangerous nature of the undertaking, the *dauntless* soldier volunteered for the assignment.

dawdle V. loiter; waste time. Inasmuch as we must meet a deadline, do not *dawdle* over this work.

dearth (dĕrth) N. scarcity. The *dearth* of skilled labor compelled the employers to open trade schools.

debase V. reduce to lower state. Do not *debase* yourself by becoming maudlin.

debauch V. corrupt; make intemperate. An irresponsible newspaper can *debauch* public ideals. debauchery, N.

debilitate V. weaken; enfeeble. Overindulgence *debilitates* character as well as physical stamina.

debonair ADJ. suave; aiming to please. The *debonair* youth was liked by all who met him because of his cheerful and obliging manner.

debutante (dĕb'-ū-tänt) N. young lady making formal entrance into society. As a *debutante*, she was often mentioned in the society columns of the newspapers.

decadence (dĕk'-) N. decay. The moral *decadence* of the people was reflected in the lewd literature of the period.

decant (-kănt') V. pour off gently. Be sure to *decant* this wine before serving it.

deciduous ADJ. falling off as of leaves. The oak is a *deciduous* tree.

declivity N. downward slope. The gentle *declivity* was sufficient to cause the brakes on his car to fail.

decorous ADJ. proper. Her *decorous* behavior was praised by her teachers. decorum, N.

ā — ale; ă — add; ä — arm; à — ask; ē — eve; ĕ — end; ê — err, her; ə — event, allow, ī — ice; ĭ — ill; ō — old; ŏ — odd; ô — orb; ōō — food; ou — out; th — thin; ū — use; ŭ — up; zh — pleasure

decoy ('-$k\widehat{oe}$) N. lure or bait. The wild ducks were not fooled by the *decoy*. also V.

decrepit ADJ. worn out by age. The *decrepit* car blocked traffic on the highway.

decry V. disparage. Do not attempt to increase your stature by *decrying* the efforts of your opponents.

deducible ADJ. derived by reasoning. If we accept your premise, your conclusions are easily *deducible*.

defalcate (-$f\breve{a}l$'-) V. misuse money held in trust. Legislation was passed to punish brokers who *defalcated* their clients' funds.

defamation N. harming a person's reputation. Such *defamation* of character may result in a libel suit.

default N. failure to act. As a result of her husband's failure to appear in court, she was granted a divorce by *default*. also V.

defeatist ADJ. attitude of one who is ready to accept defeat as a natural outcome. If you maintain your *defeatist* attitude, you will never succeed. also N.

defection N. deseertion. The children, who had made him an idol, were hurt most by his *defection* from our cause.

deference ($d\breve{e}f$'-) N. courteous regard for another's wish. In *deference* to his desires, the employers granted him a holiday.

defile V. pollute; profane. The hoodlums *defiled* the church with their scurrilous writing.

definitive ADJ. final; complete. Carl Sanburg's *Abraham Lincoln* may be regarded as the *definitive* work on the life of the Great Emancipator.

deflect V. turn aside. His life was saved when his cigarette case *deflected* the bullet.

defunct ADJ. dead; no longer in use or existence. The lawyers sought to examine the books of the *defunct* corporation.

deign ($d\bar{a}n$) V. condescend. Will he *deign* to answer your letter?

delete V. erase; strike out. If you *delete* this paragraph, the composition will have more appeal.

deleterious (-$t\bar{e}r$'-) ADJ. harmful. Workers in nuclear research must avoid the *deleterious* effects of radioactive substances.

delineation N. portrayal. He is a powerful storyteller, but he is weakest in his *delineation* of character.

delirium N. mental disorder marked by confusion. The drunkard in his *delirium* saw strange animals. delirious, ADJ.

delude V. deceive. Do not *delude* yourself into believing that he will relent.

delusion N. false belief; hallucination. This scheme is a snare and a *delusion*.

$\bar{a}$ — $\underline{a}$le; $\breve{a}$ — $\underline{a}$dd; $\ddot{a}$ — $\underline{a}$rm; $\mathring{a}$ — $\underline{a}$sk; $\bar{e}$ — $\underline{e}$ve; $\breve{e}$ — $\underline{e}$nd; $\hat{e}$ — $\underline{e}$rr, h$\underline{e}$r; ϑ — $\underline{e}$vent, all$\underline{o}$w,
$\bar{i}$ — $\underline{i}$ce; $\breve{i}$ — $\underline{i}$ll; $\bar{o}$ — $\underline{o}$ld; $\breve{o}$ — $\underline{o}$dd; $\hat{o}$ — $\underline{o}$rb; $\overline{oo}$ — f$\underline{oo}$d; ou — $\underline{ou}$t; th — $\underline{th}$in; $\bar{u}$ — $\underline{u}$se;
$\breve{u}$ — $\underline{u}$p; zh — plea$\underline{s}$ure

delusive ADJ. deceptive; raising vain hopes. Do not raise your hopes on the basis of his *delusive* promises.

demagogue N. person who appeals to people's prejudices; false leader of people. He was accused of being a *demagogue* because he made promises which aroused futile hopes in his listeners.

demean V. degrade; condescend to do. He could not *demean* himself in this matter.

demeanor N. behavior; bearing. His sober *demeanor* quieted the noisy revelers.

demise (-*mīz'*) N. death. Upon the *demise* of the dictator, a bitter dispute about succession to power developed.

demolition N. destruction. One of the major aims of the air force was the complete *demolition* of all means of transportation by bombing of rail lines and terminals.

demonic (-*món'*-) ADJ. fiendish. The Spanish Inquisition devised many *demonic* means of torture. demon, N.

demur V. delay; object. Do not *demur* at my request.

demure ADJ. serious; coy. She was *demure* and reserved.

denizen (*děn'*-) N. inhabitant. Ghosts are *denizens* of the land of the dead.

depict V. portray. In this book, the author *depicts* the slave owners as kind and benevolent masters.

depilate (*děp'*-) V. remove hair. Many women *depilate* their legs.

deplete V. reduce; exhaust. We must wait until we *deplete* our present inventory before we order replacements.

deploy V. move troops so that the battle line is extended at the expense of depth. The general *deployed* the troops along the border in order to meet the offensive of the enemy.

deposition N. testimony under oath. He made his *deposition* in the judge's chamber.

depravity N. corruption; wickedness. The *depravity* of his behavior shocked all.

deprecate (*děp'*-) V. disapprove regretfully. I must *deprecate* your attitude and hope that you will change your mind.

deprecatory ADJ. disapproving. Your *deprecatory* criticism has offended the author.

depreciate V. lessen in value. If you neglect this property, it will *depreciate*.

depredation N. plundering. After the *depredations* of the invaders, the people were penniless.

deranged ADJ. insane. He was mentally *deranged*.

derelict ADJ. abandoned. The *derelict* craft was a menace to navigation.

ā — ale; ă — add; ä — arm; å — ask; ē — eve; ĕ — end; ê — err, her; ə — event, allow, ī — ice; ĭ — ill; ō — old; ŏ — odd; ô — orb; ōō — food; ou — out; th — thin; ū — use; ŭ — up; zh — pleasure

also N.

deride v. scoff at. The people *derided* his grandiose schemes.

derision N. ridicule. They greeted his proposal with *derision* and refused to consider it seriously.

dermatologist N. physician who treats the skin and its diseases. I advise you to consult a *dermatologist* about your acne.

derogatory ADJ. expressing a low opinion. I resent your *derogatory* remarks.

descant v. discuss fully. He was willing to *descant* upon any topic of conversation, even when he knew very little about the subject under discussion.

descry (-skrī′) v. catch sight of. In the distance, we could barely *descry* the enemy vessels.

desecrate v. profane; violate the sanctity of. The soldiers *desecrated* the temple.

desiccate v. dry up. A tour of this smokehouse will give you an idea of how the pioneers used to *desiccate* food in order to preserve it.

despicable (dĕs′-) ADJ. contemptible. Your *despicable* remarks call for no reply.

despise v. scorn. I *despise* your attempts at a reconciliation at this time.

despoil v. plunder. If you do not yield, I am afraid the enemy will *despoil* the buildings.

ETYMOLOGY 8.

CUR (to care)
  curator person in charge
  sinecure position without responsibility
  secure safe
CURR, CURS (to run)
  excursion journey
  cursory brief
  precursor forerunner
CY (state of being) noun suffix (occurrence event
  democracy a democratic state
  obstinacy state of being stubborn
  accuracy state of being accurate
DA, DAT (to give)
  data facts, statistics
  mandate command

ā — ale; ă — add; ä — arm; å — ask; ē — eve; ĕ — end; ê — err, her; ə — event, allow,
ī — ice; ĭ — ill; ō — old; ŏ — odd; ô — orb; ōō — food; ou — out; th — thin; ū — use;
ŭ — up; zh — pleasure

date given time

DE (down, away) prefix

debase lower in value

decadence deterioration

decant pour off

DEB, DEBIT (to owe)

debt something owed

indebtedness debt

debenture bond

DEMO (people)

democracy rule of the people

demagogue (false) leader of the people

epidemic widespread disease (among the people)

DERM (skin)

epidermis skin

pachyderm thick-skinned quadruped

dermatology study of skin and its disorders

TEST — Word List 8 — Antonyms

Each of the questions below consists of a word printed in bold, followed by five words or phrases numbered 1 to 5. Choose the numbered word or phrase which is most nearly opposite in meaning to the word in bold and write the number of your choice on your answer paper.

141. **cryptic** 1. tomblike 2. secret 3. famous 4. candid 5. coded
142. **dank** 1. dry 2. guiltless 3. warm 4. babbling 5. reserved
143. **cupidity** 1. anxiety 2. tragedy 3. generosity 4. entertainment 5. love
144. **dastard** 1. illegitimacy 2. hero 3. presence 4. warmth 5. idol
145. **curtail** 1. mutter 2. lengthen 3. express 4. burden 5. shore
146. **dauntless** 1. stolid 2. weak 3. irrelevant 4. peculiar 5. particular
147. **cynical** 1. trusting 2. effortless 3. conclusive 4. gallant 5. vertical
148. **debilitate** 1. bedevil 2. repress 3. strengthen 4. animate 5. deaden
149. **debonair** 1. awkward 2. windy 3. balmy 4. sporty 5. stormy

ā — ale; ă — add; ä — arm; å — ask; ē — eve; ĕ — end; ê — err, her; ə — event, allow, ī — ice; ĭ — ill; ō — old; ŏ — odd; ô — orb; o͞o — food; ou — out; th — thin; ū — use; ŭ — up; zh — pleasure

150. declivity 1. trap 2. quadrangle 3. quarter 4. activity 5. upward slope

151. derogatory 1. roguish 2. immediate 3. opinionated 4. praising 5. conferred

152. decrepit 1. momentary 2. emotional 3. suppressed 4. youthful 5. unexpected

153. depravity 1. goodness 2. sadness 3. heaviness 4. tidiness 5. seriousness

154. defection 1. determination 2. joining 3. invitation 4. affection 5. cancellation

155. deranged 1. sane 2. announced 3. neighborly 4. alphabetical 5. arranged

156. defalcate 1. abscond 2. elope 3. observe 4. panic 5. use money held in trust properly

157. desecrate 1. desist 2. integrate 3. confuse 4. intensify 5. consecrate

158. defile 1. manicure 2. ride 3. purify 4. assemble 5. order

159. despicable 1. steering 2. worthy of esteem 3. inevitable 4. featureless 5. incapable

160. deleterious 1. delaying 2. experimental 3. harmless 4. graduating 5. glorious

---

Word List 9   despotism-diverse

despotism N. tyranny. The people rebelled against the *despotism* of the king.

destitute ADJ. extremely poor. The illness left the family *destitute.*

desuetude (dĕs'wə-) N. disused condition. The machinery in the idle factory was in a state of *desuetude.*

desultory (dĕs'-) ADJ. aimless; jumping around. The animals' *desultory* behavior indicated that they had no awareness of their predicament.

detergent N. cleansing agent. Many new *detergents* have replaced soap.

detonation N. explosion. The *detonation* could be heard miles away. detonate, V.

detraction N. slandering; aspersion. He is offended by your frequent *detractions* from his ability as a leader.

detriment N. harm; damage. Your acceptance of his support will ultimately

---

ā — ale; ă — add; ä — arm; å — ask; ē — eve; ĕ — end; ê — err, her; ə — event, allow,
ī — ice; ĭ — ill; ō — old; ŏ — odd; ô — orb; ōō — food; ou — out; th — thin; ū — use;
ŭ — up; zh — pleasure

prove to be a *detriment* rather than an aid to your cause.

deviate (dēv'-) v. turn away from. Do not *deviate* from the truth.

devious ADJ. going astray; erring. His *devious* behavior puzzled his friends.

devoid ADJ. lacking. He was *devoid* of any personal desire for gain in his endeavor to secure improvement in the community

devolve v. deputize; pass to others. It *devolved* upon us, the survivors, to arrange peace terms with the enemy.

devout ADJ. pious. The *devout* man prayed daily.

dexterous ADJ. skillful. The magician was so *dexterous* that we could not follow him as he performed his tricks.

diabolical ADJ. devilish. This scheme is so *diabolical* that I must reject it.

diadem (dī'- -) N. crown. The king's *diadem* was on display at the museum.

dialectic N. art of debate. I am not skilled in *dialectic* and, therefore, cannot answer your arguments as forcefully as I wish.

diaphanous (dī-ăf'-) ADJ. sheer; transparent. They admired her *diaphanous* and colorful dress.

dichotomy (dī-kŏt'-) N. branching into two parts. Your demand that I respond with either a "yes" or a "no" presupposes a *dichotomy* of choice on this issue that I do not accept.

dictum N. authoritative and weighty statement. He repeated the statement as though it were the *dictum* of the most expert worker in the group.

diffidence N. shyness. You must overcome your *diffidence* if you intend to become a salesman. diffident, ADJ.

diffusion N. wordiness; spreading in all directions. Your composition suffers from a *diffusion* of ideas; try to be more compact. diffuse, ADJ. and v.

digressive ADJ. wandering away from the subject. His book was marred by his many *digressive* remarks.

dilapidation N. state of ruin or disrepair through neglect. We felt that the *dilapidation* of the building could be corrected by several coats of paint.

dilate v. expand. In the dark, the pupils of your eyes *dilate*.

dilatory (dĭl'-) ADJ. delaying. Your *dilatory* tactics may compel me to cancel the contract.

dilemma N. problem; choice of two unsatisfactory alternatives. In this *dilemma*, he knew no one to whom he could turn for advice.

dilettante N. aimless follower of the arts; amateur; dabbler. He was not serious in his painting; he was, rather, a *dilettante*.

diminution N. lessening; reduction in size. The blockaders hoped to achieve victory as soon as the *diminution* of the enemy's supplies became

ā — ale; ă — add; ä — arm; å — ask; ē — eve; ĕ — end; ê — err, her; ə — event, allow,
ī — ice; ĭ — ill; ō — old; ŏ — odd; ô — orb; ōō — food; ou — out; th — thin; ū — use;
ŭ — up; zh — pleasure

serious.

dint N. means; effort. By *dint* of much hard work, the volunteers were able to bring the raging forest fire under control.

dipsomaniac N. one who has a strong craving for intoxicating liquor. The picture "The Lost Weekend" was an excellent portrayal of the struggles of the *dipsomaniac*.

dire ADJ. warning of disaster. People ignored his *dire* predictions of an approaching depression.

dirge N. musical lament. The funeral *dirge* stirred us to tears.

disavowal N. denial; disclaiming. His *disavowal* of his part in the conspiracy was not believed by the jury.

discernible ADJ. distinguishable; perceivable. The ships in the harbor were not *discernible* in the fog.

discerning ADJ. mentally quick and observant; having insight. The *discerning* interrogator noticed many discrepancies in his testimony.

disclaim V. disown; renounce claim to. If I grant you this privilege, will you *disclaim* all other rights?

discomfit V. put to rout; defeat; disconcert. This ruse will *discomfit* the enemy.   discomfiture, N.

disconcert V. confuse; upset; embarrass. The lawyer was *disconcerted* by the evidence produced by his adversary.

disconsolate ADJ. sad. The death of his wife left him *disconsolate*.

discordant ADJ. unharmonious; conflicting. He tried to unite the *discordant* factions.

discrete ADJ. separate; unconnected. The universe is composed of *discrete* bodies.

discretion N. prudence; circumspection; individual judgment. Use your *discretion* in this matter.

discursive ADJ. digressing; rambling. They were annoyed and bored by his *discursive* remarks.

disdain V. treat with scorn or contempt. You make enemies of all whom you *disdain*.

disgruntle V. make discontented. The passengers were *disgruntled* by the numerous delays.

disheveled (dĭ-shĕv'-) ADJ. untidy. Your *disheveled* appearance will hurt your chances in this interview.

disingenuous ADJ. not candid; calculating. Although he seemed eager, his remarks indicated that he was *disingenuous*.

disinterested ADJ. unprejudiced. The only *disinterested* person in the room was the judge.

ā — ale; ă — add; ä — arm; à — ask; ē — eve; ĕ — end; ê — err, her; ə — event, allow; ī — ice; ĭ — ill; ō — old; ŏ — odd; ô — orb; ōō — food; ou — out; th — thin; ū — use; ŭ — up; zh — pleasure

disjointed ADJ. disconnected. His remarks were so *disjointed* that we could not follow his reasoning.

dismember V. cut into small parts. When the Austrian Empire was *dismembered*, several new countries were established.

disparage V. belittle. Do not *disparage* anyone's contribution; these little gifts add up to large sums.

disparate ADJ. basically different; unrelated. It is difficult, if not impossible, to organize these *disparate* elements into a coherent whole.

disparity N. difference; condition of inequality. The *disparity* in their ages made no difference at all.

dispersion N. scattering. The *dispersion* of this group throughout the world may be explained by their expulsion from their homeland.

dispirited ADJ. lacking in spirit. The coach used all the tricks at his command to buoy up the enthusiasm of his team which had become *dispirited* at the loss of its star player.

disport V. amuse. The popularity of Florida as a winter resort is constantly increasing; each year, thousands more *disport* themselves at Miami and Palm Beach.

disputatious (-*tā'*-) ADJ. argumentative; fond of argument. People avoided discussing contemporary problems with him because of his *disputatious* manner.

disquisition N. a formal systematic inquiry; an explanation of the results of a formal inquiry. In his *disquisition*, he outlined the steps he had taken in reaching his conclusions.

dissection (*dĭ-sĕk'*-) N. analysis; cutting apart in order to examine. The *dissection* of frogs in the laboratory is particularly unpleasant to some students.

dissemble V. disguise; pretend. Even though you are trying to *dissemble* your motive in joining this group, we can see through your pretense.

disseminate V. scatter (like seeds). The invention of the radio helped propagandists to *disseminate* their favorite doctrines with ease.

dissertation N. formal essay. In order to earn a graduate degree from many universities, a candidate is frequently required to prepare a *dissertation* on some scholarly subject.

dissimulate V. pretend; conceal by feigning. She tried to *dissimulate* her grief by her gay attire.

dissipate V. squander. The young man quickly *dissipated* his inheritance.

dissolute ADJ. loose in morals. The *dissolute* life led by these people is indeed shocking.

dissonance N. discord. Some contemporary musicians deliberately use

ā — ale; ă — add; ä — arm; à — ask; ē — eve; ĕ — end; ê — err, her; ə — event, allow, ī — ice; ĭ — ill; ō — old; ŏ — odd; ô — orb; ōō — food; ou — out; th — thin; ū — use; ŭ — up; zh — pleasure

dissonance to achieve certain effects.

dissuade (dĭs-wād') v. advise against. He tried unsuccessfully to *dissuade* his friend from joining the conspirators.   dissuasion, N.

distend v. expand; swell out. I can tell when he is under stress by the way the veins *distend* on his forehead.

distortion N. twisting out of shape. It is difficult to believe the newspaper accounts of this event because of the *distortions* and exaggerations written by the reporters.

distrait (-rā') ADJ. absent-minded. Because of his concentration on the problem, the professor often appeared *distrait* and unconcerned about routine.

distraught ADJ. upset; distracted by anxiety. The *distraught* parents searched the ravine for their lost child.

diurnal (dī-ĕrn'-) ADJ. daily. A farmer cannot neglect his *diurnal* tasks at any time; cows, for example, must be milked regularly.

diva (dē'-) N. operatic singer; prima donna. Although world famous as a *diva*, she did not indulge in fits of temperament.

diverge (dĭ'-) v. vary; go in different directions from the same point. The spokes of the wheel *diverge* from the hub.

diverse ADJ. differing in some characteristics; various. There are *diverse* ways of approaching this problem.

ETYMOLOGY 9.

DI, DIURN (day)
>**diary**   day book
>**diurnal**   pertaining to daytime

DIA (across) prefix
>**diagonal**   across a figure
>**diameter**   across a circle
>**diagram**   outline drawing (writing across)

DIC, DICT (to say)
>**abdicate**   renounce
>**diction**   speech
>**verdict**   statement of jury

DIS, DIF (not) prefix
>**discord**   lack of harmony
>**differ**   disagree (carry apart)
>**distrust**   lack of trust

ā — ale; ă — add; ä — arm; à — ask; ē — eve; ĕ — end; ê — err, her; ə — event, allow, ī — ice; ĭ — ill; ō — old; ŏ — odd; ô — orb; ōō — food; ou — out; th — thin; ū — use; ŭ — up; zh — pleasure

---

TEST — Word List 9 — Synonyms and Antonyms

Each of the questions below consists of a word printed in bold, followed by five words or phrases numbered 1 to 5. Choose the numbered word or phrase which is most nearly the same as or the opposite of the word in bold and write the number of your choice on your answer paper.

161. **disingenous** 1. uncomfortable 2. eventual 3. naïve 4. complex 5. enthusiastic
162. **destitute** 1. reckless 2. dazzling 3. rich 4. characteristic 5. explanatory
163. **dilate** 1. procrastinate 2. expand 3. conclude 4. participate 5. divert
164. **deevout** 1. quiet 2. dual 3. impious 4. loyal 5. empty
165. **diminution** 1. expectation 2. context 3. validity 4. accumulation 5. difficulty
166. **devoid** 1. latent 2. eschewed 3. full of 4. suspecting 5. evident
167. **disconsolate** 1. examining 2. thankful 3. theatrical 4. joyous 5. prominent
168. **diabolical** 1. mischievous 2. lavish 3. seraphic 4. azure 5. red
169. **disheveled** 1. recognized 2. unkempt 3. short 4. written 5. witty
170. **diffidence** 1. sharpness 2. boldness 3. malcontent 4. dialogue 5. catalog
171. **dissonance** 1. admonition 2. splendor 3. discoord 4. reflection 5. aggression
172. **distrait** 1. clever 2. industrial 3. absent-minded 4. narrow 5. crooked
173. **disinterested** 1. prejudiced 2. horrendous 3. affected 4. arbitrary 5. bored
174. **dissipate** 1. economize 2. clean 3. accept 4. anticipate 5. withdraw
175. **disjointed** 1. satisfied 2. carved 3. understood 4. connected 5. evicted
176. **distend** 1. bloat 2. adjust 3. exist 4. materialize 5. finish

ā — ale; ă — add; ä — arm; â — ask; ē — eve; ĕ — end; ê — err, her; a — event, allow; ĭ — ice; ĭ — ill; ō — old; ŏ — odd; ô — orb; oo — food; ou — out; th — thin; ū — use; ŭ — up; zh — pleasure

177. **dispirited** 1. current 2. dented 3. drooping 4. removed 5. dallying
178. **diurnal** 1. containing 2. daily 3. weekly 4. monthly 5. annual
179. **disparity** 1. resonance 2. elocution 3. relief 4. difference 5. symbolism
180. **dilatory** 1. narrowing 2. procrastinating 3. enlarging 4. portentous 5. sour

---

Word List 10   diversity-enigma

diversity N. variety; dissimilitude. The *diversity* of colleges in this country indicates that many levels of ability are being cared for.

divest (dĭ-) v. strip; deprive. He was *divested* of his power to act.

divination N. foreseeing the future with aid of magic. I base my opinions not on any special gift of *divination* but on the laws of probability.

divulge v. reveal. I will not tell you this news because I am sure you will *divulge* it prematurely.

docile ADJ. obedient; easily managed. As *docile* as he seems today, that old lion was once a ferocious, snarling beast.

docket N. program, as for trial; book where such entries are made. The case of Smith vs. Jones was entered in the *docket* for July 15.   also v.

doff v. take off. He *doffed* his hat to the lady.

doggerel N. poor verse. Although we find occasional snatches of genuine poetry in his work, most of his writing is mere *doggerel*.

dogmatic ADJ. arbitrary; dictatorial. Do not be so *dogmatic* about that statement; it can be easily refuted.

dolorous (dŏl'-) ADJ. sorrowful. He found the *dolorous* lamentations of the bereaved family emotionally disturbing and he left as quickly as he could.

dolt N. stupid person. I thought I was talking to a mature audience; instead, I find myself addressing a pack of *dolts* and idiots.

domicile N. home. Although his legal *domicile* was in New York City, his work kept him away from his residence for many years.   also v.

dormant ADJ. sleeping; lethargic; torpid. Sometimes *dormant* talents in our friends surprise those of us who never realized how gifted our acquaintances really were.   dormancy, N.

dorsal ADJ. relating to the back of an animal. A shark may be identified by its

---

ā — ale; ă — add; ä — arm; â — ask; ē — eve; ĕ — end; ê — err, her; a — event, allow,
ĭ — ice; ĭ — ill; ō — old; ŏ — odd; ô — orb; ōō — food; ou — out; th — thin; ū — use;
ŭ — up; zh — pleasure

dorsal fin which projects above the surface of the ocean.

dotage (*dōt'-*) N. senility. In his *dotage,* the old man bored us with long tales of events in his childhood.

doughty (*dout'-*) ADJ. courageous. Many folk tales have sprung up about this *doughty* pioneer who opened up the New World for his followers.

dour (*dōor*) ADJ. sullen; stubborn. The man was *dour* and taciturn.

dregs N. sediment; worthless residue. The *dregs* of society may be observed in this slum area of the city.

droll (*drōl*) ADJ. queer and amusing. He was a popular guest because his *droll* anecdotes were always entertaining.

dross (*drŏss*) N. waste matter; worthless impurities. Many methods have been devised to separate the valuable metal from the *dross.*

drudgery N. mmenial work. Cinderella's fairy godmother rescued her from a life of *drudgery.*

dubious ADJ. doubtful. He has the *dubious* distinction of being the lowest ranked member of his class.

duplicity N. double-dealing; hypocrisy. People were shocked and dismayed when they learned of his *duplicity* in this affair for he had always seemed honest and straightforward.

duress (*-ĕs'*) N. forcible restraint, especially unlawfully. The hostages were held under *duress* until the prisoners' demands were met.

earthy ADJ. unrefined; coarse. His *earthy* remarks often embarrassed the ladies in his audience.

ebullient (*-būl'-*) ADJ. showing excitement; overflowing with enthusiasm. His *ebullient* nature could not be repressed; he was always laughing and gay.   ebullience, N.

eccentricity N. oddity; idiosyncrasy. Some of his friends tried to account for his rudeness to strangers as the *eccentricity* of genius.   eccentric, ADJ.

ecclesiastic ADJ. pertaining to the church. The minister donned his *ecclesiastic* garb and walked to the pulpit.   also N.

ecstasy N. rapture; trancelike joy. The announcement that the war had ended brought on an *ecstasy* that resulted in many uncontrolled celebrations.

edify V. instruct; correct morally. Although his purpose was to *edify* and not to entertain his audience, many of his listeners were amused and not enlightened.

educe (*a dūs'*) V. draw forth; elicit. He could not *educe* a principle that would encompass all the data.

eerie (*ē'rĭ*) ADJ. weird. In that *eerie* setting, it was easy to believe in ghosts and

ā — ale; ă — add; ä — arm; á — ask; ē — eve; ĕ — end; ê — err, her; a — event, allow, ī — ice; ĭ — ill; ō — old; ŏ — odd; ô — orb; ōō — food; ou — out; th — thin; ū — use; ŭ — up; zh — pleasure

other supernatural beings.

efface v. rub out. The coin had been handled so many times that its date had been *effaced*.

effectual ADJ. efficient. If we are to succeed in this endeavor, we must seek *effectual* means of securing our goals.

effeminate ADJ. having womanly traits. His voice was high-pitched and *effeminate*.

effervesce (-věs´) v. bubble over; show excitement. Some of us cannot stand the way she *effervesces* over trifles.

effete (ĕ-fēt´) ADJ. worn out; exhausted; barren. The literature of the age reflected the *effete* condition of the wriiters; no new ideas were forthcoming.

efficacy (ĕf´-) N. power to produce desired effect. The *efficacy* of the drug depends on the regularity of the dosage.   efficacious, ADJ.

effigy (ĕf´-ə-jē) N. dummy. The mob showed its irritation by hanging the judge in *effigy*.

efflorescent ADJ. flowering; realizing full power or quality. Her *efflorescent* beauty was the talk of the town.

effrontery N. shameless boldness. He had the *effrontery* to insult the guest.

effulgent (-fŭl´-) ADJ. brilliantly radiant. The *effulgent* rays of the rising sun lit the sky.

effusion N. pouring forth. The critics objected to his literary *effusion* because it was too flowery.

effusive ADJ. pouring forth; gushing. Her *effusive* manner of greeting her friends finally began to irritate them.

egoism N. excessive interest in oneself; belief that one should be interested in oneself rather than in others. His *egoism* prevented him from seeing the needs of his colleagues.

egotism N. conceit; vanity. We found his *egotism* unwarranted and irritating.

egregious (ə-grē´-jəs) ADJ. gross; shocking. He was an *egregious* liar.

egress (ēg´-) N. exit. Barnum's sign "To the *Egress*" fooled many people who thought they were going to see an animal and instead found themselves in the street.

ejaculation N. exclamation. He could not repress his *ejaculation* of surprise when he heard the news.

elation N. a rise in spirits; exaltation. She felt no *elation* at finding the purse.

elegiacal (ĕ-lə-jī´-) ADJ. like a lament; mournful. The essay on the lost crew was *elegiacal* in mood.   elegy, N.

elicit (-lĭ´-sĭt) v. draw out by discussion. The detectives tried to *elicit* where he had hidden his loot.

ā — ale; ă — add; ä — arm; à — ask; ē — eve; ě — end; ê — err, her; ə — event, allow. ī — ice; ĭ — ill; ō — old; ŏ — odd; ô — orb; ōō — food; ou — out; th — thin; ū — use; ŭ — up; zh — pleasure

elucidate V. explain; enlighten. He was called upon to *elucidate* the disputed points in his article.

elusive ADJ. evasive; baffling; hard to grasp. His *elusive* dreams of wealth were costly to those of his friends who supported him financially.

elusory ADJ. tending to deceive expectations; elusive. He argued that the project was an *elusory* one and would bring disappointment to all.

emaciated ADJ. thin and wasted. His long period of starvation had left him wan and *emaciated*.

emanate V. issue forth. A strong odor of sulphur *emanated* from the spring.

emancipate V. set free. At first, the attempts of the Abolitionists to *emancipate* the slaves were unpopular in New England as well as in the South.

embellish V. adorn. His handwriting was *embellished* with flourishes.

embezzlement N. stealing. The bank teller confessed his *embezzlement* of the funds.

emblazon V. deck in brilliant colors. *Emblazoned* on his shield was his family coat of arms.

embroil V. throw into confusion; involve in strife; entangle. He became *embrroiled* in the heated discussion when he tried to arbitrate the dispute.

emend V. correct. The editor *emended* tthe manuscript by deleting the passages which he thought inappropriate to the text.

emetic (-mĕt'-) N. substance causing vomiting. The use of an *emetic* like mustard is helpful in cases of poisoning.

eminent ADJ. high; loftty. After his appointment to this *eminent* position, he seldom had time for his former friends.

emolument (-mŏl'-) N. salary; compensation. In addition to the *emolument* this position offers, you must consider the social prestige it carries with it.

emulate (ĕm'-) V. rival; imitate. As long as our political leaders *emulate* the virtues of the great leaders of this country, we shall flourish.

enamored (-năm'-) ADJ. in love. Narcissus became *enamored* of his own beauty.

enclave N. territory enclosed within another land. The Vatican is an independent *enclave* in Italy.

encomiastic ADJ. praising; eulogistic. Some critics believe that his *encomiastic* statements about Napoleon were inspired by his desire for material advancement rather than by an honest belief in the Emperor's genius.   encomium, N.

encompass V. surround. Although we were *encompassed* by enemy forces, we were cheerful for we were well stocked and could withstand a

ā — ale; ă — add; ä — arm; à — ask; ē — eve; ĕ — end; ê — err, her; ə — event, allow.
i — ice; ĭ — ill; ō — old; ŏ — odd; ô — orb; oo — food; ou — out; th — thin; ū — use;
ŭ — up; zh — pleasure

siege until our allies joined us.

encroachment N. gradual intrusion. The *encroachment* of the factories upon the neighborhood lowered the value of the real estate.

encumber V. burden. Some people *encumber* themselves with too much luggage when they go on short trips.

endearment N. fond statement. Your gifts and *endearments* cannot make me forget your earlier insolence.

endive (*ĕn'-dīv*) N. species of leafy plant used in salads. The salad contained *endive* in addition to the ingredients she usually used.

endue V. provide with some quality; endow. He was *endued* with a lion's courage.

energize V. invigorate; make forceful and active. We shall have to *energize* our activities by getting new members to carry on.

enervate V. weaken; unnerve. The vigor of his opponent's attack *enervated* the young politician.

engender V. cause; produce. This editorial will *engender* racial intolerance unless it is denounced.

engross V. occupy fully. The boy was *engrossed* in his studies.

enhance V. advance; improve. This corsage of flowers will *enhance* the beauty of your attire.

enigma (*-nĭg'-*) N. puzzle. Despite all attempts to decipher the code, it remained an *enigma*. *enigmatic*, ADJ.

ETYMOLOGY 10.

DOC, DOCT (to teach)
> **docile** meek (teachable)
> **document** something that provides evidence
> **doctor** learned man (originally, teacher)

DOM, DOMIN (to rule)
> **dominate** having power over
> **domain** land under rule
> **dominant** prevailing

DUC, DUCT (to lead)
> **viaduct** arched roadway
> **aqueduct** artificial waterway
> **education** training (leading out)

DYNAM (power, strength)
> **dynamic** powerful

ā — ale; ă — add; ä — arm; å — ask; ē — eve; ĕ — end; ê — err, her; ə — event, allow, ī — ice; ĭ — ill; ō — old; ŏ — odd; ô — orb; ōō — food; ou — out; th — thin; ū — use; ŭ — up; zh — pleasure

dynamite powerful explosive
dynamo engine to make electrical power

EGO (I, self)

egoist person who is self-interested
egotist self-centered person
egocentric revolving about self

TEST — Word List 10 — Synonyms

Each of the questions below consists of a word printed in bold, followed by five words or phrases numbered 1 to 5. Choose the numbered word or phrase which is most nearly similar in meaning to the word in bold and write the number of your choice on your answer paper.

181. **elusive** 1. deadly 2. eloping 3. evasive 4. simple 5. petrified
182. **edify** 1. mystify 2. suffice 3. improve 4. erect 5. entertain
183. **dormant** 1. active 2. absurd 3. hibernating 4. unfortunate 5. permanent
184. **egress** 1. entrance 2. bird 3. exit 4. double 5. progress
185. **dubious** 1. external 2. straight 3. sIncere 4. doubtful 5. filling in
186. **dogmatic** 1. benign 2. canine 3. impatient 4. petulant 5. arbitrary
187. **elated** 1. debased 2. respectful 3. drooping 4. gay 5. charitable
188. **droll** 1. rotund 2. amusing 3. fearsome 4. tiny 5. strange
189. **doff** 1. withdraw 2. take off 3. remain 4. control 5. start
190. **effigy** 1. requisition 2. organ 3. charge 4. accordiion 5. dummy
191. **dour** 1. sullen 2. ornamental 3. grizzled 4. lacking speech 5. international
192. **divulge** 1. look 2. ornamental 3. deride 4. reveal 5. harm
193. **efface** 1. countenance 2. encourage 3. recognize 4. blackball 5. rub out
194. **dotage** 1. senility 2. silence 3. sensitivity 4. interest 5. generosity
195. **emaciated** 1. garrulous 2. primeval 3. vigorous 4. disparate 5. thin

---

ā — āle; ă — ădd; ä — ärm; â — âsk; ē — ēve; ĕ — ĕnd; ê — êrr, hêr; ə — əvent, əllow, ī — īce; ĭ — ĭll; ō — ōld; ŏ — ŏdd; ô — ôrb; ōō — fōōd; ou — out; th — thin; ū — ūse; ŭ — ŭp; zh — pleasure

196. enhance   1. improve   2. doubt   3. scuff   4. gasp   5. agree
197. embellish   1. doff   2. don   3. balance   4. adorn   5. equalize
198. enervate   1. weaken   2. sputter   3. arrange   4. scrutinize   5. agree
199. emend   1. cherish   2. repose   3. correct   4. assure   5. worry
200. eminent   1. purposeful   2. high   3. delectable   4. curious   5. urgent

---

Word List 11   ennui-extrovert

ennui (ŏn-wē′) N. boredom. The monotonous routine of hospital life induced a feeling of *ennui* which made him moody and irritable.

enormity N. hugeness (in a bad sense). He did not realize the *enormity* of his crime until he saw what suffering he had caused.

enrapture V. please intensely. The audience was *enraptured* by the freshness of the voices and the excellent orchestration.

ensconce (-skŏns′) V. settle comfortably. The parents thought that their children were *ensconced* safely in the private school and decided to leave for Europe.

enthrall V. capture; make slave. From the moment he saw her picture, he was *enthralled* by her beauty.

entity N. real thing. As soon as the Charter was adopted, the United Nations became an *entity* and had to be considered as a factor in world diplomacy.

entree (ŏn′-trā) N. entrance. Because of his wealth and social position, he had *entree* into the most exclusive circles.

entrepreneur N. business man; contractor. Opponents of our present tax program argue that it discourages *entrepreneurs* from trying new fields of business activity.

environ (-vī′-) V. enclose; surround. In medieval days, Paris was *environed* by a wall.   environs, N.

ephemeral (-fĕm′-) ADJ. short-lived; fleeting. The May fly is an *ephemeral* creature.

epicure N. connoisseur of food and drink. *Epicures* frequent this restaurant because it features exotic wines and dishes.

epicurean N. person who devotes himself to pleasures of the senses, especially to food. This restaurant is famous for its menu which can cater to the most exotic whim of the *epicurean*.   also ADJ.

ā — ale; ă — add; ä — arm; å — ask; ē — eve; ĕ — end; ê — err, her; ə — event, allow, ī — ice; ĭ — ill; ō — old; ŏ — odd; ô — orb; ōō — food; ou — out; th — thin; ū — use; ŭ — up; zh — pleasure

epigram N. witty thought or saying, usually short. Poor Richard's *epigrams* made Benjamin Franklin famous.

epilogue N. short speech at conclusion of dramatic work. The audience was so disappointed in the play that many did not remain to hear the *epilogue*.

epitaph N. inscription in memory of a dead person. In his will, he dictated the *epitaph* he wanted placed on his tombstone.

epithet N. descriptive word or phrase. Homer's writings are replete with such *epithets* as "rosy-fingered dawn."

epitome (ĭ-pĭt'-ō-mē) N. summary; concise abstract. This final book is the *epitome* of all his previous books. epitomize, V.

epoch N. period of time. The glacial *epoch* lasted for thousands of years.

equable (ĕk'-) ADJ. tranquil; steady; uniform. After the hot summers and cold winters of New England, he found the climate of the West Indies *equable* and pleasant.

equanimity N. calmness of temperament. In his later years, he could look upon the foolishness of the world with *equanimity* and humor.

equestrian N. rider on horseback. These paths in the park are reserved for *equestrians* and their steeds. also ADJ.

equinox N. period of equal days and nights; the beginning of spring and autumn. The vernal *equinox* is usually marked by heavy rainstorms.

equipage (ĕk'-) N. horse-drawn carriage. The *equipage* drew up before the inn.

equity N. fairness; justice. Our courts guarantee *equity* to all.

equivocal (-kwĭv'-) ADJ. doubtful; ambiguous. Macbeth was misled by the *equivocal* statements of the witches.

equivocate V. lie; mislead; attempt to conceal the truth. The audience saw through his attempts to *equivocate* on the subject under discussion and ridiculed his remarks.

erode V. eat away. The limestone was *eroded* by the dripping water.

errant ADJ. wandering. Many a charming tale has been written about the knights-*errant* who helped the weak and punished the guilty during the Age of Chivalry.

erudite (ĕr'-ū-dĭt) ADJ. learned; scholarly. His *erudite* writing was difficult to read because of the many allusions which were unfamiliar to most readers. erudition, N.

escapade (ĕs'-ka-pād) N. prank; flighty conduct. The headmaster could not regard this latest *escapade* as a boyish joke and expelled the young man.

ā — ale; ă — add; ä — arm; à — ask; ē — eve; ĕ — end; ê — err, her; ə — event, allow, ī — ice; ĭ — ill; ō — old; ŏ — odd; ô — orb; ōo — food; ou — out; th — thin; ū — use; ŭ — up; zh — pleasure

eschew (ĕs-chōō') v. avoid. He tried to *eschew* all display of temper.

escutcheon (-kŭch'-) N. shield-shaped surface on which coat of arms is placed. His traitorous acts placed a shameful blot on the family *escutcheon*.

esoteric (-tĕr'-) ADJ. known only to the chosen few. Those students who had access to his *esoteric* discussions were impressed by the scope of his thinking.

espionage (ĕs' pĭ-) N. spying. In order to maintain its power, the government developed a system of *espionage* which penetrated every household.

esprit de corps (ĕs-prē' de kôr) N. comradeship; spirit. West Point cadets are proud of their *esprit de corps*.

estranged ADJ. separated. The *estranged* wife sought a divorce.

ethereal ADJ. light; heavenly; fine. Visitors were impressed by her *ethereal* beauty, her delicate charm.

ethnic ADJ. relating to races. Intolerance between *ethnic* groups is deplorable and usually is based on lack of information.   ethnology, N.

eulogistic ADJ. praising. To everyone's surprise, the speech was *eulogistic* rather than critical in tone.

eulogy N. praise. All the *eulogies* of his friends could not remove the sting of the calumny heaped upon him by his enemies.

euphemism N. mild expression in place of an unpleasant one. The expression, "He passed away" is a *euphemism* for "He died."

euphonious ADJ. pleasing in sound. Italian and Spanish are *euphonious* languages and therefore easily sung.

evanescent ADJ. fleeting; vanishing. In the *evanescent* rays of the sunset, the entire western skyline was bathed in an orange-red hue.

evasive ADJ. not frank; eluding. Your *evasive* answers convinced the judge that you were withholding important evidence.   evade, v.; evasion, N.

evince v. show clearly. When he tried to answer the questions, he *evinced* his ignorance of the subject matter.

evoke v. call forth. He *evoked* memories of childhood when he sang the sweet lullabies.

ewer (ū-ər) N. water pitcher. The primitive conditions of the period were symbolized by the porcelain *ewer* and basin in the bedroom.

exaction N. exorbitant demand; extortion. The colonies rebelled against the *exactions* of the mother country.

exasperate v. vex. Johnny often *exasperates* his mother with his pranks.

exchequer N. treasury. He had been Chancellor of the *Exchequer* before his

---

ā — ale; ă — add; ä — arm; å — ask; ē — eve; ĕ — end; ê — err, her; ə — event, allow,
ī — ice; ĭ — ill; ō — old; ŏ — odd; ô — orb; ōō — food; ou — out; th — thin; ū — use;
ŭ — up; zh — pleasure

untimely death.

exculpate V. clear from blame. He was *exculpated* of the crime when the real criminal confessed.

execrable (*ĕx'*-) ADJ. very bad. The anecdote was in *execrable* taste.

exemplary (-*ĕm'*-) ADJ. serving as a model; outstanding. Her *exemplary* behavior was praised at commencement.

exhort (*ĕg-zôrt'*) V. urge. The evangelist will *exhort* all sinners in his audience to reform.

exhume V. dig out of the ground; remove from grave. Because of the rumor that he had been poisoned, his body was *exhumed* in order that an autopsy might be performed.

exigency (*ĕx'-ĭj-*) N. urgent situation. In this *exigency,* we must look for aid from our allies.

exiguous (-*ĭg'*-) ADJ. small; minute. Grass grew there, an *exiguous* outcropping among the rocks.

exodus N. departure. The *exodus* from the hot and stuffy city was particularly noticeable on Friday evenings.

exonerate V. acquit; exculpate. I am sure this letter will *exonerate* you.

exorbitant ADJ. excessive. The people grumbled at his *exorbitant* prices but paid them because he had a monopoly.

exottic ADJ. not native; strange. Because of his *exotic* headdress, he was followed in the streets by small children who laughed at his strange appearance.

expatiate (-*pā'-shē-āt*) V. talk at length; At this time, please give us a brief resumé of your work; we shall permit you to *expatiate* later.

expatriate N. exile; someone who has withdrawn from native land. Henry James was an American *expatriate* who settled in England.

expediency N. that which is advisable or practical. He was guided by *expediency* rather than by ethical considerations.   expedient, ADJ.

expeditiously ADV. rapidly and efficiently. Please adjust this matter as *expeditiously* as possible as it is delaying important work.

expiate (*ĕx'-pĭ-āt*) V. make amends for (a sin). He tried to *expiate* his crimes by a full confession to the authorities.

expostulation N. remonstrance. Despite the teacher's scoldings and *expostulations,* the class rèmained unruly.

expunge V. cancel; remove. If you behave, I will *expunge* this notation from your record card.

expurgate V. clean; remove offensive parts of a book. The editors felt that certain passages in the book had to be *expurgated* before it could

ā — ale; ă — add; ä — arm; â — ask; ē — eve; ĕ — end; ê — err, her; ə — event, allow, ĭ — ice; ĭ — ill; ō — old; ŏ — odd; ô — orb; ōō — food; ou — out; th — thin; ū — use; ŭ — up; zh — pleasure

be used in the classroom.

extant (*ĕx'-*) ADJ. still in existence. Although the authorities suppressed the book, many copies are *extant* and may be purchased at exorbitant prices.

extemporaneous ADJ. not planned; impromptu. Because his *extemporaneous* remarks were misinterpreted, he decided to write all his speeches in advance.

extenuate V. weaken; mitigate. It is easier for us to *extenuate* our own shortcomings than those of others.

extirpate V. root up. We must *extirpate* and destroy this monstrous philosophy.

extol V. praise; glorify. The astronauts were *extolled* as the pioneers of the Space Age.

extort V. wring from; get money by threats, etc. The blackmailer *extorted* money from his victim.

extradition N. surrender of prisoner by one state to another. The lawyers opposed the *extradition* of their client on the grounds that for more than five years he had been a model citizen.

extraneous ADJ. not essential; external. Do not pad your paper with *extraneous* matters; stick to essential items only.

extricate V. free; disentangle. He found that he could not *extricate* himself from the trap.

extrinsic ADJ. external; not inherent; foreign. Do not be fooled by *extrinsic* causes. We must look for the intrinsic reason.

extrovert N. person interested mostly in external objects and actions. A good salesman is usually an *extrovert* who likes to mingle with people.

ETYMOLOGY 11.

ERG, URG (work)
  energy power
  ergatocracy rule of the workers
  metallurgy art of working in metal
ERR (to wander)
  error mistake
  erratic not reliable, not constant
  knight-errant wandering knight
EU (good, well, beautiful) prefix
  eulogize praise

ā — ale; ă — add; ä — arm; å — ask; ē — eve; ĕ — end; ê — err, her; ə — event, allow,
ī — ice; ĭ — ill; ō — old; ŏ — odd; ô — orb; ōō — food; ou — out; th — thin; ū — use;
ŭ — up; zh — pleasure

euphemism   substitution of pleasant way of saying something blunt or unpleasant

eupeptic   having good digestion

EX (out) prefix

expel   drive out

exit   way out

extirpate   root out

EXTRA (beyond, outside) prefix

extraordinary   exceptional

extracurricular   beyond the items in the curriculum

extraterritorial   beyond the territory of a nation

Test — Word List 11 — Antonyms

Each of the questions below consists of a word printed in bold, followed by five words or phrases numbered 1 to 5. Choose the numbered word or phrase which is most nearly opposite in meaning to the word in bold and write the number of your choice on your answer paper.

201. exodus   1. neglect   2. consent   3. entry   4. gain   5. retreat
202. exasperate   1. confide   2. formalize   3. placate   4. betray   5. bargain
203. equivocal   1. mistaken   2. quaint   3. azure   4. clear   5. universal
204. exhume   1. decipher   2. dig   3. integrate   4. admit   5. inter
205. evasive   1. frank   22. correct   3. empty   4. fertile   5. watchful
206. equanimity   1. agitation   2. stirring   3. volume   4. identity   5. luster
207. ephemeral   1. sensuous   2. passing   3. popular   4. distasteful   5. eternal
208. euphonious   1. strident   2. lethargic   3. literary   4. significant   5. musical
209. equable   1. flat   2. decisive   3. stormy   4. rough   5. scanty
210. execrable   1. innumerable   2. philosophic   3. physical   4. excellent   5. meditative
211. eulogistic   1. pretty   2. critical   3. brief   4. stern   5. free
212. ennui   1. hate   2. excitement   3. seriousness   4. humility   5. kindness
213. exculpate   1. accuse   2. prevail   3. acquit   4. ravish   5. accumulate

ā — ale; ă — add; ä — arm; â — ask; ē — eve; ĕ — end; ê — err, her; a — event, allow; ī — ice; ĭ — ill; ō — old; ŏ — odd; ô — orb; ōō — food; ou — out; th — thin; ū — use; ŭ — up; zh — pleasure

214. **erudite** 1. professorial 2. stately 3. short 4. unknown 5. ignorant
215. **exonerate** 1. forge 2. accuse 3. record 4. doctor 5. reimburse
216. **extrovert** 1. clown 2. hero 3. ectomorph 4. neurotic 5. introvert
217. **exorbitant** 1. moderate 2. partisan 3. military 4. barbaric 5. expensive
218. **extrinsic** 1. reputable 2. inherent 3. swift 4. ambitious 5. cursory
219. **extraneous** 1. needless 2. decisive 3. essential 4. effective 5. expressive
220. **extemporaneous** 1. rehearsed 2. hybrid 3. humiliating 4. statesmanlike 5. picturesque

---

Word List 12   extrude-fluster

extrude V. force or push out. Much pressure is required to *extrude* these plastics.

exuberant ADJ. abundant; effusive; lavish. His speeches were famous for his *exuberant* language and vivid imagery.

exude V. discharge; give forth. The maple syrup is obtained from the sap that *exudes* from the trees in early spring. exudation, N.

fabricate V. build; lie. She *fabricated* a clever tale, but we knew better than to believe her.

façade (fä-sähd′) N. front of the building. The *façade* of the church had often been photographed by tourists.

facet (fă′-sĕt) N. small plane surface (of a gem); a side. The stone-cutter decided to improve the rough diamond by providing it with several *facets*.

facetious ADJ. humorous; jocular. Your *facetious* remarks are not appropriate at this serious moment.

facile (fă′-sĭl) ADJ. easy; expert. Because he was a *facile* speaker, he never refused a request to address an organization.

facilitate V. make less difficult. He tried to *facilitate* matters at home by getting a part-time job.

faction N. party; clique; dissension. The quarrels and bickering of the two

ā — ale; ă — add; ä — arm; à — ask; ē — eve; ĕ — end; ê — err, her; a — event, allow, ī — ice; ĭ — ill; ō — old; ŏ — odd; ô — orb; ōō — food; ou — out; th — thin; ū — use; ŭ — up; zh — pleasure

small *factions* within the club disturbed the majority of the members.

factitious ADJ. artificial; sham. Hollywood actressees often create *factitious* tears by using glycerine.

factious ADJ. inclined to form factions; causing dissension. Your statement is *factious* and will upset the harmony that now exists.

factotum (-tōt'-) handyman; person who does all kinds of work. Although we had hired him as a messenger, we soon began to use him as a general *factotum* around the office.

fain ADV. gladly. The knight said, "I would *fain* be your protector."

fallacious (-lā'-) ADJ. misleading. Your reasoning must be *fallacious* because it leads to a ridiculous answer.

fallible ADJ. liable to err. I know I am *fallible*, but I feel confident that I am right this time.

fallow ADJ. plowed but not sowed; uncultivated. Farmers have learned that it is advisable to permit land to lie *fallow* every few years.

fanaticism N. excessive zeal. He could not control the *fanaticism* of his followers.

fancied ADJ. imagined; unreal. You are resenting *fancied* insults. No one has ever said such things about you. fancy, V.

fancier N. breeder or dealer of animals. The dog *fancier* exhibited his prize collie at the annual kennel club show.

fanciful ADJ. whimsical; visionary. This is a *fanciful* scheme because it does not consider the facts.

fantastic ADJ. unreal; grotesque; whimsical. Your fears are *fantastic* because no such animal as you have described exists.

fastidious ADJ. difficult to please; squeamish. The waitresses disliked serving him his dinner because of his very *fastidious* taste.

fatalism N. belief that events are determined by forces beyond one's control. With unwavering *fatalism*, he accepted the hardships which beset him. fatalistic, ADJ.

fatuous ADJ. foolish; inane. He is far too intelligent to utter such *fatuous* remarks.

fauna (fäw'-) N. animals of a period or region. The scientist could visualize the *fauna* of the period by examining the skeletal remains and the fossils.

faux pas (fō´pä) N. an error or slip (in manners or behavior). Your tactless remark during dinner was a *faux pas*.

fawning ADJ. courting favor by cringing and flattering. He was constantly

---

ā — ale; ă — add; ä — arm; à — ask; ē — eve; ĕ — end; ê — err, her; ə — event, allow, ī — ice; ĭ — ill; ō — old; ŏ — odd; ô — orb; ōō — food; ou — out; th — thin; ū — use; ŭ — up; zh — pleasure

surrounded by a group of *fawning* admirers who hoped to win some favor.

fealty (fē'-əl-) N. loyalty; faithfulness. The feudal lord demanded *fealty* of his vassals.

feasible ADJ. practicable. This is an entirely *feasible* proposal. I suggest we adopt it.

fecundity N. fertility; fruitfulness. The *fecundity* of his mind is illustrated by the many vivid images in his poems.

feign (fān) V. pretend. Lady Macbeth *feigned* illness in the courtyard.

feint (fānt) N. trick; shift; sham blow. The boxer was fooled by his opponent's *feint* and dropped his guard.   also V.

felicitous ADJ. apt; suitably expressed; well-chosen. He was famous for his *felicitous* remarks and was called upon to serve as master-of-ceremonies at many a banquet.

fell ADJ. cruel; deadly. Henley writes of the "*fell* clutch of circumstance" in his poem "Invictus."

ferment (fĕr'-) N. agitation; commotion. The entire country was in a state of *ferment*.

ferret V. drive or hunt out of hiding. He *ferreted* out their secret.

fervent ADJ. ardent; hot. She laughed at his *fervent* love letters.

fervid ADJ. ardent. His *fervid* enthusiasm inspired all of us to undertake the dangerous mission.

fervor N. glowing ardor. Their kiss was full of the *fervor* of first love.

fester V. generate pus. The wound from the splinter in her finger began to *fester*.

fete (fāt) V. honor at a festival. The returning hero was *feted* at a community supper and dance.   also N.

fetid (fĕt'-ĭd) ADJ. malodorous. The neglected wound became *fetid*.

fetish (fĕt'-) N. object supposed to possess magical powers; an object of special devotion. The native wore a *fetish* around his neck to ward off evil spirits.

fetter V. shackle. The prisoner was *fettered* to the wall.

fiasco (fē-ăs'-cō) N. total failure. Our ambitious venture ended in a *fiasco*.

fiat (fē'-) N. command. I cannot accept government by *fiat*; I feel that I must be consulted.

fickle ADJ. changeable; unfaithful. He discovered she was *fickle*.

fictitious ADJ. imaginary. Although this book purports to be a biography of George Washington, many of the incidents are *fictitious*.

fidelity N. loyalty. A dog's *fidelity* to his owner is one of the reasons why that

ā — ale; ă — add; ä — arm; â — ask; ē — eve; ĕ — end; ê — err, her; ə — event, allow, ī — ice; ĭ — ill; ō — old; ŏ — odd; ô — orb; ōō — food; ou — out; th — thin; ū — use; ŭ — up; zh — pleasure

animal is a favorite household pet.

figment N. invention; imaginary thing. That incident is a *figment* of your imagination.

filch V. steal. The boys *filched* apples from the fruitstand.

filial ADJ. pertaining to a son or daughter. Many children forget their *filial* obligations and disregard the wishes of their parents.

finale (fĭ-nä´-lē) N. conclusion. It is not until we reach the *finale* of this play that we can understand the author's message.

finesse (fĭ-nĕs´) N. delicate skill. The *finesse* and adroitness of the surgeon impressed the observers in the operating room.

finicky ADJ. too particular; fussy. The old lady was *finicky* about her food.

finite (fī´-nīt) ADJ. limited. It is difficult for humanity with its *finite* existence to grasp the infinite.

fissure (fĭsh´-ər) N. crevice. The mountain climbers secured foot-holds in tiny *fissures* in the rock.

fitful ADJ. spasmodic; intermittent. After several *fitful* attempts, he decided to postpone the start of the project until he felt more energetic.

flaccid (flăk´-sĭd) ADJ. flabby. His sedentary life had left him with *flaccid* muscles.

flagellate (flă´-jĕl-) V. flog; whip. The Romans used to *flagellate* criminals with a whip that had three knotted strands.

flagging ADJ. weak; drooping. The encouraging cheers of the crowd lifted the team's *flagging* spirit.

flagrant (flā´-) ADJ. conspicuously wicked. We cannot condone such *flagrant* violations of the rules.

flail V. thresh grain by hand; strike or slap. In medieval times, warriors *flailed* their foes with metal balls attached to handles.

flair N. talent. He has an uncanny *flair* for discovering new artists before the public has become aware of their existence.

flamboyant (-bôy´-) ADJ. ornate. Modern architecture has discarded the *flamboyant* trimming on buildings and emphasizes simplicity of line.

flaunt V. display ostentatiously. She is not one of those actresses who *flaunt* their physical charms; she can act.

flay V. strip off skin; plunder. The criminal was condemned to being *flayed* alive.

fleck V. spot. Her cheeks, *flecked* with tears, were testimony to the hours of weeping.

fledgling ADJ. inexperienced. While it is necessary to provide these *fledgling*

ā — ale; ă — add; ä — arm; å — ask; ē — eve; ĕ — end; ê — err, her; a — event, allow, ī — ice; ĭ — ill; ō — old; ŏ — odd; ô — orb; ōō — food; ou — out; th — thin; ū — use; ŭ — up; zh — pleasure

poets with an opportunity to present their work, it is not essential that we admire everything they write.   also N.

flick N. light stroke as with a whip. The horse needed no encouragement; one *flick* of the whip was all the jockey had to apply to get the animal to run at top speed.

flippancy N. trifling gaiety. Your *flippancy* at this serious moment is offensive.

flora N. plants of a region or era. Because she was a botanist, she spent most of her time studying the *flora* of the desert.

florid ADJ. flowery, ruddy. His complexion was even more *florid* than usual because of his anger.

flotilla (-*tĭl'*-) N. small fleet. It is always an exciting and interesting moment when the fishing *flotilla* returns to port.

flotsam (*flŏt'*-) N. drifting wreckage. Beachcombers eke out a living by salvaging the *flotsam* and jetsam of the sea.

flout V. reject; mock. The headstrong youth *flouted* all authority; he refused to be curbed.

fluctuation N. wavering. Meteorologists watch the *fluctuations* of the barometer in order to predict the weather.

fluency N. smoothness of speech. He spoke French with *fluency* and ease.

fluster V. confuse; befuddle with liquor. The teacher's sudden question *flustered* him and he stammered his reply.

ETYMOLOGY 12.

FAC, FIC, FEC, FECT (to make, to do)
- **factory**   place where things are made
- **fiction**   manufactured story
- **affect**   to cause to change

FALL, FALS (to deceive)
- **fallacious**   faulty
- **infallible**   not prone to error, perfect
- **falsify**   lie

FER, LAT (to bring, to bear)
- **transfer**   bring from one place to another
- **coniferous**   bearing cones, as pine trees

FIC (making, creating) adjective suffix
- **terrific**   creating terror
- **soporific**   making sleepy

ā — ale; ă — add; ä — arm; â — ask; ē — eve; ĕ — end; ê — err, her; ə — event, allow, ī — ice; ĭ — ill; ō — old; ŏ — odd; ô — orb; ōō — food; ou — out; th — thin; ū — use; ŭ — up; zh — pleasure

TEST — Word List 12 — Synonyms and Antonyms

Each of the questions below consists of a word printed in bold, followed by five words or phrases numbered 1 to 5. Choose the numbered word or phrase which is most nearly the same as or the opposite of the word in bold and write the number of your choice on your answer paper.

221. **finite** 1. bounded 2. established 3. affirmative 4. massive 5. finicky

222. **fiasco** 1. cameo 2. mansion 3. pollution 4. success 5. gamble

223. **flair** 1. conflagration 2. inspiration 3. bent 4. egregiousness 5. magnitude

224. **flamboyant** 1. old-fashioned 2. restrained 3. impulsive 4. cognizant 5. eloquent

225. **fanciful** 1. imaginative 2. knowing 3. elaborate 4. quick 5. lusty

226. **fecundity** 1. prophecy 2. futility 3. fruitfulness 4. need 5. dormancy

227. **fell** 1. propitious 2. illiterate 3. catastrophic 4. futile 5. inherent

228. **fiat** 1. motor 2. degree 3. lesion 4. suture 5. order

229. **fledgling** 1. popular 2. loose 3. expert 4. colorful 5. flaying

230. **factitious** 1. genuine 2. magnificent 3. polished 4. puny 5. ridiculous

231. **fidelity** 1. brotherhood 2. parentage 3. treachery 4. conscience 5. consistency

232. **flail** 1. succeed 2. harvest 3. knife 4. strike 5. resent

233. **florid** 1. ruddy 2. rusty 3. ruined 4. patient 5. poetic

234. **fatuous** 1. fatal 2. natal 3. terrible 4. sensible 5. tolerable.

235. **ferment** 1. stir up 2. fill 3. ferret 4. mutilate 5. banish

236. **fickle** 1. fallacious 2. tolerant 3. loyal 4. hungry 5. stupid

237. **exude** 1. prevent 2. ooze 3. manage 4. protrude 5. insure

238. **feasible** 1. theoretical 2. impatient 3. constant 4. present 5. impractical

239. **feign** 1. deserve 2. condemn 3. condone 4. attend 5. pretend

240. **filch** 1. milk 2. purloin 3. itch 4. cancel 5. resent

---

ā — ale; ă — add; ä — arm; â — ask; ē — eve; ĕ — end; ê — err, her; ə — event, allow, i — ice; ĭ — ill; ō — old; ŏ — odd; ô — orb; ōō — food; ou — out; th — thin; ū — use; ŭ — up; zh — pleasure

Word List 13   flux-float

flux N. flowing; series of changes. While conditions are in such a state of *flux*, I do not wish to commit myself too deeply in this affair.

foible N. weakness; slight fault. We can overlook the *foibles* of our friends.

foist V. insert improperly; palm off. I will not permit you to *foist* such ridiculous ideas upon the membership of this group.

foment (-*mĕnt'*) V. stir up; instigate. This report will *foment* dissension in the club.

foolhardy ADJ. rash. Don't be *foolhardy*. Get the advice of experienced people before undertaking this venture.

foppish ADJ. vain about dress and appearance. He tried to imitate the *foppish* manner of the young men of the court.

foray (*fô'*-) N. raid. The company staged a midnight *foray* against the enemy outpost.

forbearance N. patience. We must use *forbearance* in dealing with him because he is still weak from his illness.

foreboding N. premonition of evil. Caesar ridiculed his wife's *forebodings* about the Ides of March.

forensic (-*rĕn'-sĭk*) ADJ. suitable to debate or courts of law. In his best *forensic* manner, the lawyer addressed the jury.

formidable (*fôr'*-) ADJ. menacing; threatening. We must not treat the battle lightly for we are facing a *formidable* foe.

forte (*fôrt*-) N. strong point or special talent. I am not eager to play this rather serious role, for my *forte* is comedy.

fortitude N. bravery; courage. He was awarded the medal for his *fortitude* in the battle.

fortuitous ADJ. accidental; by chance. There is no connection between these two events; their timing is extremely *fortuitous*.

foster V. rear; encourage. According to the legend, Romulus and Remus were *fostered* by a she-wolf.   also ADJ.

fractious (*frăk'-shəs*) ADJ. unruly. The *fractious* horse unseated its rider.

frailty N. weakness. Hamlet says, "*Frailty*, thy name is woman."

franchise N. right granted by government. The city issued a *franchise* to the company to operate surface transit lines on the streets for ninety-nine years.

frantic ADJ. wild. At the time of the collision, many people became *frantic* with fear.

ā — ale; ă — add; ä — arm; à — ask; ē — eve; ĕ — end; ê — err, her; ə — event, allow, i — ice; ĭ — ill; ō — old; ŏ — odd; ô — orb; oo — food; ou — out; th — thin; ū — use; ŭ — up; zh — pleasure

fraudulent ADJ. cheating; deceitful. The government seeks to prevent *fraudulent* and misleading advertising.

fraught (frôt) ADJ. filled. Since this enterprise is *fraught* with danger, I will ask for volunteers who are willing to assume the risks.

fray N. brawl. The three musketeers were in the thick of the *fray*.

freebooter N. buccaneer. This town is a rather dangerous place to visit as it is frequented by pirates, *freebooters,* and other plunderers.

frenetic ADJ. frenzied; frantic. His *frenetic* activities convinced us that he had no organized plan of operation.

frenzied ADJ. madly excited. As soon as they smelled smoke, the *frenzied* animals proceed to and fro in their cages.

fresco N. painting on plaster (usually fresh). The cathedral is visited by many tourists who wish to admire the *frescoes* by Giotto.

freshet N. sudden overflow, usually of a stream. Motorists were warned that spring *freshets* had washed away several small bridges and that long detours would be necessary.

friction N. clash in opinion; rubbing against. At this time when harmony is essential, we cannot afford to have any *friction* in our group.

frieze (frēz) N. ornamental band on a wall. The *frieze* of the church was adorned with sculpture.

frigid ADJ. intensely cold. Alaska is in the *frigid* zone.

fritter V. waste. He could not apply himself to any task and *frittered* away his time in idle conversation.

frolicsome ADJ. prankish; gay. The *frolicsome* puppy tried to lick the face of its owner.

froward (frō'-) ADJ. disobedient; perverse; stubborn. Your *froward* behavior has alienated many of us who might have been your supporters.

frowzy ADJ. slovenly; unkempt; dirty. Her *frowzy* appearance and her cheap decorations made her appear ludicrous in this group.

fructify V. bear fruit. This tree should *fructify* in three years.

frugality N. thrift. In these difficult days, we must live with *frugality*. frugal, ADJ.

fruition (frōō-ĭ'-) N. bearing of fruit; fulfillment; realization. This building marks the *fruition* of all our aspirations and years of hard work.

frustrate V. thwart; defeat. We must *frustrate* his ruthless plan to seize control of the government.

fulminate V. thunder; explode. The people against whom he *fulminated* were innocent of any wrongdoing.

fulsome ADJ. disgustingly excessive. His *fulsome* praise of the dictator annoyed his listeners.

ā — ale; ă — add; ä — arm; à — ask; ē — eve; ĕ — end; ê — err, her; ə — event, allow,
ī — ice; ĭ — ill; ō — old; ŏ — odd; ô — orb; ōō — food; ou — out; th — thin; ū — use;
ŭ — up; zh — pleasure

functionary N. official. As his case was transferred from one *functionary* to another, he began to despair of ever reaching a settlement.

funereal (-nēr'-ē-əl) ADJ. sad; solemn. I fail to understand why there is such a *funereal* atmosphere; we have lost a battle, not a war.

furor (fū'-rôr) N. frenzy; great excitement. The story of his embezzlement of the funds created a *furor* on the stock exchange.

furtive (fêr'-tŭv) ADJ. stealthy. The boy gave a *furtive* look at his classmate's test paper.

fusion N. union; coalition. The opponents of the political party in power organized a *fusion* movement.

fustian (fŭs'-) ADJ. pompous; bombastic. Several in the audience were deceived by his *fustian* style; they mistook pomposity for erudition.

gadfly N. animal-biting fly; an irritating person. Like a *gadfly*, he irritated all the guests at the hotel; within forty-eight hours, everyone regarded him as an annoying busybody.

gaff N. hook; barbed fishing spear. When he attempted to land the sailfish, he was so nervous that he dropped the *gaff* into the sea.   also V.

gainsay V. deny. He could not *gainsay* the truth of the report.

galleon N. large sailing ship. The Spaniards pinned their hopes on the *galleon*, the large warship; the British on the smaller and faster pinnace.

galvanize V. stimulate by shock; stir up. The entire nation was *galvanized* into strong military activity by the news of the attack on Pearl Harbor.

gambol V. skip; leap playfully. Watching children *gamboling* in the park is a pleasant experience.

gamester (gām'-stěr) N. gambler. An inveterate *gamester*, he was willing to wager on the outcome of any event, even one which involved the behavior of insects.

gamut (găm'-) N. entire range. In this performance, the leading lady was able to demonstrate the complete *gamut* of her acting ability.

gape (gāp) V. open widely. The huge pit *gaped* before him; if he stumbled, he would fall in.

garbled ADJ. mixed up; based on false or unfair selection. The *garbled* report confused many readers who were not familiar with the facts. garble, V.

garish (găr'-) ADJ. gaudy. She wore a *garish* rhinestone necklace.

garner V. gather; store up. He hoped to *garner* the world's literature in one library.

garnish V. decorate. Parsley was used to *garnish* the boiled potato.   also N.

garrulity (-rōō'-) N. talkativeness. Her *garrulity* cost her many an invitation by hosts who feared she would totally monopolize an evening's

ā —ale; ă —add; ä —arm; à —ask; ē —eve; ě —end; ê —err, her; ə —event, allow,
ī —ice; ĭ —ill; ō —old; ŏ —odd; ô —orb; ōō —food; ou —out; th —thin; ū —use;
ŭ —up; zh —pleasure

conversation. **garrulous,** ADJ.

gauntlet N. leather glove, challenge. Now that we have been challenged, we must take up the *gauntlet* and meet our adversary fearlessly.

gazette N. official periodical publication. He read the *gazettes* regularly for the announcement of his promotion.

generality N. vauge statement. This report is filled with *generalities;* you must be more specific in your statements.

geniality N. cheerfulness; kindliness; sympathy. This restaurant is famous and popular because of the *geniality* of the proprietor who tries to make everyone happy.

genre (zhŏn'-rə) N. style of art illustrating scenes of common life. His painting of fisherfolk at their daily tasks is an excellent illustration of *genre* art.

genteel ADJ. well-bred; elegant. We are looking for a man with a *genteel* appearance who can inspire confidence by his cultivated manner.

gentility N. those of privileged class; refinement. Her family was proud of its *gentility*.

gentry N. people of standing; class of people just below nobility. The local *gentry* did not welcome the visits of the summer tourists and tried to ignore their presence in the community.

germane (-mān') ADJ. pertinent; bearing upon the case at hand. The lawyer objected that the testimony being offered was not *germane* to the case at hand.

gesticulation N. motion; gesture. Operatic performers are trained to make exaggerated *gesticulations* because of the large auditoriums in which they appear.

ghastly ADJ. horrible. The murdered man was a *ghastly* sight.

gibber (jĭb'-) V. speak foolishly. The demented man *gibbered* incoherently.

gibbet (jĭb'-) N. gallows. The bodies of the highwaymen were left dangling from the *gibbet* as a warning to other would-be transgressors.

gibe (jīb) V. mock. As you *gibe* at their superstitious beliefs, do you realize that you, too, are guilty of similarly foolish thoughts?

gig (gĭg) N. two-wheeled carriage. As they drove down the street in their new *gig,* drawn by the dappled mare, they were cheered by the people who recognized them.

gist (jĭst) N. essence. She was asked to give the *gist* of the essay in two sentences.

glaze V. cover with a thin and shiny surface. The freezing rain *glazed* the streets and made driving hazardous.

glean V. gather leavings. After the crops had been harvested by the machines,

ā — ale; ă — add; ä — arm; â — ask; ē — eve; ĕ — end; ê — err, her; ə — event, allow, ĭ — ice; ĭ — ill; ō — old; ŏ — odd; ô — orb; ōō — food; ou — out; th — thin; ū — use; ŭ — up; zh — pleasure

the peasants were permitted to *glean* the wheat left in the fields.

glib ADJ. fluent. He is a *glib* speaker.

gloaming N. twilight. The snow began to fall in the *gloaming* and continued all through the night.

gloat V. express evil satisfaction; view malevolently. As you *gloat* over all your ill-gotten wealth, do you think of the many victims you have defrauded?

ETYMOLOGY 13.

FY (to make) verb suffix
  magnify   make greater
  petrify   make into stone
  beautify   make beautiful

GAM (marriage)
  monogamy   marriage to one person
  bigamy   marriage to two people at the same time
  polygamy   having many spouses at the same time

GEN, GENER (class, race)
  genus   group of biological species with similar characteristics
  generic   characteristic of a class
  gender   class organized according to sex

TEST — Word List 13 — Synonyms

Each of the questions below consists of a word printed in bold, followed by five words or phrases numbered 1 to 5. Choose the numbered word or phrase which is most nearly similar in meaning to the word in bold and write the number of your choice on your answer paper.

241. **garnish** 1. paint 2. garner 3. adorn 4. abuse 5. banish
242. **frugality** 1. foolishness 2. extremity 3. indifference 4. enthusiasm 5. economy
243. **foray** 1. excursion 2. contest 3. ranger 4. intuition 5. fish
244. **gadfly** 1. humorist 2. nuisance 3. scholar 4. bum 5. thief
245. **foolhardy** 1. strong 2. unwise 3. brave 4. futile 5. erudite
246. **glib** 1. slippery 2. fashionable 3. antiquated 4. articulate 5. anticlimactic

ā — ale; ă — add; ä — arm; à — ask; ē — eve; ĕ — end; ê — err, her; ə — event, allow, ī — ice; ĭ — ill; ō — old; ŏ — odd; ô — orb; oo — food; ou — out; th — thin; ū — use; ŭ — up; zh — pleasure

247. franchise   1. subway   2. kiosk   3. license   4. reason   5. fashion
248. furtive   1. underhanded   2. coy   3. blatant   4. quick   5. abortive
249. garner   1. prevent   2. assist   3. collect   4. compute   5. consult
250. gist   1. chaff   2. summary   3. expostulation   4. expiation   5. chore
251. foster   1. speed   2. fondle   3. become infected   4. raise   5. roll
252. foppish   1. scanty   2. radical   3. orthodox   4. dandyish   5. magnificent
253. furor   1. excitement   2. worry   3. flux   4. anteroom   5. lover
254. germane   1. bacteriological   2. Middle European   3. prominent   4. warlike   5. relevant
255. fritter   1. sour   2. chafe   3. dissipate   4. cancel   5. abuse.
256. garish   1. sordid   2. flashy   3. prominent   4. lusty   5. thoughtful
257. formidable   1. dangerous   2. outlandish   3. grandiloquent   4. impenetrable   5. vulnerable
258. garrulity   1. credulity   2. senility   3. loquaciousness   4. speciousness   5. artistry
259. forment   1. spoil   2. instigate   3. interrogate   4. settle   5. maintain
260. galleon   1. liquid measure   2. ship   3. armada   4. company   5. printer's proof

---

Word List 14   glossy-homily

glossy ADJ. smooth and shining. I want this photograph printed on *glossy* paper.

glut V. overstock; fill to excess. The many manufacturers *glutted* the market and could not find purchasers for the many articles they had produced.

glutinous (gl$\overline{oo}$'-) ADJ. sticky; viscous. Molasses is a *glutinous* substance.

gluttonous ADJ. greedy for food. The *gluttonous* boy ate all the cookies. glutton, N.

gnarled (närld) ADJ. twisted. The *gnarled* oak tree had been a landmark for years and was mentioned in several deeds.

gnome (n$\overline{o}$m) N. dwarf; underground spirit. In medieval mythology, *gnomes* were the special guardians and inhabitants of subterranean mines.

goad V. urge on. He was *goaded* by his friends until he yielded to their wishes.

ā — ale; ă — add; ä — arm; à — ask; ē — eve; ĕ — end; ê — err, her; ə — event, allow.
ī — ice; ĭ — ill; ō — old; ŏ — odd; ô — orb; o͞o — food; ou — out; th — thin; ū — use;
ŭ — up; zh — pleasure

gorge V. stuff oneself. The gluttonous guest *gorged* himself with food as though he had not eaten for days.

gory ADJ. bloody. The audience shuddered as it listened to the details of the *gory* massacre.

gossamer (gŏs'-) ADJ. sheer; like cobwebs. Nylon can be woven into *gossamer* or thick fabrics.   also N.

gouge (gouj) V. tear out. In that fight, all the rules were forgotten; the adversaries bit, kicked, and tried to *gouge* each other's eyes out.

gourmand (gôr-mŏnd') N. epicure; person who takes excessive pleasure in fine food. The *gourmand* liked the French cuisine.

gourmet (gôr-mā') N. epicure; connoisseur of food and drink. The *gourmet* stated that this was the best onion soup he had ever tasted.

granary (grăn'-) N. storehouse for grain. We have reason to be thankful for our crops were good and our *granaries* are full.

grandiloquent ADJ. pompous; bombastic; using high-sounding language. The politician could never speak simply; he was always *grandiloquent*.

grandiose (grăn'-dē-ōs) ADJ. imposing; impressive. His *grandiose* manner impressed those who met him for the first time.

granulate V. form into grains. Sugar that has been *granulated* dissolves more readily than lump sugar.   granule, N.

graphic ADJ. pertaining to the art of delineating; vividly described. I was particularly impressed by the *graphic* presentation of the storm.

gratis (grăt'-) ADV. free. The company offered to give one package *gratis* to every purchaser of one of their products.   also ADJ.

gratuitous)-tū'-) ADJ. given freely; unwarranted. I resent your *gratuitous* remarks because no one asked for them.   gratuity, N.

gregarious (grə-găr'-) ADJ. sociable. He was not *gregarious* and preferred to be alone most of the time.

grisly ADJ. ghastly. She shuddered at the *grisly* sight.

grotto N. small cavern. The Blue *Grotto* on Capri can be entered only by small boats rowed by natives through a natural opening in the rocks.

gruel N. liquid food made by boiling oatmeal, etc., in milk or water. Our daily allotment of *gruel* made the meal not only monotonous but also unpalatable.

grueling ADJ. exhausting. The marathon is a *grueling* race.

gruesome ADJ. grisly. People screamed when his *gruesome* appearance was flashed on the screen.

gruff ADJ. rough-mannered. Although he was blunt and *gruff* with most people, he was always gentle with children.

ā — ale; ă — add; ä — arm; á — ask; ē — eve; ĕ — end; ê — err, her; ə — event, allow,
ī — ice; ĭ — ill; ō — old; ŏ — odd; ô — orb; ōō — food; ou — out; th — thin; ū — use;
ŭ — up; zh — pleasure

guffaw (gŭf-fô') N. boisterous laughter. The loud *guffaws* that came from the closed room indicated that the members of the committee had not yet settled down to serious business.

guile (gīl) N. deceit; duplicity. He achieved his high position by *guile* and treachery.

guileless ADJ. without deceit. He is naïve, simple and *guileless;* he cannot be guilty of fraud.

guise N. appearance; costume. In the *guise* of a plumber, the detective investigated the murder case.

gullible ADJ. easily deceived. He preyed upon the *gullible* who believed his stories of easy wealth.

gustatory ADJ. affecting the sense of taste. This food is particularly *gustatory* because of the spices it contains.

gusto N. enjoyment; enthusiasm. He accepted the assignment with such *gusto* that I feel he would have been satisfied with a smaller salary.

gusty ADJ. windy. The *gusty* weather made sailing precarious.

guttural ADJ. pertaining to the throat. *Guttural* sounds are produced in the throat or in the back of the tongue and palate.

habiliments (-bĭl'-ə-) N. garb; clothing. Although not a minister, David Belasco used to wear clerical *habiliments*.

hackneyed ADJ. commonplace; trite. The English teacher criticized his story because of its *hackneyed* plot.

haggard ADJ. wasted away; gaunt. After his long illness, he was pale and *haggard*.

haggle V. argue about prices. I prefer to shop in a store that has a one-price policy because, whenever I *haggle* with a shopkeeper, I am never certain that I paid a fair price for the articles I purchased.

halcyon (hăl'-sē-) ADJ. calm; peaceful. A peaceful look came over his face as he recalled the *halcyon* days of his youth.

hallowed ADJ. blessed; consecrated. He was laid to rest in *hallowed* ground.

hallucination N. delusion. His *hallucination* was so vivid that he cried out in anguish. hallucination, v..

hamper V. obstruct. The minority party agreed not to *hamper* the efforts of the leaders to secure a lasting peace.

hap N. chance; luck. In his poem "Hap," Thomas Hardy objects to the part chance plays in our lives.

haphazard ADJ. random; by chance. His *haphazard* reading left him unacquainted with authors of the books.

hapless ADJ. unfortunate. This *hapless* creature had never known a moment's pleasure.

ā — ale; ă — add; ä — arm; á — ask; ē — eve; ĕ — end; ê — err, her; ə — event, allow, ī — ice; ĭ — ill; ō — old; ŏ — odd; ô — orb; ōō — food; ou — out; th — thin; ū — use; ŭ — up; zh — pleasure

harangue (-răng') N. noisy speech. In his lengthy *harangue*, the principal berated the offenders.

harass (hă'-) V. annoy by repeated attacks. She used to *harass* her husband by her continual demands for fine attire.

harbinger (här'bǐn-jěr) N. forerunner. The crocus is an early *harbinger* of spring.

harping N. tiresome dwelling on a subject. Her constant *harping* on the good times she had had before her marriage angered her husband. harp, V.

harridan N. shrewish hag. Most people avoided the *harridan* because they feared her abusive and vicious language.

harrow V. break up ground after plowing; torture. I don't want to *harrow* you at this time by asking you to recall the details of your unpleasant experience.

harry V. raid. The guerilla band *harried* the enemy nightly.

haughtiness N. pride; arrogance. I resent his *haughtiness* because he is no better than we are.   haughty, ADJ.

hauteur (ō-têr') N. haughtiness. His snobbishness is obvious to all who witness his *hauteur* when he talks to those whom he considers his social inferiors.

hawser N. large rope. The ship was tied to the pier by a *hawser*.

hazardous ADJ. dangerous. Your occupation is too *hazardous* for insurance companies to consider your application.

hazy ADJ. slightly obscure. In *hazy* weather, you cannot see the top of this mountain.

hedonism (hē'-) N. belief that pleasure is the sole aim in life. *Hedonism* and asceticism are opposing philosophies of human behavior.

heedless ADJ. not noticing; disregarding. He drove on, *heedless* of the warnings placed at the side of the road that it was dangerous.

heinous (hā'-) ADJ. atrocious; hatefully bad. Hitler's *heinous* crimes will never be forgotten.

heresy N. opinion contrary to popular belief; opinion contrary to accepted religion. Your remarks are pure *heresy*.

heretic N. person who maintains opinions contrary to the doctrines of the church. She was punished by the Spanish Inquisition because she was a *heretic*.

hermitage N. home of a hermit. Even in his remote *hermitage* he could not escape completely from the world.

heterogeneous (-jēn'-) ADJ. dissimilar. in *heterogeneous* groupings, we have motley collections, while in homogeneous groupings we have

ā — ale; ă — add; ä — arm; å — ask; ē — eve; ĕ — end; ê — err, her; ə — event, allow,
ī — ice; ǐ — ill; ō — old; ŏ — odd; ô — orb; ōō — food; ou — out; th — thin; ū — use;
ŭ — up; zh — pleasure

people or things which have common traits.

hiatus (hī-āt'-) N. gap; pause. There was a *hiatus* of twenty years in the life of Rip Van Winkle.

hibernal (hī-bêr'-) ADJ. wintry. Bears prepare for their long *hibernal* sleep by overeating.

hibernate v. sleep throughout the winter. Bears are one of the many species of animals that *hibernate*.

hierarchy N. body divided into ranks. It was difficult to step out of one's place in this *hierarchy*.

hieroglyphics N. picture writing. The discovery of the Rosetta Stone enabled scholars to read the ancient Egyptian *hieroglyphics*.

hilarity N. boisterous mirth. This *hilarity* is improper on this solemn day of mourning.

hindmost ADJ. farthest behind. You could always find him in the *hindmost* lines when a battle was being waged.

hireling N. one who serves for hire (usually contemptuously). In a matter of such importance, I do not wish to deal with *hirelings;* I must meet with the chief.

hirsute (hêr-soot') ADJ. hairy. He was a *hirsute* individual with a heavy black beard.

histrionic ADJ. theatrical. He was proud of his *histrionic* ability and wanted to play the role of Hamlet.   histrionics, N.

hoary ADJ. white with age. The man was *hoary* and wrinkled.

hogshead N. large barrel. On the trip to England, the ship carried munitions; on its return trip, *hogsheads* filled with French wines and Scotch liquors.

holocaust N. destruction by fire. Citizens of San Francisco remember that the destruction of the city was caused not by the earthquake but by the *holocaust* that followed.

holster N. pistol case. Even when he was not in uniform, he carried a *holster* and pistol under his arm.

homespun ADJ. doméstic; made at home. *Homespun* wit like *homespun* cloth is often coarse and plain.

homily N. sermon; serious warning. His speeches were always *homilies*, advising his listeners to repent and reform.

ETYMOLOGY 14.

GRAPH, GRAM (writing)

ā — ale; ă — add; ä — arm; à — ask; ē — eve; ĕ — end; ê — err, her; ə — event, allow, ī — ice; ĭ — ill; ō — old; ŏ — odd; ô — orb; oo — food; ou — out; th — thin; ū — use; ŭ — up; zh — pleasure

epigram   a pithy statement
telegram   an instantaneous message over great distances
stenography   shorthand (writing narrowly)

GREG (flock, herd)
gregarious   tending to group together as in a herd
aggregate   group, total
egregious   out of the group; now used in a bad sense as wicked

HELI, HELIO (sun)
heliotrope   flower that faces the sun
heliograph   instrument that uses sun's rays to send signals
helium   element abundant in sun's atmosphere

TEST — Word List 14 — Antonyms

Each of the questions below consists of a word printed in bold, followed by five words or phrases numbered 1 to 5. Choose the numbered word or phrase which is most nearly opposite in meaning to the word in bold and write the number of your choice on your answer paper.

261. **grandiose**   1. false   2. ideal   3. proud   4. simple   5. functional
262. **hibernal**   1. wintry   2. summerlike   3. local   4. seasonal   5. springlike
263. **gregarious**   1. antisocial   2. anticipatory   3. glorious   4. horrendous   5. similar
264. **gratuitous**   1. warranted   2. frank   3. ingenuous   4. frugal   5. pithy
265. **hapless**   1. cheerful   2. consistent   3. fortunate   4. considerate   5. shapely
266. **heterogeneous**   1. orthodox   2. pagan   3. unlike   4. similar   5. banished
267. **gusto**   1. noise   2. panic   3. fancy   4. gloom   5. distaste
268. **gusty**   1. calm   2. noisy   3. fragrant   4. routine   5. gloomy
269. **haphazard**   1. fortuitous   2. indifferent   3. deliberate   4. accidental   5. conspiring
270. **hirsute**   1. scaly   2. bald   3. erudite   4. quiet   5. long
271. **gullible**   1. incredulous   2. fickle   3. tantamount   4. easy   5. stylish
272. **granulate**   1. crystallize   2. store   3. crush   4. magnify   5. sweeten

ā — ale; ă — add; ä — arm; à — ask; ē — eve; ĕ — end; ê — err, her; ə — event, allow, ī — ice; ĭ — ill; ō — old; ŏ — odd; ô — orb; ōō — food; ou — out; th — thin; ū — use; ŭ — up; zh — pleasure

273. **gourmet** 1. cook 2. maitre de 3. glutton 4. epicure 5. author
274. **halcyon** 1. pacific 2. prior 3. subsequent 4. puerile 5. martial
275. **gnome** 1. fairy 2. giant 3. pygmy 4. native 5. alien
276. **hilarity** 1. gloom 2. heartiness 3. weakness 4. casualty 5. paucity
277. **hackneyed** 1. carried 2. original 3. banal 4. timely 5. oratorical
278. **heretic** 1. sophist 2. believer 3. interpreter 4. pacifist 5. owner
279. **grisly** 1. unsavory 2. doubtful 3. untidy 4. pleasant 5. bearish
280. **haggard** 1. shrewish 2. inspired 3. plump 4. maidenly 5. vast

---

Word List 15 homogeneous-incarnate

homogeneous (-*jēn'*-) ADJ. of the same kind. Educators try to put pupils of similar abilities into classes because they believe that this *homogeneous* grouping is advisable.   homogeneity, N.

homonym N. word similar in sound but different in meaning and spelling. Pear and pair are *homonyms*.

horticultural ADJ. pertaining to cultivation of gardens. When he bought his house, he began to look for flowers and decorative shrubs, and began to read books dealing with *horticultural* matters.

hostelry (*hŏs'*-) N. inn. Travelers interested in economy should stay at *hostelries* and pensions rather than fashionable hotels.

hubbub N. confused uproar. The market place was a scene of *hubbub* and excitement; in all the noise, we could not distinguish particular voices.

humane (-*mān'*) ADJ. kind. His *humane* and considerate treatment of the unfortunate endeared him to all.

humdrum ADJ. dull; monotonous. After his years of adventure, he could not settle down to a *humdrum* existence.

humid ADJ. damp. He could not stand the *humid* climate and moved to a drier area.

humility N. humbleness of spirit. He spoke with a *humility* and lack of pride which impressed his listeners.

humus N. substance formed by decaying vegetable matter. In order to improve his garden, he spread *humus* over his lawn and flower beds.

ā — ale; ă — add; ä — arm; ȧ — ask; ē — eve; ĕ — end; ê — err, her; ə — event, allow,
ī — ice; ĭ — ill; ō — old; ŏ — odd; ô — orb; o͞o — food; ou — out; th — thin; ū — use;
ŭ — up; zh — pleasure

hybrid N. mongrel; mixed breed. Mendel's formula explains the appearance of *hybrids* and pure species in breeding.   also ADJ.

hypercritical ADJ. excessively exacting. You are *hypercritical* in your demands for perfection; we all make mistakes.

hypochondriac (hī-pō-kŏn'-) N. person unduly worried about his health; worrier without cause about illness. The doctor prescribed chocolate pills for his patient who was a *hypochondriac*.

hypocritical (hĭp-ō-) ADJ. pretending to be virtuous; deceiving. I resent his *hypocritical* posing as a friend for I know he is interested only in his own advancement.

hypothetical ADJ. based on assumptions or hypotheses. Why do we have to consider *hypothetical* cases when we have actual case histories which we may examine?   hypothesis, N.

iconoclastic ADJ. attacking cherished traditions. George Bernard Shaw's *iconoclastic* plays often startled people.

ideology N. ideas of a group of people. That *ideology* is dangerous to this country because it embraces violent philosophies.

idiom N. special usage in language. I could not understand their *idiom* because literal translation made no sense.

idiosyncrasy N. peculiarity; eccentricity. One of his personal *idiosyncrasies* was his habit of rinsing all cutlery given him in a restaurant.

idolatry (ī-dol') N. worship of idols; excessive admiration. Such *idolatry* of singers of popular ballads is typical of the excessive enthusiasm of youth.

igneous (ĭg'-) ADJ. produced by fire; volcanic. Lava, pumice, and other *igneous* rocks are found in great abundance around Mount Vesuvius near Naples.

ignoble (ĭg-nō'-) ADJ. of lowly origin; unworthy. This plan is inspired by *ignoble* motives and I must, therefore, oppose it.

ignominious (-mĭn'-) ADJ. disgraceful. The country smarted under the *ignominious* defeat and dreamed of the day when it would be victorious.   ignominy, N.

illimitable ADJ. infinite. Man, having explored the far reaches of the earth, is reaching out into *illimitable* space.

illusion N. misleading vision. It is easy to create an optical *illusion* in which lines of equal length appear different.   illusory, ADJ.

imbecility N. weakness of mind. I am amazed at the *imbecility* of the readers of these trashy magazines.

imbibe V. drink in. The dry soil *imbibed* the rain quickly.

ā — ale; ă — add; ä — arm; å — ask; ē — eve; ĕ — end; ê — err, her; ə — event, allow,
ī — ice; ĭ — ill; ō — old; ŏ — odd; ô — orb; ōō — food; ou — out; th — thin; ū — use;
ŭ — up; zh — pleasure

imbroglio (-brōl'-yō) N. a complicated situation; perplexity; entanglement. He was called in to untangle the *imbroglio* but failed to bring harmony to the situation.

imbue V. saturate; fill. His visits to the famous Gothic cathedrals *imbued* him with feelings of awe and reverence.

immaculate ADJ. pure; spotless. The West Point cadets were *immaculate* as they lined up for inspection.

imminent ADJ. impending; near at hand. The *imminent* battle will determine our success or failure in this conflict.

immobility N. state of being immovable. Modern armies cannot afford the luxury of *immobility* as they are vulnerable to attack while standing still.

immolate V. offer as a sacrifice. The tribal king offered to *immolate* his daughter to quiet the angry gods.

immune ADJ. exempt. He was fortunately *immune* to the disease and could take care of the sick.

immutable ADJ. unchangeable. Scientists are constantly seeking to discover the *immutable* laws of nature.

impair V. worsen; diminish in value. This arrest will *impair* his reputation in the community.

impale V. pierce. He was *impaled* by the spear hurled by his adversary.

impasse N. predicament from which there is no escape. In this *impasse*, all turned to prayer as their last hope.

impassive ADJ. without feeling; not affected by pain. The American Indian has been depicted as an *impassive* individual, undemonstrative and stoical.

impeach V. charge with crime in office; indict. The angry congressman wanted to *impeach* the President.

impeccable ADJ. faultless. He was proud of his *impeccable* manners.

impecunious ADJ. without money. Now that he was wealthy, he gladly contributed to funds to assist the *impecunious* and the disabled.

impending ADJ. nearing; approaching. The entire country was saddened by the news of his *impending* death.

impenitent ADJ. not repentant. We could see by his brazen attitude that he was *impenitent*.

imperious ADJ. domineering. His *imperious* manner indicated that he had long been accustomed to assuming command.

impermeable ADJ. impervious; not permitting passage through its substance. This new material is *impermeable* to liquids.

ā — ale; ă — add; ä — arm; å — ask; ē — eve; ĕ — end; ê — err, her; ə — event, allow,
ī — ice; ĭ — ill; ō — old; ŏ — odd; ô — orb; ōō — food; ou — out; th — thin; ū — use;
ŭ — up; zh — pleasure

impertinent ADJ. insolent. I regard your remarks as *impertinent* and resent them.

imperturbability N. calmness. We are impressed by his *imperturbability* in this critical moment and are calmed by it.

impervious ADJ. not penetrable; not permitting passage through. You cannot change their habits for their minds are *impervious* to reasoning.

impetuous ADJ. violent; hasty; rash. We tried to curb his *impetuous* behavior because we felt that in his haste he might offend some people.

impetus (ĭm'-) N. moving force. His fear of the city was the *impetus* for moving to the suburbs.

impiety (-pī'-ə-tē) N. irreverence; wickedness. We cannot forgive such an act of *impiety*.

impious (ĭm'-pē-əs) ADJ. irreverent. The congregation was offended by his *impious* remarks.

implacable (-plā'-) ADJ. incapable of being pacified. Madame Defarge was the *implacable* enemy of the Evremonde family.

implication N. that which is hinted at or suggested. If I understand the *implications* of your remark, you do not trust our captain.

implicit ADJ. understood but not stated. It is *implicit* that you will come to our aid if we are attacked.

impolitic (-pŏl'-) ADJ. not wise. I think it is *impolitic* to raise this issue at the present time because the public is too angry.

import (ĭm'-) N. significance. I feel that you have not grasped the full *import* of the message sent to us by the enemy.

importune V. beg earnestly. I must *importune* you to work for peace at this time.   importunate, ADJ.

imprecate (ĭm'-) V. curse; pray that evil will befall. To *imprecate* Hitler's atrocities is not enough; we must insure against any future practice of genocide.

impregnable (-prĕg'-) ADJ. invulnerable. Until the development of the airplane as a military weapon, the fort was considered *impregnable*.

impromptu (-prŏmp'-) ADJ. without previous preparation. His listeners were amazed that such a thorough presentation could be made in an *impromptu* speech.

impropriety (-prī'-) N. state of being inappropriate. Because of the *impropriety* of his costume, he was denied entrance into the dining room.

improvident (-prŏv'-) ADJ. thriftless. He was constantly being warned to mend his *improvident* ways and begin to ''save for a rainy day.''

ā — ale; ă — add; ä — arm; à — ask; ē — eve; ĕ — end; ê — err, her; ə — event, allow, ī — ice; ĭ — ill; ō — old; ŏ — odd; ô — orb; ōō — food; ou — out; th — thin; ū — use; ŭ — up; zh — pleasure

improvise V. compose on the spur of the moment. He would sit at the piano and *improvise* for hours on themes from Bach and Handel.

impugn (-*pūn'*) V. doubt; challenge; gainsay. I cannot *impugn* your honesty without evidence.

impunity N. freedom from punishment. The bully mistreated everyone in the class with *impunity* for he felt that no one would dare retaliate.

imputation N. charge; reproach. You cannot ignore the *imputations* in his speech that you are the guilty party.

inanimate ADJ. lifeless. She was asked to identify the still and *inanimate* body.

inadvertence N. oversight; carlessness. By *inadvertence*, he omitted two questions on the examination.

inalienable ADJ. not to be taken away; nontransferable. *The Declaration of Independence* mentions the *inalienable* rights that all of us possess.

inane (*ĭ-nān'*) ADJ. silly; senseless. Such comments are *inane* because they do not help us solve our problem.   inanity, N.

inarticulate ADJ. speechless; producing indistinct speech. He became *inarticulate* with rage and uttered sounds without meaning.

incapacitate V. disable. During the winter, many people were *incapacitated* by respiratory ailments.

incarcerate V. imprison. The warden will *incarcerate* the felon.

incarnate ADJ. endowed with flesh; personified. Your attitude is so fiendish that you must be a devil *incarnate*.

ETYMOLOGY 15.

IL, ILE (pertaining to, capable of) adjective suffix
    puerile pertaining to a child
    ductile capable of being led
    civil pertaining to a citizen

TEST — Word List 15 — Synonyms and Antonyms

Each of the following questions consists of a word printed in bold, followed by five words or phrases numbered 1 to 5. Choose the numbered word or phrase which is most nearly the same as or the opposite of the word in bold and write the number of your choice on your answer paper.

ā — ale; ă — add; ä — arm; à — ask; ē — eve; ĕ — end; ê — err, her; ə — event, allow; ī — ice; ĭ — ill; ō — old; ŏ — odd; ô — orb; ōō — food; ou — out; th — thin; ū — use; ŭ — up; zh — pleasure

281. **immutable** 1. silent 2. changeable 3. articulate 4. loyal 5. varied
282. **incarcerate** 1. inhibit 2. acquit 3. account 4. imprison 5. force
283. **importune** 1. export 2. plead 3. exhibit 4. account 5. visit
284. **inalienable** 1. inherent 2. repugnant 3. closed to immigration 4. full 5. accountable
285. **impetuous** 1. rash 2. inane 3. just 4. flagrant 5. redolent
286. **impromptu** 1. prompted 2. appropriate 3. rehearsed 4. foolish 5. vast
287. **immolate** 1. debate 2. scour 3. sacrifice 4. sanctify 5. ratify
288. **impervious** 1. impenetrable 2. vulnerable 3. chaotic 4. cool 5. perfect
289. **impeccable** 1. unmentionable 2. quotable 3. blinding 4. faulty 5. hampering
290. **hypercritical** 1. intolerant 2. false 3. extreme 4. inarticulate 5. cautious
291. **impassive** 1. active 2. demonstrative 3. perfect 4. anxious 5. irritated
292. **impair** 1. separate 2. make amends 3. make worse 4. falsify 5. cancel
293. **immaculate** 1. chastened 2. chewed 3. sullied 4. angered 5. beaten
294. **impolitic** 1. campaigning 2. advisable 3. hopeless 4. legal 5. fortunate
295. **hubbub** 1. bedlam 2. fury 3. cap 4. axle 5. wax
296. **impecunious** 1. affluent 2. afflicted 3. affectionate 4. affable 5. afraid
297. **hypothetical** 1. logical 2. fantastic 3. wizened 4. assumed 5. acromatic
298. **hybrid** 1. product 2. species 3. mixture 4. fish 5. genus
299. **impunity** 1. violation 2. liability 3. joke 4. play on words 5. canard
300. **inane** 1. passive 2. wise 3. intoxicated 4. mellow 5. silent

---

Word List 16   incendiary-intellect

incendiary N. arsonist. The fire spread in such an unusual manner that the fire

ā — ale; ă — add; ä — arm; â — ask; ē — eve; ĕ — end; ê — err, her; ə — event, allow.
ī — ice; ĭ — ill; ō — old; ŏ — odd; ô — orb; o͞o — food; ou — out; th — thin; ū — use;
ŭ — up; zh — pleasure

department chiefs were certain that it had been set by an *incendiary*. also N.

incentive N. spur; motive. Pupils who dislike school must be given an *incentive* to learn.

incessant ADJ. uninterrupted. The crickets kept up an *incessant* chirping which disturbed our attempts to fall asleep.

inchoate (*ĭn'-kō-*) ADJ. recently begun; rudimentary; elementary. Before the Creation, the world was an *inchoate* mass.

incipient ADJ. beginning; in an early stage. I will go to sleep early for I want to break an *incipient* cold.

incisive (*-sī'-sŭv*) ADJ. cutting; sharp. His *incisive* remarks made us see the fallacy in our plans.

incite V. arouse to action. The demagogue *incited* the mob to take action into its own hands.

inclement ADJ. stormy; unkind. I like to read a good book in *inclement* weather.

inclusive ADJ. tending to include all. This session will run from January 10 to February 15 *inclusive*.

incognito (*-cŏg'-*) ADJ. with identity concealed; using an assumed name. The monarch enjoyed traveling through the town *incognito* and mingling with the populace.

incommodious (*-mō'-*) ADJ. not spacious. In their *incommodious* quarters, they had to improvise for closet space.

incompatible ADJ. inharmonious. The married couple argued incessantly and finally decided to separate because they were *incompatible*.

incongruity (*-grū'-*) N. lack of harmony; absurdity. The *incongruity* of his wearing sneakers with his formal attire amused the observers.

inconsequential (*-quĕn'-*) ADJ. of trifling significance. Your objections are *inconsequential* and may be disregarded.

incontrovertible (*-vêrt'-*) ADJ. indisputable. We must yield to the *incontrovertible* evidence which you have presented and free your client.

incorporeal (*-pô'-rĭ-*) ADJ. immaterial; without a material body. We must devote time to the needs of our *incorporeal* mind as well as our corporeal body.

incorrigible (*-cŏr'-*) ADJ. uncorrectable. Because he was an *incorrigible* criminal, he was sentenced to life imprisonment.

incredulity (*-dū'-lĭ-*) N. tendency to disbelief. Your *incredulity* in the face of all the evidence is hard to understand.

increment N. increase. This job has an annual *increment* in salary until you

---

ā — ale; ă — add; ä — arm; â — ask; ē — eve; ĕ — end; ê — err, her; a — event, allow.
ī — ice; ĭ — ill; ō — old; ŏ — odd; ô — orb; ōō — food; ou — out; th — thin; ū — use;
ŭ — up; zh — pleasure

reach the maximum of $18,000 a year.

incriminate v. accuse. The evidence gathered against the racketeers *incriminates* some high public officials as well.

incubate v. hatch; scheme. Inasmuch as our supply of electricity is cut off, we shall have to rely on the hens to *incubate* these eggs.

incubus N. burden; mental care; nightmare. The *incubus* of financial worry helped bring on his nervous breakdown.

inculcate v. teach. In an effort to *inculcate* religious devotion, the officials ordered that the school day begin with the singing of a hymn.

incumbent N. office holder. The newly elected public official received valuable advice from the present *incumbent*.   also ADJ.

incursion N. temporary invasion. The nightly *incursions* and hit and run raids of our neighbors across the border tried the patience of the country to the point where we decided to retaliate in force.

indefatigable (-făt'-) ADJ. tireless. He was *indefatigable* in his constant efforts to raise funds for the Red Cross.

indemnify v. make secure against loss; compensate for loss. The city will *indemnify* all home owners whose property is spoiled by this project.

indenture v. bind servant or apprentice to master. Many immigrants could come to America only after they had *indentured* themselves for several years.   also N.

indict (-dīt') v. charge. If the grand jury *indicts* the suspect, he will go to trial.

indigenous (-dĭj'-ĕ-) ADJ. native. Tobacco is one of the *indigenous* plants which the early explorers found in this country.

indigent (ĭn'-) ADJ. poor. Because he was *indigent*, he was sent to the welfare office.

indignity N. offensive or insulting treatment. Although he seemed to accept the *indignities* heaped upon him cheerfully, he was inwardly very angry.

indisputable (-dĭs'-) ADJ. too certain to be disputed. In the face of these *indisputable* statements, I withdraw my complaint.

indite v. write; compose. Cyrano *indited* many letters for Christian.

indolence N. laziness. The sultry weather in the tropics encourages a life of *indolence*.

indomitable ADJ. unconquerable. The founders of our country had *indomitable* will power.

indubitably ADV. beyond a doubt. Because his argument was *indubitably* valid, the judge accepted it.

indulgent ADJ. humoring; yielding; lenient. An over-*indulgent* parent may

ā — ale; ă — add; ä — arm; à — ask; ē — eve; ĕ — end; ê — err, her; ə — event, allow, ī — ice; ĭ — ill; ō — old; ŏ — odd; ô — orb; ōō — food; ou — out; th — thin; ū — use; ŭ — up; zh — pleasure

spoil the child.

ineffable ADJ. unutterable; cannot be expressed in speech. Such *ineffable* joy must be experienced; it cannot be described.

inept ADJ. unsuited; absurd; incompetent. The constant turmoil in the office proved that he was an *inept* administrator.

inexorable (-*ĕx'*-) ADJ. relentless; unyielding; implacable. The governor is *inexorable;* he will not suspend the sentence.

infallible ADJ. unerring. We must remember that none of us is *infallible*.

infamous (ĭn'-) ADJ. notoriously bad. Jesse James was an *infamous* outlaw.

inference N. conclusion drawn from data. I want you to check this *inference* because it may have been based on insufficient information.

infinitesimal ADJ. very small. In the twentieth century, physicists have made their greatest discoveries about the characteristics of *infinitesimal* objects like the atom and its parts.

infirmity N. weakness. His greatest *infirmity* was lack of will power.

inflated ADJ. enlarged (with air or gas). After the balloons were *inflated*, they were distributed among the children.

influx N. flowing into. The *influx* of refugees into the country has taxed the relief agencies severely.

infraction N. violation. Because of his many *infractions* of school regulations, he was suspended by the dean.

infringe V. violate; encroach. I think your machine *infringes* on my patent.

ingenuous (-*jĕn'-ū*-) ADJ. naive; young; unsophisticated. These remarks indicate that you are *ingenuous* and unaware of life's harsher realities.

ingrate N. ungrateful person. You are an *ingrate* since you have treated my gifts with scorn.

ingratiate (-*grā'*-) V. become popular with. He tried to *ingratiate* himself into her parents' good graces.

inherent (-*hēr'*-) ADJ. firmly established by nature or habit. His *inherent* love of justice compelled him to come to their aid.

inhibit V. prohibit; restrain. The child was not *inhibited* in his responses.   inhibition, N.

inimical (ĭn-ĭm'-) ADJ. unfriendly; hostile. She felt that they were *inimical* and were hoping for her downfall.

iniquitous ADJ. unjust; wicked. I cannot approve of the *iniquitous* methods you used to gain your present position.   iniquity, N.

inkling N. hint. This came as a complete surprise to me as I did not have the slightest *inkling* of your plans.

innate ADJ. inborn. His *innate* talent for music was soon recognized by his

ā — ale; ă — add; ä — arm; à — ask; ē — eve; ĕ — end; ê — err, her; ə — event, allow, ī — ice; ĭ — ill; ō — old; ŏ — odd; ô — orb; ōo — food; ou — out; th — thin; ū — use; ŭ — up; zh — pleasure

parents.

innocuous ADJ. harmless. Let him drink it; it is *innocuous*.

innovation N. change; introduction of something new. He loved *innovations* just because they were new.

innuendo (*ĭn-nū-ĕn'-*) N. hint; insinuation. I resent the *innuendoes* in your statement more than the statement itself.

inordinate ADJ. unrestrained; excessive. She had an *inordinate* fondness for candy.

insatiable ADJ. not easily satisfied; greedy. His thirst for knowledge was *insatiable;* he was always in the library.

inscrutable ADJ. incomprehensible; not to be discovered. Your motives are *inscrutable*.

insensate (*-sĕn'-*) ADJ. without feeling. He lay there as *insensate* as a log.

insidious ADJ. treacherqus; stealthy; sly. The cancer cell is *insidious* because it works secretly within our body for our defeat.

insinuate V. hint; imply. What are you trying to *insinuate* by that remark?

insipid ADJ. tasteless; dull. I am bored by your *insipid* talk.

insolent ADJ. haughty and contemptuous. I resent your *insolent* manner.

insolvency N. bankruptcy; lack of ability to repay debts. When rumors of his *insolvency* reached his creditors, they began to press him for payment of the money due them.

insomnia N. wakefulness; inability to sleep. He refused to join us for a midnight cup of coffee because he claimed it gave him *insomnia*.

instigate V. urge; start; provoke. I am afraid that this statement will *instigate* a revolt.

insular ADJ. like an island; narrow-minded. In an age of such rapid means of communication, we cannot afford to be hemmed in by such *insular* ideas.

insuperable ADJ. insurmountable; invincible. In the face of *insuperable* difficulties they maintained their courage and will to resist.

insurgent ADJ. rebellious. We will not discuss reforms until the *insurgent* troops have returned to their homes.

integrate V. make whole; combine; make into one unit. He tried to *integrate* all their activities into one program.

integrity N. wholeness; purity; uprightness. He was a man of great *integrity*.

intellect N. higher mental powers. He thought college would develop his *intellect*.

ā — ale; ă — add; ä — arm; à — ask; ē — eve; ĕ — end; ê — err, her; ə — event, allow,
ī — ice; ĭ — ill; ō — old; ŏ — odd; ô — orb; ōō — food; ou — out; th — thin; ū — use;
ŭ — up; zh — pleasure

ETYMOLOGY 16.

IN (in, into, upon, toward) prefix
>> **incursion** invasion
>> **insidious** treacherous

IN (not, without) prefix
>> **inconsequential** not significant
>> **inimical** hostile, not friendly
>> **insipid** tasteless

TEST — Word List 16 — Synonyms

>> Each of the questions below consists of a word printed in bold, followed by five words or phrases numbered 1 to 5. Choose the numbered word or phrase which is most nearly similar in meaning to the word in bold and write the number of your choice on your answer paper.

301. incentive 1. objective 2. goad 3. stimulation 4. beginning 5. simulation

302. indubitably 1. flagrantly 2. doubtfully 3. carefully 4. carelessly 5. certainly

303. inconsequential 1. disorderly 2. insignificant 3. subsequent 4. insufficient 5. preceding

304. insinuate 1. resist 2. suggest 3. report 4. rectify 5. lecture

305. incorrigible 1. narrow 2. straight 3. inconceivable 4. unreliable 5. unreformable

306. ingenuous 1. clever 2. stimulating 3. naive 4. wily 5. cautious

307. indolence 1. sloth 2. poverty 3. latitude 4. aptitude 5. anger

308. innocuous 1. not capable 2. not dangerous 3. not eager 4. not frank 5. not peaceful

309. insipid 1. witty 2. flat 3. wily 4. talkative 5. lucid

310. incompatible 1. capable 2. reasonable 3. faulty 4. indifferent 5. alienated

311. incriminate 1. exacerbate 2. involve 3. intimidate 4. lacerate 5. prevaricate

312. infirmity 1. disability 2. age 3. inoculation 4. hospital 5. unity

ā — ale; ă — add; ä — arm; à — ask; ē — eve; ĕ — end; ê — err, her; ə — event, allow.
ĭ — ice; ĭ — ill; ō — old; ŏ — odd; ô — orb; o͞o — food; ou — out; th — thin; ū — use;
ŭ — up; zh — pleasure

313. **infallible**   1. final   2. unbelievable   3. perfect   4. inaccurate   5. inquisitive

314. **indigent**   1. lazy   2. pusillanimous   3. penurious   4. affluent   5. contrary

315. **inclement**   1. unfavorable   2. abandoned   3. kindly   4. selfish   5. active

316. **integrate**   1. tolerate   2. unite   3. flow   4. copy   5. assume

317. **inimical**   1. antagonistic   2. anonymous   3. fanciful   4. accurate   5. seldom

318. **inculcate**   1. exculpate   2. educate   3. exonerate   4. prepare   5. embarrass

319. **indignity**   1. pomposity   2. bombast   3. obeisance   4. insult   5. message

320. **insensate**   1. aggrieved   2. unconcerned   3. angered   4. patent   5. prehensile

---

Word List 17   intelligentsia-levity

intelligentsia N. the intelligent and educated classes (often used derogatorily). He preferred discussions about sports and politics to the literary conversations of the *intelligentsia*.

inter (-*tĕr′*) v. bury. They are going to *inter* the body tomorrow.

interim N. meantime. The company will not consider our proposal until next week; in the *interim*, let us proceed as we have in the past.

interment (-*tĕr′-*) N. burial. *Interment* will take place in the church cemetery at 2 P.M. Wednesday.

interminable ADJ. endless. Her telephone conversation seemed *interminable*.

intermittent ADJ. periodic; on and off. Our picnic was marred by *intermittent* rains.

intimate v. hint. She *intimated* rather than stated her preferences.

intimidation (-*dā′-*) N. fear. The dictator ruled by *intimidation*.

intransigent ADJ. refusing any compromise. The strike settlement has collapsed because both sides are *intransigent*.

intrepid (-*trĕp′-*) ADJ. fearless. For his *intrepid* conduct in battle he was promoted.

intrinsic ADJ. belonging to a thing in itself; inherent. Although the *intrinsic* value of this award is small, I shall always cherish it.

ā — ale; ă — add; ä — arm; å — ask; ē — eve; ĕ — end; ê — err, her; ə — event, allow;
ī — ice; ĭ — ill; ō — old; ŏ — odd; ô — orb; ōō — food; ou — out; th — thin; ū — use;
ŭ — up; zh — pleasure

introvert N. one who is introspective; inclined to think more about oneself. In his poetry, he reveals that he is an *introvert* by his intense interest in his own problems.

intrude V. trespass, enter as an uninvited person. He hesitated to intrude on their conversation.

intuition N. power of knowing without reasoning. She claimed to know the truth by *intuition*. intuitive, ADJ.

inundate V. overflow; flood. The tremendous waves *inundated* the town.

inured ADJ. accustomed; hardened. He became *inured* to the Alaskan cold.

invective N. abuse. He had expected criticism but not the *invective* which greeted his proposal.

inveigle (-vē´-) V. lead astray; wheedle. He was *inveigled* into joining the club.

inverse ADJ. opposite. There is an *inverse* ratio between the strength of light and its distance.

inveterate ADJ. deep-rooted; habitual. He is an *inveterate* smoker.

invidious ADJ. designed to create ill-will or envy. We disregarded her *invidious* remarks because we realized how jealous she was.

inviolability (-vī´-) N. security from being destroyed, corrupted, or profaned. They respected the *inviolability* of her faith and did not try to change her manner of living.

invulnerable ADJ. incapable of injury. Achilles was *invulnerable* except in his heel.

iota (ī-ō´-tä) N. very small quantity. He hadn't an *iota* of common sense.

irascible (ĭ-ras´-ĭbĺ) ADJ. irritable; easily angered. His *irascible* temper frightened me.

iridescent (-dĕs´-) ADJ. exhibiting rainbowlike colors. He admired the *iridescent* hues of the oil that floated on the surface of the water.

ironical (-rŏn´-) ADJ. resulting in an unexpected and contrary manner. It is *ironical* that his success came when he least wanted it. irony, N.

irreconcilable ADJ. incompatible; not able to be resolved. The separated couple was *irreconcilable*.

irrelevant (-rĕl´-) ADJ. not applicable; unrelated. This statement is *irrelevant* and should be disregarded by the jury.

irremediable (-mē´-di-) ADJ. incurable; uncorrectable. The error he made was *irremediable*.

irreparable (rĕp´-) ADJ. not able to be corrected or repaired. Your apology cannot atone for the *irreparable* damage you have done to his reputation.

irreverent ADJ. lacking proper respect. The worshippers resented his *irreverent* remarks about their faith.

ā — ale; ă — add; ä — arm; â — ask; ē — eve; ĕ — end; ê — err, her; ə — event, allow,
ī — ice; ĭ — ill; ō — old; ŏ — odd; ô — orb; ōō — food; ou — out; th — thin; ū — use;
ŭ — up; zh — pleasure

irrevocable (-*rĕv'*-) ADJ. unalterable. Let us not brood over past mistakes since they are *irrevocable*.

iterate (*ĭt'*-) V. utter a second time; repeat. I will *iterate* the warning I have previously given to you.

itinerant (*ī-tĭn'*-) ADJ. wandering; traveling. He was an *itinerant* peddler.

jaded ADJ. fatigued; surfeited. He looked for exotic foods to stimulate his *jaded* appetite.

jargon N. language used by special group; gibberish. We tried to understand the *jargon* of the peddlers in the market place but could not find any basis for comprehension.

jaundiced ADJ. yellowed; prejudiced; envious. He gazed at the painting with *jaundiced* eyes.

jeopardy (*jĕp'*-) N. exposure to death or danger. He cannot be placed in double *jeopardy*.

jettison V. throw overboard. In order to enable the ship to ride safely through the storm, the captain had to *jettison* much of his cargo.

jingoism N. extremely aggressive and militant patriotism. We must be careful to prevent a spirit of *jingoism* from spreading at this time; the danger of a disastrous war is too great.

jocose (-*kōs'*) ADJ. given to joking. The salesman was a *jocose* person.

jocular ADJ. said or done in jest. Do not take my *jocular* remarks seriously.

jocund ADJ. merry. Santa Claus is always gay and *jocund*.

jubilation N. rejoicing. There was great *jubilation* when the armistice was announced.

judicious ADJ. wise; determined by sound judgment. I believe that this plan is not *judicious;* it is too risky.

junket N. a merry feast or picnic. The opposition claimed that his trip to Europe was merely a political *junket*.

junto (*ŭn'*-*tō*) N. group of men joined on political intrigue; cabal. As soon as he learned of its existence, the dictator ordered the execution of all of the members of the *junto*.

ken N. range of knowledge. I cannot answer your question since this matter is beyond my *ken*.

kiosk (*kē'*-*ŏsk*) N. summer-house; open pavilion. She waited at the subway *kiosk*.

kismet N. fate. *Kismet* is the Arabic word for "fate."

kith N. familiar friends. He always helped both his *kith* and kin.

kleptomaniac N. person who has a compulsive desire to steal. They discovered that the *kleptomaniac* was a wealthy customer when they caught her stealing some cheap trinkets.

ā — ale; ă — add; ä — arm; â — ask; ē — eve; ĕ — end; ê — err, her; ə — event, allow, ī — ice; ĭ — ill; ō — old; ŏ — odd; ô — orb; ōō — food; ou — out; th — thin; ū — use; ŭ — up; zh — pleasure

knavery N. rascality. We cannot condone such *knavery* in public officials.

knell N. tolling of a bell at a funeral; sound of the funeral bell. "The curfew tolls the *knell* of parting day."

knoll N. little round hill. Robert Louis Stevenson's grave is on a *knoll* in Samoa.

labyrinth N. maze. Tom and Betty were lost in the *labyrinth* of secret caves.

lacerate (lăs'-êr-) V. mangle; tear. Her body was *lacerated* in the automobile crash.

lackadaisical ADJ. affectedly languid. He was *lackadaisical* and indifferent about his part in the affair.

lackey N. footman; toady. The duke was followed by his *lackeys.*

laconic ADJ. brief and to the point. Will Rogers' *laconic* comments on the news made him world-famous.

laggard ADJ. slow; sluggish. The sailor had been taught not to be *laggard* in carrying out orders.

lagniappe (lă-nyăp') N. trifling present given to a customer. The butcher threw in some bones for the dog as a *lagniappe.*

lagoon N. shallow body of water near a sea; lake. They enjoyed their swim in the calm *lagoon.*

laity (lā'-ĭ-tĭ) N. laymen; persons not connected with the clergy. The *laity* does not always understand the clergy's problems.

lambent ADJ. flickering; softly radiant. They sat quietly before the *lambent* glow of the fireplace.

laminated ADJ. made of thin plates or scales. Banded gneiss is a *laminated* rock.

lampoon V. ridicule. This article *lampoons* the pretensions of some movie moguls.   also N.

languid ADJ. weary; sluggish; listless. Her siege of illness left her *languid* and pallid.

languish V. lose animation; lose strength. In some stories, love-lorn damsels *languish* and pine away.

lapidary N. worker in precious stones. He employed a *lapidary* to cut the large diamond.

largess (lär'-gĕs) N. generous gift. Lady Bountiful distributed *largess* to the poor.

lascivious ADJ. lustful. The *lascivious* books were confiscated and destroyed.

lassitude N. languor; weariness. The hot, tropical weather created a feeling of *lassitude* and encouraged drowsiness.

latent (lā'-) ADJ. dormant; hidden. His *latent* talent was discovered by accident.

ā — ale; ă — add; ä — arm; å — ask; ē — eve; ĕ — end; ê — err, her; ə — event, allow, ī — ice; ĭ — ill; ō — old; ŏ — odd; ô — orb; ōō — food; ou — out; th — thin; ū — use; ŭ — up; zh — pleasure

lateral ADJ. coming from the side. In order to get good plant growth, the gardener must pinch off all *lateral* shoots.

latitude N. freedom from narrow limitations. I think you have permitted your son too much *latitude* in this matter.

laudatory ADJ. expressing praise. The critics' *laudatory* comments helped to make her a star.

lave (*lāv*) V. wash. The running water will *lave* away all stains.

lavish ADJ. liberal; wasteful. The actor's *lavish* gifts pleased her.

lecherous ADJ. impure in thought and act; lustful; unchaste. He is a *lecherous* and wicked old man.

lesion N. unhealthy change in structure; injury. Many *lesions* are the result of disease.

lethal ADJ. deadly. It is unwise to leave *lethal* weapons where children may find them.

lethargic (*lə-thär'-*) ADJ. drowsy; dull. The stuffy room made him *lethargic*.

levity N. lightness. Such *levity* is improper on this serious occasion.

ETYMOLOGY 17.

INTER (between, among) prefix
> **intervene**   come between
> **international**   between nations
> **interjection**   a statement thrown in

IST (one who practices) noun suffix
> **humorist**   one who provides humor
> **specialist**   one who engages in a specialty
> **optimist**   one who is hopeful

IT, ITINER (journey, road)
> **exit**   way out
> **itinerary**   plan of journey
> **itinerant**   traveling from place to place

ITY (state of being) noun suffix
> **annuity**   state of being yearly
> **credulity**   state of being gullible
> **sagacity**   wisdom

IZE, ISE (to make) verb suffix
> **victimize**   to make a victim
> **rationalize**   to reason
> **harmonize**   to make peaceful

ā — ale; ă — add; ä — arm; â — ask; ē — eve; ĕ — end; ê — err, her; ə — event, allow, ī — ice; ĭ — ill; ō — old; ŏ — odd; ô — orb; ōō — food; ou — out; th — thin; ū — use; ŭ — up; zh — pleasure

JAC, JACT, JEC (to throw)
>**projectile** missile; something thrown forward
>**trajectory** path taken by thrown object
>**reject** throw back

JUR, JURAT (to swear)
>**abjure** renounce
>**perjure** to testify falsely
>**jury** group of men sworn to seek the truth

LABOR, LABORAT (to work)
>**laboratory** place where work is done
>**collaborate** work together with others
>**laborious** difficult

LEG, LECT (to choose, to read)
>**election** choice
>**legible** able to read
>**eligible** able to be selected

LEG (law)
>**legislature** law-making body
>**legitimate** lawful
>**legal** lawful

TEST — Word List 17 — Antonyms

Each of the questions below consists of a word printed in bold, followed by five words or phrases numbered 1 to 5. Choose the numbered word or phrase which is most nearly opposite in meaning to the word in bold and write the number of your choice on your answer paper.

321. intermittent 1. heavy 2. fleeting 3. constant 4. fearless 5. responding

322. irreverent 1. related 2. mischievous 3. respecting 4. pious 5. violent

323. inundate 1. abuse 2. deny 3. swallow 4. treat 5. drain

324. laconic 1. milky 2. verbose 3. wicked 4. flagrant 5. derelict

325. inter 1. exhume 2. amuse 3. relate 4. frequent 5. abandon

326. latent 1. hidden 2. forbidding 3. execrable 4. early 5. obvious

327. intransigent 1. stationary 2. yielding 3. incorruptible 4. magnificent 5. grandiose

ā — ale; ă — add; ä — arm; â — ask; ē — eve; ĕ — end; ê — err, her; ə — event, allow, ī — ice; ĭ — ill; ō — old; ŏ — odd; ô — orb; ōō — food; ou — out; th — thin; ū — use; ŭ — up; zh — pleasure

328. **jaded** 1. upright 2. stimulated 3. aspiring 4. applied 5. void
329. **levity** 1. bridge 2. dam 3. praise 4. blame 5. solemnity
330. **inveterate** 1. inexperienced 2. sophisticated 3. professional 4. wicked 5. ascetic
331. **lampoon** 1. darken 2. praise 3. abandon 4. sail 5. fly
332. **irrelevant** 1. lacking piety 2. fragile 3. congruent 4. pertinent 5. varied
333. **intrepid** 1. cold 2. hot 3. understood 4. callow 5. craven
334. **intrinsic** 1. extrinsic 2. abnormal 3. above 4. abandoned 5. basic
335. **lackadaisical** 1. monthly 2. possessing time 3. ambitious 4. pusillanimous 5. intelligent
336. **lethargic** 1. convalescent 2. beautiful 3. enervating 4. invigorating 5. interrogating
337. **inured** 1. accustomed 2. fitted 3. intestate 4. futile 5. inexperienced
338. **jaundiced** 1. whitened 2. inflamed 3. quickened 4. aged 5. unbiased
339. **kith** 1. outfit 2. strangers 3. brothers 4. ceramics tool 5. quality
340. **laudatory** 1. dirtying 2. disclaiming 3. defamatory 4. inflammatory 5. debased

---

Word List 18   lewd—mendicant

lewd ADJ. lustful. They found his *lewd* stories objectionable.

lexicon N. dictionary. I cannot find this word in any *lexicon* in the library. lexicographer, N.

liaison (*lē-ā-zŏn'*) ADJ. officer who acts as go-between for two armies. As *liaison* officer, he had to avoid offending the leaders of the two armies.

libelous ADJ. defamatory; injurious to the good name of a person. He sued the newspaper because of its *libelous* story.

libertine N. debauched person, roué. Although she was aware of his reputation as a *libertine*, she felt she could reform him and help him break his dissolute way of life.

libidinous (*-bĭd'-*) ADJ. lustful. They objected to his *libidinous* behavior.

ā — ale; ă — add; ä — arm; â — ask; ē — eve; ĕ — end; ê — err, her; ə — event, allow,
ī — ice; ĭ — ill; ō — old; ŏ — odd; ô — orb; ōō — food; ou — out; th — thin; ū — use;
ŭ — up; zh — pleasure

libretto N. text of an opera. The composer of an opera's music is remembered more frequently than the author of its *libretto*.

licentious ADJ. wanton; lewd; dissolute. The *licentious* monarch helped bring about his country's downfall.

lieu (*lōō*) N. instead. They accepted his check in *lieu* of cash.

limn (*lǐm*) V. portray; describe vividly. He was never satisfied with his attempts to *limn* her beauty on canvas.

limpid ADJ. clear. A *limpid* stream ran through his property.

linguistic ADJ. pertaining to language. The modern tourist will encounter very little *linguistic* difficulty as English has become an almost universal language.

liquidate V. settle accounts; clear up. He was able to *liquidate* all his debts in a short period of time.

lithe (*lǐth*) ADJ. flexible; supple. Her figure was *lithe* and willowy.

litigation N. lawsuit. Try to settle this amicably; I do not want to start *litigation*.

livid ADJ. lead-colored; black and blue; enraged. His face was so *livid* with rage that we were afraid that he might have an attack of apoplexy.

loath (*lōth*) ADJ. averse; reluctant. They were both *loath* for him to go.

loathe V. detest. We *loathed* the wicked villain.

lode N. metal-bearing vein. If this *lode* which we have discovered extends for any distance, we have found a fortune.

longevity (-*jěv'*-) N. long life. The old man was proud of his *longevity*.

lope V. gallop slowly. As the horses *loped* along, we had an opportunity to admire the ever-changing scenery.

loquacious ADJ. talkative. She is very *loquacious* and can speak on the telephone for hours.

lout N. clumsy person. The delivery boy is an awkward *lout*.

lucent ADJ. shining. The moon's *lucent* rays silvered the river.

lucid ADJ. bright; easily understood. His explanation was *lucid* and to the point.

lucrative ADJ. profitable. He turned his hobby into a *lucrative* profession.

lucre N. money. Preferring *lucre* to fame, he wrote stories of popular appeal.

lugubrious ADJ. mournful. The *lugubrious* howling of the dogs added to our sadness.

luminous ADJ. shinging; issuing light. The sun is a *luminous* body.

lunar ADJ. pertaining to the moon. *Lunar* craters can be plainly seen with the aid of a small telescope.

lurid ADJ. wild; sensational. The *lurid* stories he told shocked his listeners.

luscious ADJ. pleasing to taste or smell. The ripe peach was *luscious*.

luster N. shine; gloss. The soft *luster* of the silk in the dim light was pleasing.

ā — <u>a</u>le; ă — <u>a</u>dd; ä — <u>a</u>rm; å — <u>a</u>sk; ē — <u>e</u>ve; ĕ — <u>e</u>nd; ê — <u>e</u>rr, h<u>e</u>r; ə — <u>e</u>vent, all<u>o</u>w,
ī — <u>i</u>ce; ĭ — <u>i</u>ll; ō — <u>o</u>ld; ŏ — <u>o</u>dd; ô — <u>o</u>rb; ōō — f<u>oo</u>d; ou — <u>ou</u>t; th — <u>th</u>in; ū — <u>u</u>se;
ŭ — <u>u</u>p; zh — plea<u>s</u>ure

lustrous ADJ. shining. Her large and *lustrous* eyes gave a touch of beauty to an otherwise drab face.

luxuriant ADJ. fertile; abundant; ornate. Farming was easy in this *luxuriant* soil.

macabre (-ä'-) ADJ. gruesome; grisly. The city morgue is a *macabre* spot for the uninitiated.

macerate V. waste away. Cancer *macerated* his body.

Machiavellian (mä-kē-ə-věl'-) ADJ. crafty; double dealing. I do not think he will be a good ambassador because he is not accustomed to the *Machiavellian* maneuverings of foreign diplomats.

machinations (măk-ĭ-nā'-) N. schemes. I can see through your wily *machinations*.

madrigal N. pastoral song. His program of folk songs included several *madrigals* which he sang to the accompaniment of a lute.

maelstrom (māl'-) N. whirlpool. The canoe was tossed about in the *maelstrom*.

magnanimous ADJ. generous. The philanthropist was most *magnanimous*.

magnate N. person of prominence or influence. The steel *magnate* decided to devote more time to city politics.

magniloquent ADJ. boastful; pompous. In their stories of the trial, the reporters ridiculed the *magniloquent* speeches of the defense attorney.

magnitude N. greatness; extent. It is difficult to comprehend the *magnitude* of his crime.

maim V. mutilate; injure. The hospital could not take care of all who had been wounded or *maimed* in the railroad accident.

malediction N. curse. The witch uttered *maledictions* against her captors.

malefactor N. criminal. We must try to bring these *malefactors* to justice.

malevolent ADJ. wishing evil. We must thwart his *malevolent* schemes.

malicious ADJ. dictated by hatred or spite. The *malicious* neighbor spread the gossip.

malign (-līn') V. speak evil of; defame. Because of her hatred of the family, she *maligns* all who are friendly to them.

malignant (-lĭg'-) ADJ. having an evil influence; virulent. This is a *malignant* disease; we may have to use drastic measures to stop its spread.

malingerer (-lĭng'-gér-) N. one who feigns illness to escape duty. The captain ordered the sergeant to punish all *malingerers*.

mall N. public walk. The *Mall* in Central Park has always been a favorite spot for Sunday strollers.

malleable (măl'-) ADJ. capable of being shaped by pounding. Gold is a *malleable* metal.

ā — ale; ă — add; ä — arm; á — ask; ē — eve; ĕ — end; ê — err, her; ə — event, allow, ī — ice; ĭ — ill; ō — old; ŏ — odd; ô — orb; ōō — food; ou — out; th — thin; ū — use; ŭ — up; zh — pleasure

mammoth ADJ. gigantic. The *mammoth* corporations of the twentieth century are a mixed blessing.

mandatory ADJ. obligatory. These instructions are *mandatory;* any violation will be severely punished.

maniacal (-nī'-) ADJ. raving mad. His *maniacal* laughter frightened us.

manifest ADJ. understandable; clear. His evil intentions were *manifest* and yet we could not stop him.

manifesto N. declaration; statement of policy. This statement may be regarded as the *manifesto* of the party's policy.

manipulate V. operate with the hands. Hou do you *manipulate* these puppets?

marauder N. raider; intruder. The sounding of the alarm frightened the *marauders*.

marital ADJ. pertaining to marriage. After the publication of his book on *marital* affairs, he was often consulted by married people on the verge of divorce.

maritime ADJ. bordering on the sea; nautical. Canada's *Maritime* Provinces depend on the sea for their wealth.

marrow N. soft tissue filling bones. The frigid cold chilled the traveler to the *marrow*.

martial ADJ. warlike. The sound of *martial* music is always inspiring.

martinet N. strict disciplinarian. The commanding officer was a *martinet* who observed each regulation to the letter.

masticate V. chew. We must *masticate* our food carefully and slowly in order to avoid stomach disorders.

maternal ADJ. motherly. Many animals display *maternal* instincts only while their offspring are young and helpless.

matricide N. murder of a mother by a child. A crime such as *matricide* is inconceivable.

matrix (mā'-) N. mold or die. The cast around the *matrix* was cracked.

maudlin ADJ. effusively sentimental. I do not like such *maudlin* pictures. I call them tear-jerkers.

mausoleum (-lē'-) N. monumental tomb. His body was placed in the family *mausoleum*.

mauve (mōv) ADJ. pale purple. The *mauve* tint in the lilac bush was another indication that spring had finally arrived.

maxim N. proverb; a truth pithily stated. Aesop's fables illustrate moral *maxims*.

meander V. to wind or turn in its course. It is difficult to sail up this stream because of the way it *meanders* through the countryside.

meddlesome ADJ. interfering. He felt his marriage was suffering because of

ā — ale; ă — add; ä — arm; à — ask; ē — eve; ĕ — end; ê — err, her; ə — event, allow, ī — ice; ĭ — ill; ō — old; ŏ — odd; ô — orb; ōō — food; ou — out; th — thin; ū — use; ŭ — up; zh — pleasure

his *meddlesome* mother-in-law.

mediate v. settle a dispute through the services of an outsider. Let us *mediate* our differences rather than engage in a costly strike.

medicore ADJ. ordinary; commonplace. We were disappointed because he gave a rather *mediocre* performance in this role.

meditation N. reflection; thought. She reached her decision only after much *meditation*.

medley N. mixture. The band played a *medley* of Gershwin tunes.

melee (*mā-lā'*) N. fight. The captain tried to ascertain the cause of the *melee* which had broken out among the crew members.

mellifluous ADJ. flowing smoothly; smooth. Italian is a *mellifluous* language.

memento N. token; reminder. Take this book as a *memento* of your visit.

memorialize v. commemorate. Let us *memorialize* his great contribution by dedicating this library in his honor.

mendacious (*-dā'-*) ADJ. lying; false. People soon learned to discount his *mendacious* stories.

mendicant N. beggar. From the moment we left the ship, we were surrounded by *mendicants* and peddlers.

ETYMOLOGY 18.

LIB, LIBR, LIBER (book)
>> **library** collection of books
>> **libretto** the "book" of a musical play
>> **libel** slander (originally found in a little book)

LOQU, LOCUT (to talk)
>> **soliloquy** speech by one individual
>> **loquacious** talkative
>> **elocution** speech

LUC (light)
>> **elucidate** enlighten
>> **lucid** clear
>> **translucent** allowing some light to pass through

MAL (bad)
>> **malevolent** evil (wishing bad)
>> **malediction** curse (state of saying evil)
>> **malefactor** evil-doer

MAN (hand)
>> **manufacture** create (make by hand)

ā — ale; ă — add; ä — arm; â — ask; ē — eve; ĕ — end; ê — err, her; ə — event, allow,
ī — ice; ĭ — ill; ō — old; ŏ — odd; ô — orb; ōō — food; ou — out; th — thin; ū — use;
ŭ — up; zh — pleasure

> **manuscript**   writing by hand
> **emancipate**   free (to let go from the hand)

MAR (sea)

> **maritime**   connected with seafaring
> **submarine**   undersea craft
> **mariner**   seaman

TEST — Word List 18 — Synonyms and Antonyms

Each of the questions below consists of a word printed in bold, followed by five words or phrases numbered 1 to 5. Choose the numbered word or phrase which is most nearly the same as or the opposite of the word in bold and write the number of your choice on your answer paper.

341. **magnitude** 1. realization 2. fascination 3. enormity 4. gratitude 5. interference

342. **maniacal** 1. demoniac 2. saturated 3. sane 4. sanitary 5. handcuffed

343. **loquacious** 1. taciturn 2. sentimental 3. soporific 4. soothing 5. sedate

344. **malefactor** 1. quail 2. law breaker 3. beneficiary 4. banker 5. female agent

345. **mellifluous** 1. porous 2. honeycombed 3. strong 4. strident 5. viscous

346. **limpid** 1. erect 2. turbid 3. tangential 4. timid 5. weary

347. **mediocre** 1. average 2. bitter 3. medieval 4. industrial 5. agricultural

348. **macabre** 1. musical 2. frightening 3. chewed 4. wicked 5. exceptional

349. **malign** 1. intersperse 2. vary 3. emphasize 4. frighten 5. eulogize

350. **lithe** 1. stiff 2. limpid 3. facetious 4. insipid 5. vast

351. **lurid** 1. dull 2. duplicate 3. heavy 4. grotesque 5. intelligent

352. **malevolent** 1. kindly 2. vacuous 3. ambivalent 4. volatile 5. primitive

353. **manifest** 1. limited 2. obscure 3. faulty 4. varied 5. vital

354. **loath** 1. loose 2. evident 3. deliberate 4. eager 5. tiny

355. **malediction** 1. misfortune 2. hap 3. fruition 4. correct pronunciation 5. benediction

ā — ale; ă — add; ä — arm; å — ask; ē — eve; ĕ — end; ê — err, her; ə — event, allow;
ī — ice; ĭ — ill; ō — old; ŏ — odd; ô — orb; oo — food; ou — out; th — thin; ū — use;
ŭ — up; zh — pleasure

356. **magniloquent** 1. loquacious 2. bombastic 3. rudimentary 4. qualitative 5. minimizing

357. **lugubrious** 1. frantic 2. cheerful 3. burdensome 4. oily 5. militant

358. **malleable** 1. brittle 2. blatant 3. brilliant 4. brownish 5. basking

359. **martial** 1. bellicose 2. celibate 3. divorced 4. quiescent 5. planetary

360. **livid** 1. alive 2. mundane 3. positive 4. purplish 5. vast

---

Word List 19   menial-nadir

menial ADJ. suitable for servants; low. I cannot understand why a person of your ability and talent should engage in such *menial* activities. also N.

mentor N. teacher. During this very trying period, he could not have had a better *mentor* for the teacher was sympathetic and understanding.

mercantile ADJ. concerning trade. I am more interested in the opportunities available in the *mercantile* field than I am in the legal profession.

mercenary ADJ. interested in money or gain. I am certain that your action was prompted by *mercenary* motives. also N.

mercurial ADJ. fickle; changing. He was of a *mercurial* temperament and therefore unpredictable.

meretricious (měr-ĭ-trĭ'-) ADJ. flashy; tawdry. Her jewels were inexpensive but not *meretricious*.

meringue (mě-rāng') N. a pastry decoration made of white of eggs. The lemon *meringue* pie is one of our specialties.

mesa (mā' sàh) N. high, flat-topped hill. The *mesa*, rising above the surrounding countryside, was the most conspicuous feature of the area.

metallurgical ADJ. pertaining to the art of removing metals from ores. During the course of his *metallurgical* research, the scientist developed a steel alloy of tremendous strength.

metamorphosis N. change of form. The *metamorphosis* of caterpillar to butterfly is typical of many such changes in animal life.

metaphysical ADJ. pertaining to speculative philosophy. The modern poets have gone back to the fanciful poems of the *metaphysical* poets of the seventeenth century for many of their images. metaphysics, N.

ā — ale; ă — add; ä — arm; à — ask; ē — eve; ĕ — end; ê — err, her; a — event, allow,
ī — ice; ĭ — ill; ō — old; ŏ — odd; ô — orb; ōō — food; ou — out; th — thin; ū — use;
ŭ — up; zh — pleasure

mete (*mēt*) v. measure; distribute. He tried to be impartial in his efforts to *mete* out justice.

meticulous ADJ. excessively careful. He was *meticulous* in checking his accounts.

metropolis N. large city. Every evening this terminal is filled with the thousands fo commuters who are going from this *metropolis* to their homes in the suburbs.

mettle N. courage; spirit. When challenged by the other horses in the race, the thoroughbred proved its *mettle* by its determination to hold the lead.

mews N. group of stables built around a courtyard. Let us visit the *mews* to inspect the newly-purchased horse.

mien (*mēn*) N. demeanor; bearing. She had the gracious *mien* of a queen.

migrant ADJ. changing its habitat; wandering. These *migrant* birds return every spring.

migratory ADJ. wandering. The return of the *migratory* birds to the northern sections of this country is a harbinger of spring.

militate v. work against. Your record of lateness and absence will *militate* against your changes of promotion.

mincing ADJ. affectedly dainty. Yum-Yum walked across the stage with *mincing* steps.

mirage (*-rähj'*) N. unreal reflection; optical illusion. The lost prospector was fooled by a *mirage* in the desert.

misadventure N. mischance; ill luck. The young explorer met death by *misadventure*.

misanthrope N. one who hates mankind. We thought the hermit was a *misanthrope* because he shunned our society.

misapprehension N. error; misunderstanding. To avoid *misapprehension*, I am going to ask all of you to repeat the instructions I have given.

miscegenation N. intermarriage between races. Some states passed laws against *miscegenation*.

miscellany N. mixture of writings on various subjects. This is an interesting *miscellany* of nineteenth-century prose.

mischance N. ill luck. By *mischance*, he lost his week's salary.

miscreant N. wretch; villain. His kindness to the *miscreant* amazed all of us who had expected to hear severe punishment pronounced.

misdemeanor N. minor crime. The culprit pleaded guilty to a *misdemeanor* rather than face trial for a felony.

misgivings N. doubts. Hamlet described his *misgivings* to Horatio but decided to fence with Laertes despite his forboding of evil.

ā — ale; ă — add; ä — arm; á — ask; ē — eve; ĕ — end; ê — err, her; ə — event, allow, ī — ice; ĭ — ill; ō — old; ŏ — odd; ô — orb; ōō — food; ou — out; th — thin; ū — use; ŭ — up; zh — pleasure

mishap (*mĭs'-*) N. accident. With a little care you could have avoided this *mishap*.

misnomer N. wrong name; incorrect designation. His tyrannical conduct proved to all that his nickname, King Eric the Just, was a *misnomer*.

misogynist N. hater of women. She accused him of being a *misogynist* because he had been a bachelor all his life.

missile N. object to be thrown. Scientists are experimenting with guided *missiles*.

mite N. very small object or creature; small coin. The criminal was so heartless that he even stole the widow's *mite*.

mitigate V. appease. He did nothing to *mitigate* her wrath.

mobile ADJ. movable; not fixed. The *mobile* blood bank operated by the Red Cross visited our neighborhood today.   mobility, N.

mode (*mōd*) N. prevailing style. She was not used to their lavish *mode* of living.

modicum N. limited quantity. His story is based on a *modicum* of truth.

modish ADJ. fashionable. She always discarded all garments which were no longer *modish*.

modulation N. toning down; changing from one key to another. When she spoke, it was with quiet *modulation* of voice.

moiety N. half; part. There is a slight *moiety* of the savage in her personality which is not easily perceived by those who do not know her well.

mollify V. soothe. We tried to *mollify* the hysterical child by promising her many gifts.

molt V. shed or cast off hair or feathers. The male robin *molted* in the spring.

molten ADJ. melted. The city of Pompeii was destroyed by volcanic ash rather than by *molten* lava flowing from Mount Vesuvius.

momentous ADJ. very important. On this *momentous* occasion, we must be very solemn.

monetary ADJ. pertaining to money. She was in complete charge of all *monetary* matters affecting the household.

monotheism N. belief in one God. Abraham was the first to proclaim his belief in *monotheism*.

moodiness N. fits of depression or gloom. We could not discover the cause of his recurrent *moodiness*.

moot (*mōot*) ADJ. debatable. Our tariff policy is a *moot* subject.

morbid ADJ. given to unwholesome thought; gloomy. These *morbid* speculations are dangerous; we must lighten our thinking by emphasis on more pleasant matters.

ā — ale; ă — add; ä — arm; å — ask; ē — eve; ĕ — end; ê — err, her; ə — event, allow, ī — ice; ĭ — ill; ō — old; ŏ — odd; ô — orb; ōō — food; ou — out; th — thin; ū — use; ŭ — up; zh — pleasure

mordant ADJ. biting; sarcastic; stinging. Actors feared the critic's *mordant* pen.

mores (*mō′ rāz*) N. customs. The *mores* of Mexico are those of Spain with modifications.

moribund ADJ. at the point of death. The doctors called the family to the bedside of the *moribund* patient.

morose (-*rōs′*) ADJ. ill-humored; sullen. When we first meet Hamlet, we find him *morose* and depressed.

mortician N. undertaker. The *mortician* prepared the corpse for burial.

mortify V. humiliate; punish the flesh. She was so *mortified* by her blunder that she ran to her room in tears.

mote N. small speck. The tiniest *mote* in the eye is very painful.

motif (*mō-tēf′*) N. theme. This simple *motif* runs throughout the entire score.

motley ADJ. parti-colored; mixed. The captain had gathered a *motley* crew to sail the vessel.

mountebank N. charlatan; boastful pretender. The patent medicine man was a *mountebank*.

muddle V. confuse; mix up. His thoughts were *muddled* and chaotic.

muggy ADJ. warm and damp. August in New York City is often *muggy*.

mulct (*mŭlkt*) V. defraud a person of something. The lawyer was accused of trying to *mulct* the boy of his legacy.

multiform ADJ. having many forms. Snowflakes are *multiform* but always hexagonal.

multilingual ADJ. having many languages. Because they are bordered by four countries, the Swiss people are *multilingual*.

multiplicity N. state of being numerous. He was appalled by the *multiplicity* of details he had to complete before setting out on his mission.

mundane ADJ. worldly as opposed to spiritual. He was concerned only with *mundane* matters, especially the daily stock market quotations.

munificent ADJ. very generous. The *munificent* gift was presented to the bride.

murkiness N. darkness; gloom. The *murkiness* and fog of the waterfront that evening depressed me.

muse V. ponder. He *mused* about the beauty of the statue.

musky ADJ. having the odor of musk. She left a trace of *musky* perfume behind her.

musty ADJ. stale; spoiled by age. The attic was dark and *musty*.

mutable ADJ. changing in form; fickle. His opinions were *mutable* and easily influenced by anyone who had any powers of persuasion.

mutilate V. maim. The torturer threatened to *mutilate* his victim.

mutinous ADJ. unruly; rebellious. The captain had to use force to quiet his

ā — ale; ǎ — add; ä — arm; à — ask; ē — eve; ĕ — end; ê — err, her; ə — event, allow, ī — ice; ǐ — ill; ō — old; ŏ — odd; ô — orb; ōō — food; ou — out; th — thin; ū — use; ŭ — up; zh — pleasure

mutinous crew.

myriad N. very large number. *Myriads* of mosquitoes from the swamps invaded our village every twilight.

nadir (*nā'-*) N. lowest point. The cold spell reached its *nadir* yesterday.

ETYMOLOGY 19.

MITT, MISS (to send)
    missile projectile
    admit allow in
    dismiss send away
MON, MONIT (to warn)
    admonish warn
    premonition foreboding
    monitor watcher (warner)
MORI, MORT (to die)
    mortuary funeral parlor
    moribund dying
    immortal not dying

TEST — Word List 19 — Synonyms

Each of the questions below consists of a word printed in bold, followed by five words or phrases numbered 1 to 5. Choose the numbered word or phrase which is most nearly similar in meaning to the word in bold and write the number of your choice on your answer paper.

361. **modish** 1. sentimental 2. stylish 3. vacillating 4. contrary 5. adorned
362. **mordant** 1. dying 2. trenchant 3. fabricating 4. controlling 5. avenging
363. **mollify** 1. avenge 2. attenuate 3. attribute 4. mortify 5. appease
364. **menial** 1. intellectual 2. clairvoyant 3. servile 4. arrogant 5. laudatory
365. **moribund** 1. dying 2. appropriate 3. leather bound 4. answering 5. undertaking
366. **mirage** 1. dessert 2. illusion 3. water 4. mirror 5. statement

ā — ale; ă — add; ä — arm; á — ask; ē — eve; ĕ — end; ê — err, her; a — event, allow, ī — ice; ĭ — ill; ō — old; ŏ — odd; ô — orb; oo — food; ou — out; th — thin; ū — use; ŭ — up; zh — pleasure

367. mischance 1. opportunity 2. ordinance 3. aperture 4. anecdote 5. adversity
368. mundane 1. global 2. futile 3. spiritual 4. heretic 5. worldly
369. multilingual 1. variegated 2. polyglot 3. multilateral 4. polyandrous 5. multiplied
370. moot 1. visual 2. invisible 3. controversial 4. anticipatory 5. obsequious
371. motley 1. active 2. disguised 3. variegated 4. somber 5. sick
372. mulct 1. swindle 2. hold 3. record 4. print 5. fertilize
373. munificent 1. grandiose 2. puny 3. philanthropic 4. poor 5. gracious
374. monetary 1. boring 2. fascinating 3. fiscal 4. stationary 5. stationery
375. misanthrope 1. benefactor 2. philanderer 3. hermit 4. aesthete 5. epicure
376. mentor 1. guide 2. genius 3. talker 4. philosopher 5. stylist
377. meticulous 1. steadfast 2. remiss 3. quaint 4. painstaking 5. overt
378. muggy 1. attacking 2. fascinating 3. humid 4. characteristic 5. gelid.
379. musty 1. flat 2. necessary 3. indifferent 4. nonchalant 5. vivid
380. misdemeanor 1. felony 2. peccadillo 3. indignity 4. flat 5. illiteracy

---

Word List 20   naiveté-optometrist

naiveté (nīh-ēv′-tā) N. quality of being sophisticated. I cannot believe that such *naiveté* is unassumed in a person of her age and experience.
natal (nā′-) ADJ. pertaining to birth. He refused to celebrate his *natal* day because it reminded him of the few years he could look forward to.
natation N. swimming. The Red Cross emphasizes the need for courses in *natation*.
nauseate V. cause to become sick; fill with disgust. The foul smells began to *nauseate* him.
nave N. main body of a church. The *nave* of the cathedral was empty at this hour.

ā — ale; ă — add; ä — arm; à — ask; ē — eve; ĕ — end; ê — err, her; ə — event, allow,
ĭ — ice; ĭ — ill; ō — old; ŏ — odd; ô — orb; oo — food; ou — out; th — thin; ū — use;
ŭ — up; zh — pleasure

nebulous ADJ. cloudy; hazy. Your theories are too *nebulous;* please clarify them.

necrology N. obituary notice; list of the dead. The *necrology* of those buried in this cemetery is available in the office.

necromancy N. black magic; dealings with the dead. Because he was able to perform feats of *necromancy,* the natives thought he was in a league with the devil.

nefarious ADJ. very wicked. He was universally feared because of his many *nefarious* deeds.

negation N. denial. I must accept his argument since you have been unable to present any *negation* of his evidence.

nemesis N. revenging agent. Captain Bligh vowed to be Christian's *nemesis*.

neophyte N. recent convert; beginner. This mountain slope contains slides that will challenge experts as well as *neophytes*.

nepotism N. favoritism (to a relative). John left his position with the company because he felt that advancement was based on *nepotism* rather than ability.

nettle V. annoy; vex. Do not let him *nettle* you with his sarcastic remarks.

nexus N. connection. I fail to see the *nexus* which binds these two widely separated events.

nib N. beak; pen-point. The *nibs* of post office pens are often clotted and corroded.

nicety (*nī'-sə-tī*) N. precision; minute distinction. I cannot distinguish between such *niceties* of reasoning.

niggardly (*nĭg'-*) ADJ. meanly stingy; parsimonious. The *niggardly* pittance the widow receives from the government cannot keep her from poverty.

nocturnal ADJ. done at night. Mr. Jones obtained a watchdog to prevent the *nocturnal* raids on his chicken coops.

noisome ADJ. foul smelling; unwholesome. I never could stand the *noisome* atmosphere surrounding the slaughterhouses.

nomadic ADJ. wandering. Several *nomadic* tribes of Indians would hunt in this area each year.

nonchalance N. indifference; lack of interest. He heard the news of the tragedy with complete *nonchalance*.

noncommittal ADJ. neutral; unpledged; undecided. We were annoyed by his *noncommittal* reply for we had been led to expect definite assurances of his approval.

nonentity N. nonexistence; person of no importance. Of course you are a

ā — ale; ă — add; ä — arm; à — ask; ē — eve; ĕ — end; ê — err, her; ə — event, allow, ī — ice; ĭ — ill; ō — old; ŏ — odd; ô — orb; ōō — food; ou — out; th — thin; ū — use; ŭ — up; zh — pleasure

nonentity; you will continue to be one until you prove your value to the community.

non sequitur N. a conclusion that does not follow from the facts stated. Your term paper is full of *non sequiturs;* I cannot see how you reached the conclusions you state.

nosegay N. fragrant bouquet. These spring flowers will make an attractive *nosegay.*

nostalgia N. home-sickness; longing for the past. The first settlers found so much work to do that they had little time for *nostalgia.*

notorious ADJ. outstandingly bad; unfavorably known. Captain Kidd was a *notorious* pirate.

novice N. beginner. Even a *novice* can do good work if he follows these simple directions.

noxious ADJ. harmful. We must trace the source of these *noxious* gases.

nugatory ADJ. futile; worthless. This agreement is *nugatory* for no court will enforce it.

numismatist (*-mĭs'-*) N. person who collects coins. The *numismatist* had a splendid collection of antique coins.

nurture V. bring up; feed; educate. We must *nurture* the young so that they will develop into good citizens.

nutrient ADJ. providing nourishment. During the convalescent period, the patient must be provided with *nutrient* foods.

oaf N. stupid, awkward person. He called the unfortunate waiter a clumsy *oaf.*

obdurate ADJ. stubborn. He was *obdurate* in his refusal to listen to our complaints.

obeisance (ō-bā'-sȧns) N. bow. She made an *obeisance* as the king and queen entered the room.

obelisk N. tall column tapering and ending in a pyramid. Cleopatra's Needle is an *obelisk* in Central Park, New York City.

obese (*-bēs'*) ADJ. fat. It is advisable that *obese* people try to lose weight.

obfuscate V. confuse; muddle. Do not *obfuscate* the issues by dragging in irrelevant arguments.

obituary ADJ. death notice. I first learned of his death when I read the *obituary* column in the newspaper.

objurgate V. scold; rebuke severely. I am afraid he will *objurgate* us publicly for this offense.

oblique ADJ. slanting; deviating from the perpendicular or from a straight line. The sergeant ordered the men to march "*Oblique* right."

obliquity N. departure from right principles; perversity. His moral decadence

---

ā — ale; ă — add; ä — arm; ȧ — ask; ē — eve; ĕ — end; ê — err, her; a — event, allow,
ī — ice; ĭ — ill; ō — old; ŏ — odd; ô — orb; ōō — food; ou — out; th — thin; ū — use;
ŭ — up; zh — pleasure

was marked by his *obliquity* from the ways of integrity and honesty.

obliterate v. destroy completely. The tidal wave *obliterated* several island villages.

oblivion N. forgetfulness. His works had fallen into a state of *oblivion;* no one bothered to read them.

obloquy (ŏb'-) N. slander; disgrace; infamy. I resent the *obloquy* that you are casting upon my reputation.

obnoxious ADJ. offensive. I find your behavior *obnoxious;* please amend your ways.

obsequious (-sē'-) ADJ. slavishly attentive; servile; sycophantic. Nothing is more disgusting to me than the *obsequious* demeanor of the people who wait upon you.

obsession N. fixed idea; continued brooding. This *obsession* with the supernatural has made him unpopular with his neighbors.

obsolete ADJ. out-moded. That word is *obsolete;* do not use it.

obtrude v. push into prominence. The other members of the group object to the manner in which you *obtrude* your opinions into matters of no concern to you.

obtrusive ADJ. pushing forward. I found him a very *obtrusive* person, constantly seeking the center of the stage.

obtuse ADJ. blunt; stupid. Because he was so *obtuse*, he could not follow the teacher's reasoning and asked foolish questions.

obviate v. make unnecessary; get rid of. I hope this contribution will *obviate* any need for further collections of funds.

occult (-kŭlt') ADJ. mysterious; secret; supernatural. The *occult* rites of the organization were revealed only to members.

oculist N. physician who specializes in treatment of the eyes. In many states, an *oculist* is the only one who may apply medicinal drops to the eyes for the purpose of examing them.

odious ADJ. hateful. I find the task of punishing you most *odious*.   odium, N.

odoriferous ADJ. giving off an odor. The *odoriferous* spices stimulated his jaded appetite.

odorous ADJ. fragrant. This variety of hybrid tea rose is more *odorous* than the one you have in your garden.

officious ADJ. meddlesome; excessively trying to please. Browning informs us that the Duke resented the bough of cherries some *officious* fool brought to the Duchess.

ogle (ō'-gl) v. glance coquettishly at; make eyes at. It is improper to *ogle* the

ā — ale; ă — add; ä — arm; å — ask; ē — eve; ĕ — end; ê — err, her; a — event, allow, ī — ice; ĭ — ill; ō — old; ŏ — odd; ô — orb; ōō — food; ou — out; th — thin; ū — use; ŭ — up; zh — pleasure

passers-by.

olfactory ADJ. concerning the sense of smell. The *olfactory* organ is the nose.

oligarchy N. government by a few. The feudal *oligarchy* was supplanted by an autocracy.

ominous ADJ. threatening. The dog growled *ominously* at the stranger.

omnipotent (-nĭp'-) ADJ. all-powerful. The monarch regarded himself as *omnipotent* and responsible to no one for his acts.

omniscient (-nĭsh'-ĕnt) ADJ. all-knowing. I do not pretend to be *omniscient*, but I am positive about this item.

omnivorous (-nĭv'-) ADJ. eating both plant and animal food; devouring everything. Man is an *omnivorous* animal.

onerous (ŏn'-) ADJ. burdensome. He quit because he found the work too *onerous*. onus, N.

onomatopoeia (-pē'-yă) N. words formed in imitation of natural sounds. Words like ''rustle'' and ''gargle'' are illustrations of *onomatopoeia*.

onslaught N. vicious assault. We suffered many casualties during the unexpected *onslaught* of the enemy troops.

opalescent ADJ. iridescent. The Ancient Mariner admired the *opalescent* sheen on the water.

opaque ADJ. dark; not transparent. I want something *opaque* placed in this window so that no one will be able to watch me.

opiate N. sleep producer; deadener of pain. By such *opiates* he made the people forget their difficulties and accept their unpleasant circumstances.

opportune ADJ. timely; well-chosen. You have come at an *opportune* moment for I need a new secretary.

opprobrious ADJ. disgraceful. I find your conduct so *opprobrious* that I must exclude you from classes.

optician N. maker and seller of eyeglasses. The patient took the prescription given him by his oculist to the *optician*.

optometrist N. one who fits glasses to remedy visual defects. Although an *optometrist* is qualified to treat many eye disorders, he may not use medicines or surgery in his examinations.

ETYMOLOGY 20.

NAV (ship)

ā — ale; ă — add; ä — arm; á — ask; ē — eve; ĕ — end; ê — err, her; ə — event, allow,
ī — ice; ĭ — ill; ō — old; ŏ — odd; ô — orb; ōō — food; ou — out; th — thin; ū — use;
ŭ — up; zh — pleasure

navigate   to sail a ship
circumnavigate   sail around the world
naval   pertaining to ships

OMNI (all)

omniscient   all knowing
omnipotent   all powerful
omnivorous   eating everything

OPER (to work)

operate   to work
cooperation   working together
opera   musical drama

TEST — Word List 20 — Antonyms

Each of the questions below consists of a word printed in bold, followed by five words or phrases numbered 1 to 5. Choose the numbered word or phrase which is most nearly opposite in meaning to the word in bold and write the number of your choice on your answer paper.

381. **obsession** 1. whim 2. loss 3. phobia 4. delusion 5. feud
382. **nefarious** 1. wanton 2. lacking 3. benign 4. impious 5. futile
383. **obdurate** 1. yielding 2. fleeting 3. finite 4. fascinating 5. permanent
384. **obtuse** 1. sheer 2. transparent 3. tranquil 4. timid 5. shrewd
385. **nocturnal** 1. harsh 2. marauding 3. patrolling 4. daily 5. fallow
386. **obloquy** 1. praise 2. rectangle 3. circle 4. dialogue 5. cure
387. **neophyte** 1. veteran 2. satellite 3. aspirant 4. handwriting 5. violence
388. **opportune** 1. occasional 2. fragrant 3. fragile 4. awkward 5. neglected
389. **obese** 1. skillful 2. cadaverous 3. clever 4. unpredictable 5. lucid
390. **opiate** 1. distress 2. sleep 3. stimulant 4. laziness 5. despair
391. **notorious** 1. fashionable 2. renowned 3. infamous 4. intrepid 5. invincible
392. **odious** 1. fragrant 2. redolent 3. fetid 4. delightful 5. puny
393. **nebulous** 1. starry 2. clear 3. cold 4. fundamental 5. porous

ā — ale; ă — add; ä — arm; à — ask; ē — eve; ĕ — end; ê — err, her; ə — event, allow, ī — ice; ĭ — ill; ō — old; ŏ — odd; ô — orb; ōō — food; ou — out; th — thin; ū — use; ŭ — up; zh — pleasure

394. **omniscient** 1. sophisticated 2. ignorant 3. essential 4. trivial 5. isolated
395. **obsolete** 1. heated 2. desolate 3. renovated 4. frightful 5. automatic
396. **niggardly** 1. protected 2. biased 3. prodigal 4. bankrupt 5. placated
397. **omnipotent** 1. weak 2. democratic 3. despotic 4. passionate 5. late
398. **negation** 1. postulation 2. hypothecation 3. affirmation 4. violation 5. anticipation
399. **noisome** 1. quiet 2. dismayed 3. fragrant 4. sleepy 5. inquisitive
400. **obsequious** 1. successful 2. democratic 3. supercilious 4. ambitious 5. lamentable

---

Word List 21 opulence-perfunctory

opulence (ŏp'-ū-) N. wealth. Visitors from Europe are amazed at the *opulence* of this country.

oratorio N. dramatic poem set to music. The glee club decided to present an *oratorio* during their recital.

ordinance N. decree. Passing a red light is a violation of a city *ordinance*.

orifice (ôr'-) N. mouthlike opening; small opening. The Howe Caverns were discovered when someone observed that a cold wind was issuing from an *orifice* in the hillside.

ornate (-nāt') ADJ. excessively decorated; highly decorated. Furniture of the Baroque period can be recognized by its *ornate* carvings.

ornithologist N. scientific student of birds. Audubon's drawings of American bird life have been of interest not only to the *ornithologists* but also to the general public.

oscillate (ŏs'-ĭ-) V. vibrate pendulumlike; waver. It is interesting to note how public opinion *oscillates* between the extremes of optimism and pessimism.

ostensible ADJ. apparent; professed; pretended. Although the *ostensible* purpose of this expedition is to discover new lands, we are really interested in finding new markets for our products.

ostentatious ADJ. showy; pretentious. The real hero is never *ostentatious*.

ā — ale; ă — add; ä — arm; å — ask; ē — eve; ĕ — end; ê — err, her; ə — event, allow,
ī — ice; ĭ — ill; ō — old; ŏ — odd; ô — orb; ōō — food; ou — out; th — thin; ū — use;
ŭ — up; zh — pleasure

osteopath N. one who practices healing by manipulation. The services of an *osteopath* may be helpful in treating severe cases of sciatica.

ostracize V. exclude from public favor; ban. As soon as the newspapers carried the story of his connection with the criminals, his friends began to *ostracize* him.   ostracism, N.

overt (-vêrt') ADJ. open to view. According to the United States Constitution, a person must commit an *overt* act before he may be tried for treason.

pacifist N. one opposed to force; anti-militarist. The *pacifists* urged that we reduce our military budget and recall our troops stationed overseas.

paean (pē'-) N. song of praise or joy. They sang *paeans* to the god of spring.

palatable ADJ. agreeable; pleasing to the taste. Paying taxes can never be made *palatable*.

palatial ADJ. magnificent. He proudly showed us through his *palatial* home.

palaver (-lăv'-) N. discussion; misleading speech; chatter. In spite of all the *palaver* before the meeting, the delegates were able to conduct serious negotiations when they sat down at the conference table.

palette N. board on which painter mixes pigments. At the present time, art supply stores are selling paper *palettes* which may be discarded after use.

pallet N. small, poor bed. The weary traveler went to sleep on his straw *pallet*.

palliate V. ease pain; make less guilty or offensive. Doctors must *palliate* that which they cannot cure.

pallid ADJ. pale; wan. Because his occupation required that he work at night and sleep during the day, he had an exceptionally *pallid* complexion.

palpable ADJ. tangible; easily perceptible. I cannot understand how you could overlook such a *palpable* blunder.

palpitate V. throb; flutter. As he became excited, his heart began to *palpitate* more and more erratically.

paltry (päwl'-) ADJ. insignificant; petty. This is a *paltry* sum to pay for such a masterpiece.

panacea (-sē'-) N. cure-all; remedy for all diseases. There is no easy *panacea* that will solve our complicated international situation.

pandemonium N. wild tumult. When the ships collided in the harbor, *pandemonium* broke out among the passengers.

pander V. cater to the low desires of others. Books which *pander* to man's lowest instincts should be banned.

panegyric (-jĭr'-) N. formal praise. The modest hero blushed as he listened to

ā — ale; ă — add; ä — arm; à — ask; ē — eve; ĕ — end; ê — err, her; ə — event, allow, ī — ice; ĭ — ill; ō — old; ŏ — odd; ô — orb; oo — food; ou — out; th — thin; ū — use; ŭ — up; zh — pleasure

the *panegyrics* uttered by the speakers about his valorous act.

panorama N. comprehensive view; unobstructed view in all directions. Tourists never forget the impact of their first *panorama* of the Grand Canyon.

pantomime N. acting without dialogue. Because he worked in *pantomime*, the clown could be understood wherever he appeared.

papyrus (-*pī'*-) N. ancient paper made from stem of papyrus plant. The ancient Egyptians were among the first to write on *papyrus*.

parable N. short, simple story teaching a moral. Let us apply the lesson that this *parable* teaches to our own conduct.

paradox N. statement that looks false but is actually correct; a contradictory statement. Wordsworth's "The child is father to the man" is an example of *paradox*.

paragon N. model of perfection. The class disliked him because the teacher was always pointing to him as a *paragon* of virtue.

parallelism N. state of being parallel; similarity. There is a striking *parallelism* between the two ages.

paranoia (-*nôī'-yə*) N. chronic form of insanity marked by delusions of grandeur or persecution. The psychiatrists analyzed his ailment as *paranoia*.

paraphernalia (-*nā'*-) N. equipment; odds-and-ends. His desk was cluttered with paper, pen, ink, dictionary, and other *paraphernalia* of the writing craft.

paraphrase V. restate a passage in own words while retaining thought of author. In 250 words or less, *paraphrase* this article.

parasite N. animal or plant living on another; toady; sycophant. The tapeworm is an example of the kind of *parasite* that may infest the human body.

paregoric N. medicine that eases pain. The doctor prescribed a *paregoric* to alleviate his suffering.

pariah (*pār'*-) N. social outcast. I am not a *pariah* to be shunned and ostracized.

parlance N. language; idiom. All this legal *parlance* confuses me; I need an interpreter.

parley N. conference. The peace *parley* has not produced the anticipated truce.

parody N. humorous imitation; travesty. We enjoyed the clever *parodies* of popular songs which the chorus sang.

paroxysm N. fit or attack of pain, laughter, rage. When he heard of his son's misdeeds, he was seized by a *paroxysm* of rage.

ā — ale; ă — add; ä — arm; à — ask; ē — eve; ĕ — end; ê — err, her; ə — event, allow, ī — ice; ĭ — ill; ō — old; ŏ — odd; ô — orb; ōō — food; ou — out; th — thin; ū — use; ŭ — up; zh — pleasure

parricide N. person who murders his own father; murder of a father. The jury was shocked by the details of this vicious *parricide*.

parry v. ward off a blow. He was content to wage a defensive battle and tried to *parry* his opponent's thrusts.

parsimonious ADJ. stingy; excessively frugal. His *parsimonious* nature did not permit him to enjoy any luxuries.

partiality N. inclination; bias. As a judge, I must avoid any evidence of *partiality* when I award the prize.

parvenu N. upstart; newly-rich person. Although extremely wealthy, he was regarded as a *parvenu* by the aristocratic members of society.

passive ADJ. not active; acted upon. *Passive* resistance proved a very effective weapon.

pastoral ADJ. rural. In these stories of *pastoral* life, we find an understanding of the daily tasks of country folk.

patent ADJ. open for the public to read; obvious. It was *patent* to everyone that the witness spoke the truth.

pathetic ADJ. causing sadness, compassion, pity; touching. Everyone in the auditorium was weeping by the time he finished the *pathetic* tale.

pathos N. tender sorrow; pity; quality in art or literature that produces these feelings. A quiet tone of *pathos* ran through the novel.

patriarch (pā'-) N. father and ruler of a family or tribe. In many primitive tribes, the leader and lawmaker was the *patriarch*.

patricide N. person who murders his father; murder of a father. The words parricide and *patricide* have exactly the same meaning.

patrimony N. inheritance from father. As predicted by his critics, he spent his *patrimony* within two years of his father's death.

paucity N. scarcity. The poor test papers indicate that the members of this class have a *paucity* of intelligence.

peccadillo N. slight offense. If we examine these escapades carefully, we will realize that they are mere *peccadilloes* rather than major crimes.

peculate v. steal; embezzle. His crime of *peculating* public funds entrusted to his care is especially damnable.

pecuniary ADJ. pertaining to money. I never expected a *pecuniary* reward for my work in this activity.

pedagogue N. teacher; dull and formal teacher. He could never be a stuffy *pedagogue;* his classes were always lively and filled with humor.

pedantic ADJ. showing off learning; bookish. What you say is *pedantic* and reveals an unfamiliarity with the realities of life.   pedant, N.

pediatrician N. expert in children's diseases. The family doctor advised the parents to consult a *pediatrician* about their child's ailment.

ā — ale; ă — add; ä — arm; à — ask; ē — eve; ĕ — end; ê — err, her; ə — event, allow, ī — ice; ĭ — ill; ō — old; ŏ — odd; ô — orb; oo — food; ou — out; th — thin; ū — use; ŭ — up; zh — pleasure

pelf N. stolen property; money or wealth (in a contemptuous sense). Your possessions are only *pelf;* they will give you no lasting pleasure.

pell-mell ADV. in confusion; disorderly. The excited students dashed *pell-mell* into the stadium to celebrate the victory.

pellucid (*-lū'sĭd*) ADJ. transparent; limpid; easy to understand. After reading these stodgy philosophers, I find his *pellucid* style very enjoyable.

penance N. self-imposed punishment for sin. The Ancient Mariner said, "I have *penance* done and penance more will do."

penchant (*pĕn'-chənt*) N. strong inclination; liking. He had a strong *penchant* for sculpture.

pendant ADJ. hanging down from something. Her *pendant* earrings glistened in the light.

pendent ADJ. suspended; jutting; pending. The *pendent* rock hid the entrance to the cave.

penitent ADJ. repentant. When he realized the enormity of his crime, he became remorseful and *penitent*.

pensive ADJ. dreamily thoughtful; thoughtful with a hint of sadness. The *pensive* youth gazed at the painting for a long time and then sighed.

penumbra (*-nŭm'-*) N. partial shadow (in an eclipse). During an eclipse, we can see an area of total darkness and a lighter area which is the *penumbra.*

penurious (*-nū'-*) ADJ. stingy; parsimonious. He was a *penurious* man, averse to spending money even for the necessities of life.

penury (*pĕn'-*) N. extreme poverty. We find much *penury* and suffering in this slum area.

percussion ADJ. striking one object against another sharply. The drum is a *percussion* treatment.

perdition N. damnation; complete ruin. He was damned to eternal *perdition*.

peremptory (*pĕr-ĕmp'-*) ADJ. demanding and leaving no choice. I resent your *peremptory* attitude.

perennial (*-ĕn'-*) N. lasting. These plants are hardy *perennials* and will bloom for many years.

perfidious (*-fĭd'-*) ADJ. basely false. Your *perfidious* gossip is malicious and dangerous.

perfidy (*pər'-*) N. violation of a trust. When we learned of his *perfidy*, we were shocked and dismayed.

perforce (*-fôrs'*) ADV. of necessity. I must *perforce* leave as my train is about to start.

perfunctory ADJ. superficial; listless; not thorough. He overlooked many

ā — ale; ă — add; ä — arm; à — ask; ē — eve; ĕ — end; ê — err, her; ə — event, allow,
ī — ice; ĭ — ill; ō — old; ŏ — odd; ô — orb; ōō — food; ou — out; th — thin; ū — use;
ŭ — up; zh — pleasure

weaknesses when he inspected the factory in his *perfunctory* manner.

ETYMOLOGY 21.

PAC (peace)
        pacify   to make peaceful
        pacific   peaceful
        pacifist   person opposed to war
PEL, PULS (to drive)
        compulsion   a forcing to do
        repel   drive back
        expel   drive out, banish

TEST — Word List 21 — Synonyms and Antonyms

Each of the questions below consists of a word printed in bold, followed by five words or phrases numbered 1 to 5. Choose the numbered word or phrase which is most nearly the same as or the opposite of the word in bold and write the number of your choice on your answer paper.

401. ostentatious 1. occasional 2. flashy 3. intermittent 4. authentic 5. hospitable
402. palliate 1. smoke 2. quicken 3. substitute 4. alleviate 5. sadden
403. pandemonium 1. calm 2. frustration 3. efficiency 4. impishness 5. sophistication
404. pariah 1. village 2. suburb 3. outcast 4. disease 5. benefactor
405. papyrus 1. mountain 2. peninsula 3. paper 4. animal 5. pyramid
406. penchant 1. distance 2. imminence 3. dislike 4. attitude 5. void
407. perennial 1. flowering 2. recurring 3. centennial 4. partial 5. deciduous
408. pellucid 1. logistical 2. philandering 3. limpid 4. vagrant 5. warranted

ā — ale; ă — add; ä — arm; á — ask; ē — eve; ĕ — end; ê — err, her; ə — event, allow,
ī — ice; ĭ — ill; ō — old; ŏ — odd; ô — orb; ōō — food; ou — out; th — thin; ū — use;
ŭ — up; zh — pleasure

409. **paucity** 1. pouch 2. peace 3. quickness 4. abundance 5. nuisance
410. **panegyric** 1. medication 2. panacea 3. rotation 4. vacillation 5. praise
411. **paean** 1. serf 2. pealing 3. lien 4. lament 5. folly
412. **opulence** 1. pessimism 2. patriotism 3. potency 4. passion 5. poverty
413. **pallet** 1. bed 2. pigment board 3. bench 4. spectrum 5. quality
414. **parable** 1. equality 2. allegory 3. frenzy 4. folly 5. cuticle
415. **paranoia** 1. fracture 2. statement 3. quantity 4. benefaction 5. sanity
416. **parsimonious** 1. grammatical 2. syntactical 3. effective 4. extravagant 5. esoteric
417. **penurious** 1. imprisoned 2. captivated 3. parsimonious 4. vacant 5. abolished
418. **perfunctory** 1. official 2. thorough 3. insipid 4. vicarious 5. distinctive
419. **orifice** 1. altar 2. gun 3. guitar 4. device 5. opening
420. **paradox** 1. exaggeration 2. contradiction 3. hyperbole 4. invective 5. poetic device

---

Word List 22   perimeter–precedent (n)

perimeter N. outer boundary. To determine the *perimeter* of any quadrilateral, we add the four sides.

peripatetic (*-tĕt'-*) ADJ. walking about; moving. The *peripatetic* school of philosophy derives its name from the fact that Aristotle walked with his pupils while discussing philosophy with them.

periphery (*-rĭf'-*) N. edge, especially of a round surface. He sensed that there was something just beyond the *periphery* of his vision.

perjury N. false testimony while under oath. When several witnesses appeared to challenge his story, he was indicted for *perjury*.

permeable (*pêr'-*) ADJ. porous; allowing passage through. Glass is *permeable* to light.

permeate V. pass through; spread. The odor of frying onions *permeated* the air.

ā — ale; ă — add; ä — arm; à — ask; ē — eve; ĕ — end; ê — err, her; ə — event, allow,
ī — ice; ĭ — ill; ō — old; ŏ — odd; ô — orb; ōō — food; ou — out; th — thin; ū — use;
ŭ — up; zh — pleasure

pernicious ADJ. very destructive. He argued that these books had a *pernicious* effect on young and susceptible minds.

perpetrate V. commit an offense. Only an insane person could *perpetrate* such a horrible crime.

perpetual ADJ. everlasting. Ponce de Leon hoped to find *perpetual* youth.

persiflage (*pêr'-sĭ-flahj*) N. flippant conversation; banter. This *persiflage* is not appropriate when we have such serious problems to discuss.

perspicacious ADJ. having insight; penetrating; astute. We admired his *perspicacious* wisdom and sagacity.

pert ADJ. impertinent; forward. I think your *pert* and impudent remarks call for an apology.

pertinacious ADJ. stubborn; persistent. He is bound to succeed because his *pertinacious* nature will not permit him to quit.

pertinent ADJ. suitable; to the point. The lawyer wanted to know all the *pertinent* details.

perturb V. disturb greatly. I am afraid this news will *perturb* him.

perturbation N. agitation. I fail to understand why such an innocent remark should create such *perturbation*.

perusal (-$\overline{oo}'$-) N. reading. I am certain that you have missed important details in your rapid *perusal* of this document.   peruse, V.

pervade V. spread throughout. As the news of the defeat *pervaded* the country, a feeling of anger directed at the rulers who had been the cause of the disaster grew.

perverse ADJ. stubborn; intractable. Because of your *perverse* attitude, I must rate you as deficient in cooperation.

perversion N. corruption; turning from right to wrong. Inasmuch as he had no motive for his crimes, we could not understand his *perversion*.

perversity N. stubborn maintenance of a wrong cause. I cannot forgive your *perversity* in repeating such an impossible story.

pervious ADJ. penetrable. He has a *pervious* mind and readily accepts new ideas.

pessimism N. belief that life is basically bad or evil; gloominess. There is no reason for your *pessimism*.

pestilential ADJ. causing plague; baneful. People were afraid to explore the *pestilential* swamp.   pestilence, N.

petrify V. turn to stone. His sudden and unexpected appearance seemed to *petrify* her.

petulant (*pĕt'-$\overline{u}$*) ADJ. touchy; peevish. The feverish patient was *petulant* and restless.

phial N. small bottle. Even though it is small, this *phial* of perfume is

ā — ale; ă — add; ä — arm; à — ask; ē — eve; ĕ — end; ê — err, her; ə — event, allow,
ĭ — ice; ĭ — ill; ō — old; ŏ — odd; ô — orb; ōō — food; ou — out; th — thin; ū — use;
ŭ — up; zh — pleasure

expensive.

philander v. make love lightly; flirt. Do not *philander* with my affections because love is too serious.

philanthropist N. lover of mankind; doer of good. As he grew older, he became famous as a *philanthropist* and benefactor of the needy.

philistine (*fĭl'-ĭs-*) N. narrow-minded person; uncultured and exclusively interested in material gain. We need more men of culture and enlightenment; we have too many *philistines* among us.

philology N. study of language. The professor of *philology* advocated the use of Esperanto as an international language.

phlegmatic ADJ. calm; not easily disturbed. The nurse was a cheerful but *phlegmatic* person.

physiognomy N. face. He prided himself on his ability to analyze a person's character by studying his *physiognomy*.

pied (*pīd*) ADJ. variegated; multi-colored. The *pied* antelope may be recognized by its white face.

pillage (*pĭl'-ĭj*) v. plunder. The enemy *pillaged* the quiet village and left it in ruins.

pillory v. punish by placing in a wooden frame and subjecting to ridicule. Even though he was mocked and *pilloried*, he maintained that he was correct in his beliefs.

pinion v. restrain. They *pinioned* his arms against his body but left his legs free so that he could move about.

pinnacle N. peak. We could see the morning sunlight illuminate the *pinnacle* while the rest of the mountain lay in shadow.

pious ADJ. devout. The *pious* parents gave their children a religious upbringing.

piquant (*pē'-*) ADJ. pleasantly tart tasting; stimulating. The *piquant* sauce added to our enjoyment of the meal.   piquancy, N.

pique (*pēk*) N. irritation; resentment. She showed her *pique* by her refusal to appear with the other contestants at the end of the contest.

piscatorial ADJ. pertaining to fishing. He spent many happy hours in his *piscatorial* activities.

pithy ADJ. concise; meaty. I enjoy reading his essays because they are always compact and *pithy*.

pittance N. a small allowance or wage. He could not live on the *pittance* he received as a pension and had to look for an additional source of revenue.

placate v. pacify; conciliate. The teacher tried to *placate* the angry mother.

placid ADJ. peaceful; calm. After his vacation in this *placid* section, he felt

ā — ale; ă — add; ä — arm; á — ask; ē — eve; ĕ — end; ê — err, her; ə — event, allow,
ī — ice; ĭ — ill; ō — old; ŏ — odd; ô — orb; ōō — food; ou — out; th — thin; ū — use;
ŭ — up; zh — pleasure

soothed and rested.

plagiarism N. theft of another's idea or writings passed off as original. The editor recognized the *plagiarism* and rebuked the culprit who had presented the manuscript as original.

plaintive ADJ. mournful. The dove has a *plaintive* and melancholy call.

platitude N. trite remark; commonplace statement. His *platitudes* impressed the ignorant.

plauditory ADJ. approving; applauding. The theatrical company reprinted the *plauditory* comments of the critics in its advertisement.

plebeian (-bē'-) ADJ. common; pertaining to the common people. His speeches were aimed at the *plebeian* minds and emotions; they disgusted the more refined.

plenary (plē'-) ADJ. complete; full. The union leader was given *plenary* power to negotiate a new contract with the employers.

plenipotentiary ADJ. fully empowered. Since he was not given *plenipotentiary* powers by his government, he could not commit his country without consulting his superiors.

plethora (plĕth'-) N. excess; overabundance. She offered a *plethora* of reasons for her shortcomings.

plumb ADJ. checking perpendicularity; vertical. Before hanging wallpaper it is advisable to drop a *plumb* line from the ceiling as a guide.

podiatrist (-dī-) N. doctor who treats ailments of the feet. He consulted a *podiatrist* about his fallen arches.

podium N. pedestal; raised platform. The audience applauded as the conductor made his way to the *podium.*

poignant (pôēn'-ənt) ADJ. keen; piercing; severe. Her *poignant* grief left her pale and weak.

politic ADJ. expedient; prudent; well-devised. Even though he was disappointed, he did not think it *politic* to refuse this offer.

poltroon (-trōōn') N. coward. Only a *poltroon* would so betray his comrades at such a dangerous time.

polygamist (-lĭg'-) N. one who has more than one spouse (usually a wife) at a time. He was arrested as a *polygamist* when his two wives filed complaints about him.

polygot ADJ. speaking several languages. New York City is a *polyglot* community because of the thousands of immigrants who settled there.

pommel V. beat. The severity with which he was *pommeled* was indicated by the bruises he displayed on his head and face.

portend V. foretell; presage. The king did not know what these omens might *portend* and asked his soothsayers to interpret them.

ā — ale; ă — add; ä — arm; å — ask; ē — eve; ĕ — end; ê — err, her; ə — event, allow, ī — ice; ĭ — ill; ō — old; ŏ — odd; ô — orb; ōō — food; ou — out; th — thin; ū — use; ŭ — up; zh — pleasure

portent N. sing; omen; forewarning. He regarded the black cloud as a *portent* of evil.

portentous (*-těn'*-) ADJ. ominous; serious. I regard our present difficulties and dissatisfactions as *portentous* omens of future disaster.

portly ADJ. stately; stout. The wealthy financier was a *portly* gentleman.

posterity N. descendants; future generations. We hope to leave a better world to *posterity*.

posthumous (*pŏs'*-) ADJ. after death (as of child born after father's death or book published after author's death). The critics acclaimed him after the *posthumous* publication of his novel.

postulate N. self-evident truth. We must accept these statements as *postulates* before pursuing our discussions any further.   also V.

potentate (*pō'*-) N. monarch; sovereign. The *potentate* spent more time at Monte Carlo than he did at home with his people.

potential ADJ. expressing possibility; latent. This juvenile delinquent is a *potential* murderer.

potion N. dose (of liquid). Tristan and Isolde drink a love *potion* in the first act of the opera.

potpourri (*pō-pŏō-rē'*) N. heterogeneous mixture; medley. He offered a *potpourri* of folk songs from many lands.

poultice (*pōl'*-) N. soothing application applied to sore and inflamed portions of the body. He was advised to apply a flax-seed *poultice* to the inflammation.

practicable ADJ. feasible. The board of directors decided that the plan was *practicable* and agreed to undertake the project.

practical ADJ. based on experience; useful. He was a *practical* man and opposed to theory.

pragmatic ADJ. practical; concerned with practical values. This test should provide us with a *pragmatic* analysis of the value of this course.

prate V. speak foolishly; boast idly. Let us not *prate* about our virtues.

prattle V. babble. The little girl *prattled* endlessly about her dolls.

preamble N. introductory statement. In the *preamble* to the Constitution, the purpose of the document is set forth.

precarious ADJ. uncertain; risky. I think this stock is a *precarious* investment and advise against its purchase.

precedent (*prĕs'*-) N. something preceding in time which may be used as an authority or guide for future action. This decision sets a *precedent* for future cases of a similar nature.

ā — ale; ă — add; ä — arm; à — ask; ē — eve; ĕ — end; ê — err, her; ə — event, allow; ī — ice; ĭ — ill; ō — old; ŏ — odd; ô — orb; ōō — food; ou — out; th — thin; ū — use; ŭ — up; zh — pleasure

ETYMOLOGY 22.

PET, PETIT (to seek)
> **petition**   request
> **appetite**   craving, desire
> **compete**   vie with others

PON, POSIT (to place)
> **postpone**   place after
> **preposition**   that which goes before
> **positive**   definite, unquestioned (definitely placed)

PORT, PORTAT (to carry)
> **portable**   able to be carried
> **transport**   carry across
> **export**   carry out (of country)

TEST — Word List 22 — Synonyms

Each of the questions below consists of a word printed in bold, followed by five words or phrases numbered 1 to 5. Choose the numbered word or phrase which is most nearly similar in meaning to the word in bold and write the number of your choice on your answer paper.

421. pillage   1. hoard   2. plunder   3. versify   4. denigrate   5. confide

422. petrify   1. turn to water   2. refine   3. turn to stone   4. turn to gas   5. repeat

423. pernicious   1. practical   2. comparative   3. destructive   4. tangible   5. detailed

424. physiognomy   1. posture   2. head   3. physique   4. face   5. size

425. pertinent   1. understood   2. living   3. discontented   4. puzzling   5. relevant

426. permeate   1. enlarge   2. produce   3. prod   4. disfigure   5. spread

427. phlegmatic   1. calm   2. cryptic   3. practical   4. salivary   5. dishonest

428. pertinacious   1. sticking   2. consumptive   3. superficial   4. skilled   5. advertised

429. permeable   1. perishable   2. effective   3. plodding   4. porous   5. lasting

ā — ale; ă — add; ä — arm; à — ask; ē — eve; ĕ — end; ê — err, her; ə — event, allow, ī — ice; ĭ — ill; ō — old; ŏ — odd; ô — orb; ōō — food; ou — out; th — thin; ū — use; ŭ — up; zh — pleasure

430. **philander** 1. flirt 2. quiz 3. decline 4. profit 5. quarrel
431. **pert** 1. impertinent 2. perishable 3. moral 4. deliberate 5. stubborn
432. **peripatetic** 1. worldly 2. moving 3. disarming 4. seeking 5. inherent
433. **petulant** 1. angry 2. moral 3. declining 4. underhanded 5. touchy
434. **perpetual** 1. eternal 2. standard 3. serious 4. industrial 5. interpretive
435. **plaintive** 1. mournful 2. senseless 3. persistent 4. rural 5. evasive
436. **pinion** 1. express 2. report 3. reveal 4. submit 5. restrain
437. **placate** 1. determine 2. transmit 3. pacify 4. allow 5. define
438. **pinnacle** 1. foothills 2. card game 3. pass 4. taunt 5. peak
439. **pique** 1. pyramid 2. revolt 3. resentment 4. struggle 5. inventory
440. **pious** 1. historic 2. devout 3. multiple 4. fortunate 5. authoritative

---

Word List 23   precedent (adj.)-purview

precedent (-cē′-) ADJ. preceding in time, rank, etc. Our discussions, *precedent* to this event, certainly did not give you any reason to believe that we would adopt your proposal.

precept N. practical rule guiding conduct. "Love thy neighbor as thyself" is a worthwhile *precept*.

precipitate (-cĭp′-ĭ-tĭt) ADJ. headlong; rash. Do not be *precipitate* in this matter; investigate further.

precipitate (-cĭp′-i-tāt) v. throw headlong; hasten. We must be patient as we cannot *precipitate* these results.

precipitous ADJ. steep. This hill is difficult to climb because it is so *precipitous*.

preclude v. make impossible; eliminate. This contract does not *preclude* my being employed by others at the same time that I am working for you.

precocious ADJ. developed ahead of time. By his rather adult manner of discussing serious topics, the child demonstrated that he was *precocious*.

ā — ale; ă — add; ä — arm; â — ask; ē — eve; ĕ — end; ê — err, her; ə — event, allow; ī — ice; ĭ — ill; ō — old; ŏ — odd; ô — orb; ōō — food; ou — out; th — thin; ū — use; ŭ — up; zh — pleasure

precursor N. forerunner. Gray and Burns were *precursors* of the Romantic Movement in English literature.

predatory ADJ. plundering. The hawk is a *predatory* bird.

predilection (-lĕk'-) N. partiality; preference. Although the artist used various media from time to time, he had a *predilection* for water color.

preeminent (prē-ĕm'-) ADJ. outstanding; superior. He was *preeminent* in the field of surgery.

prefatory (prĕf'-) ADJ. introductory. The chairman made a few *prefatory* remarks before he called on the first speaker.

prelude N. introduction; forerunner. I am afraid that this border raid is the *prelude* to more serious attacks.

premonition N. forewarning. We ignored these *premonitions* of disaster because they appeared to be based on childish fears.

preponderate V. be superior in power; outweigh. I feel confident that the forces of justice will *preponderate* eventually in this dispute.

preposterous ADJ. absurd; ridiculous. The excuse he gave was *preposterous*.

presage (-sāj') V. foretell. The vultures flying overhead *presaged* the discovery of the corpse in the desert.

presentiment (-sĕn'-) N. premonition; foreboding. Hamlet felt a *presentiment* about his meeting with Laertes.

presumption N. arrogance; effrontery. She had the *presumption* to disregard our advice.

pretentious ADJ. ostentatious; ambitious. I do not feel that your limited resources will permit you to carry out such a *pretentious* program.

prevaricate V. lie. He was forced to *prevaricate* to save his life.

prim ADJ. very precise and formal; exceedingly proper. The spinster was too *prim* to attract suitors.

primordial (prĭ-mor'-) ADJ. existing at the beginning (of time); rudimentary. The Neanderthal Man is one of our *primordial* ancestors.

pristine ADJ. characteristic of earlier times; primitive; unspoiled. This area has been preserved in all its *pristine* wildness.

privy ADJ. secret; hidden; not public. We do not care for *privy* chamber government.

probity N. uprightness; incorruptibility. Everyone took his *probity* for granted; his defalcations, therefore, shocked us all.

proboscis N. long snout; nose. The elephant uses his *proboscis* to handle things and carry them from place to place.

proclivity N. inclination; natural tendency. He had a *proclivity* to grumble.

procrastinate V. postpone; delay. It is wise not to *procrastinate;* otherwise,

ā — ale; ă — add; ä — arm; à — ask; ē — eve; ĕ — end; ê — err, her; ə — event, allow,
ĭ — ice; ĭ — ill; ō — old; ŏ — odd; ô — orb; ōō — food; ou — out; th — thin; ū — use;
ŭ — up; zh — pleasure

we find ourselves bogged down in a mass of work which should have been finished long ago.

prodigal ADJ. wasteful; reckless with money. The *prodigal* son squandered his inheritance.   also N.

prodigious ADJ. marvelous; enormous. He marveled at her *prodigious* appetite.

profane v. violate; desecrate. Tourists are urged not to *profane* the sanctity of holy places by wearing improper garb.

profligate ADJ. dissipated; wasteful; licentious. In this *profligate* company, he lost all sense of decency.   also N.

profusion N. lavish expenditure; overabundant condition. Seldom have I seen food and drink served in such *profusion*.

progenitor N. ancestor. We must not forget the teachings of our *progenitors* in our desire to appear modern.

progeny N. children; offspring. He was proud of his *progeny* but regarded George as the most promising of all his children.

prognosis N. forecasted course of a disease; prediciton. If the doctor's *prognosis* is correct, the patient will be in a coma for at least twenty-four hours.

prognosticate v. predict. I *prognosticate* disaster unless we change our wasteful ways.

prolific ADJ. abundantly fruitful. He was a *prolific* writer and wrote as many as three books a year.

prolix ADJ. verbose; drawn out. His *prolix* arguments irritated the jury.   prolixity, N.

promiscuous ADJ. mixed indiscriminately; haphazard; irregular. In the opera *La Bohème*, we get a picture of the *promiscuous* life led by the young artists of Paris.

promontory N. headland. They erected a lighthouse on the *promontory* to warn approaching ships of their nearness to the shore.

promulgate v. make known by official proclamation or publication. As soon as the Civil Service Commission *promulgates* the names of the successful candidates, we shall begin to hire members of our staff.

prone ADJ. inclined to; prostrate. She was *prone* to sudden fits of anger.

propagate v. multiply; spread. I am sure disease must *propagate* in such unsanitary and crowded areas.

propensity N. natural inclination. I dislike your *propensity* to belittle every contribution he makes to our organization.

propitiate v. appease. The natives offered sacrifices to *propitiate* the gods.

propitious ADJ. favorable; kindly. I think it is advisable that we wait for a more

ā — ale; ă — add; ä — arm; å — ask; ē — eve; ĕ — end; ê — err, her; ə — event, allow,
ī — ice; ĭ — ill; ō — old; ŏ — odd; ô — orb; ōō — food; ou — out; th — thin; ū — use;
ŭ — up; zh — pleasure

propitious occasion to announce our plans.

propound v. put forth for analysis. In your discussion, you have *propounded* several questions; let us consider each one separately.

propriety N. fitness; correct conduct. I want you to behave at this dinner with *propriety;* don't embarrass me.

propulsive ADJ. driving forward. The jet plane has a greater *propulsive* power than the motor-driven plane.

prorogue v. dismiss parliament; end officially. It was agreed that the king could not *prorogue* parliament until it had been in session for at least fifty days.

prosaic (*prō-zā'-ıc*) ADJ. commonplace; dull. I do not like this author because he is so unimaginative and *prosaic*.

proscribe v. ostracize; banish; outlaw. Antony, Octavius, and Lepidus *proscribed* all those who had conspired against Julius Caesar.

prosody N. the art of versification. This book on *prosody* contains a rhyming dictionary as well as samples of the various verse forms.

prostrate v. stretch out full on ground. He *prostrated* himself before the idol.

protégé (*prō-tə-zhā'*) N. person under the protection and support of a patron. Cyrano de Bergerac refused to be a *protégé* of Cardinal Richelieu.

protocol N. diplomatic etiquette. We must run this state dinner according to *protocol* if we are to avoid offending any of our guests.

protract v. prolong. Do not *protract* this phone conversation as I expect an important business call within the next few minutes.

protrude v. stick out. His fingers *protruded* from the holes in his gloves.

provender N. dry food; fodder. I am not afraid of a severe winter because I have stored a large quantity of *provender* for the cattle.

provident ADJ. displaying foresight; thrifty; preparing for emergencies. In his usual *provident* manner, he had insured himself against this type of loss.

proviso (*-vī'-zō*) N. stipulation. I am ready to accept your proposal with the *proviso* that you meet your obligations within the next two weeks.

provocation N. cause for anger or retaliation. In order to prevent a sudden outbreak of hostilities, we must give our foe no *provocation*.

proximity N. nearness. The deer sensed the hunter's *proximity* and bounded away.

proxy N. authorized agent. Please act as my *proxy* and vote for this slate of candidates.

prurient ADJ. based on lascivious thoughts. The police attempted to close the theater where the *prurient* film was being presented.

pseudonym N. pen name. Samuel Clemens' *pseudonym* was Mark Twain.

ā — ale; ă — add; ä — arm; á — ask; ē — eve; ĕ — end; ê — err, her; ə — event, allow, ī — ice; ĭ — ill; ō — old; ŏ — odd; ô — orb; ōō — food; ou — out; th — thin; ū — use; ŭ — up; zh — pleasure

psyche (sī'-ke) N. soul; mind. It is difficult to delve into the *psyche* of a human being.

psychiatrist N. doctor who treats mental diseases. A *psychiatrist* often needs long conferences with his patient before a diagnosis can be made.

puerile ADJ.childish. His *puerile* pranks sometimes offended his serious-minded friends.

pugnacious ADJ. combative; disposed to fight. As a child he was *pugnacious* and fought with everyone.

puissant (pwĭs'-) ADJ. powerful; strong; potent. We must keep his friendship for he will make a *puissant* ally.

pulchritude N. beauty; comeliness. I do not envy the judge who has to select the best from among this collection of feminine *pulchritude*.

pulmonary ADJ.pertaining to the lungs. In his researches on *pulmonary* diseases, he discovered many facts about the lungs of animals and human beings.

pulsate V. throb. We could see the blood vessels in his temple *pulsate* as he became more angry.

punctilious ADJ. laying stress on niceties of conduct, form; precise. We must be *puntilious* in our planning of this affair for any error may be regarded as a personal affront.

pungent (pŭn'-jant) ADJ. stinging; caustic. The *pungent* aroma of the smoke made me cough.

punitive (pū'-) ADJ. punishing. He asked for *punitive* measures against the offender.

puny ADJ. insignificant; tiny; weak. Our *puny* efforts to stop the flood were futile.

purgatory N. place of spiritual expiation. In this *purgatory*, he could expect no help from his comrades.

purge V. clean by removing impurities; clear of charges. If you are to be *purged* of the charge of contempt of Congress, you must be willing to answer the questions previously asked. also N.

purloin V. steal. In the story "The *Purloined* Letter," Poe points out that the best hiding place is often the most obvious place.

purport N. intention; meaning. If the *purport* of your speech was to arouse the rabble, you succeeded admirably.

purveyor N. furnisher of foodstuffs; caterer. As *purveyor* of rare wines and viands, he traveled through France and Italy every year in search of new products to sell.

purview N. scope. The sociological implications of these inventions are beyond the *purview* of this book.

ā — ale; ă — add; ä — arm; à — ask; ē — eve; ĕ — end; ê — err, her; a — event, allow,
ī — ice; ĭ — ill; ō — old; ŏ — odd; ô — orb; ōō — food; ou — out; th — thin; ū — use;
ŭ — up; zh — pleasure

ETYMOLOGY 23.

PRAEDO, PREDA (prey)
        predacious living by prey
        predatory pillaging, plundering
PRE (before) prefix
        precocious ahead of time
        precursor forerunner
PRO (before, toward) prefix
        prognosticate to foretell
        propulsive driving forward

TEST — Word List 23 — Antonyms

Each of the questions below consists of a word printed in bold, followed by five words or phrases numbered 1 to 5. Choose the numbered word or pharase which is most nearly opposite in meaning to the word in bold and write the number of your choice on your answer paper.

441. precipitate 1. fast 2. anticipatory 3. cautious 4. considerate 5. dry

442. prim 1. informal 2. prior 3. exterior 4. private 5. cautious

443. protract 1. make circular 2. shorten 3. further 4. retrace 5. involve

444. prelude 1. intermezzo 2. overture 3. aria 4. aftermath 5. duplication

445. probity 1. regret 2. assumption 3. corruptibility 4. extent 5. upswing

446. pretentious 1. ominous 2. calm 3. unassuming 4. futile 5. volatile

447. prodigal 1. wandering 2. thrifty 3. consistent 4. compatible 5. errant

448. prosaic 1. pacified 2. reprieved 3. pensive 4. imaginative 5. rhetorical

450. puerile 1. fragrant 2. adult 3. lonely 4. feminine 5. masterly

451. pulchritude 1. ugliness 2. notoriety 3. bestiality 4. masculinity 5. servitude

---

ā — ale; ă — add; ä — arm; à — ask; ē — eve; ĕ — end; ê — err, her; ə — event, allow,
ī — ice; ĭ — ill; ō — old; ŏ — odd; ô — orb; ōō — food; ou — out; th — thin; ū — use;
ŭ — up; zh — pleasure

452. **prefatory** 1. outstanding 2. magnificent 3. conclusive 4. intelligent 5. predatory
453. **punctilious** 1. happy 2. active 3. vivid 4. careless 5. futile
454. **puissant** 1. pouring 2. fashionable 3. articulate 4. healthy 5. weak
455. **prolix** 1. stupid 2. indifferent 3. redundant 4. livid 5. pithy
456. **profane** 1. sanctify 2. desecrate 3. define 4. manifest 5. urge
457. **presumption** 1. assertion 2. activation 3. motivation 4. proposition 5. humility
458. **pristine** 1. cultivated 2. condemned 3. crude 4. cautious 5. critical
459. **prodigious** 1. infinitesimal 2. indignant 3. indifferent 4. indisposed 5. insufficient
460. **punitive** 1. large 2. vindictive 3. rewarding 4. restive 5. languishing

---

Word List 24   pusillanimous-reiterate

pusillanimous ADJ. cowardly; faint-hearted. You should be ashamed of your *pusillanimous* conduct during this dispute.

putrid ADJ. foul; rotten; decayed. The gangrenous condition of the wound was indicated by the *putrid* smell when the bandages were removed. putrescence, N.

pyromaniac N. person with an insane desire to set things on fire. The detectives searched the area for the *pyromaniac* who had set these costly fires.

quack N. charlatan; impostor. Do not be misled by the exorbitant claims of this *quack*.

quaff (*kwăhf*) V. drink with relish. As we *quaffed* our ale, we listened to the gay songs of the students in the tavern.

quail V. cower; lose heart. He was afraid that he would *quail* in the face of danger.

qualms N. misgivings. His *qualms* of conscience had become so great that he decided to abandon his plans.

quandary N. dilemma. When the two colleges to which he had applied accepted him, he was in a *quandary* as to which one he should attend.

ā — ale; ă — add; ä — arm; á — ask; ē — eve; ĕ — end; ê — err, her; ə — event, allow,
ī — ice; ĭ — ill; ō — old; ŏ — odd; ô — orb; ōō — food; ou — out; th — thin; ū — use;
ŭ — up; zh — pleasure

quay (*kē*) N. dock; landing place. Because of the captain's carelessness, the ship crashed into the *quay*.

quell V. put down; quiet. The police used fire hoses and tear gas to *quell* the rioters.

querulous ADJ. fretful; whining. His classmates were repelled by his *querulous* and complaining statements.

quibble V. equivocate; play on words. Do not *quibble;* I want a straightforward and definite answer.   also N.

quiescent (*kwī-ĕs'-*) ADJ. at rest; dormant. After this geyser erupts, it will remain *quiescent* for twenty-four hours.

quietude (*kwī'-ə-tūd*) N. tranquility. He was impressed by the air of *quietude* and peace that pervaded the valley.

quintessence N. purest and highest embodiment. These books display the *quintessence* of wit.

quip N. taunt. You are unpopular because you are too free with your *quips* and sarcastic comments.

quirk N. startling twist; caprice. By a *quirk* of fate, he found himself working for the man whom he had discharged years before.

qui vive (*kē vēv'*) N. wide awake; expectant. Let us be on the *qui vive*.

quixotic (*kwĭks-ot'-*) ADJ. idealistic but impractical. He is constantly presenting these *quixotic* schemes.

quizzical ADJ. bantering; comical; humorously serious. Will Rogers' *quizzical* remarks endeared him to his audiences.

rabid (*răb'-*) ADJ. like a fanatic; furious. He was a *rabid* follower of the Dodgers and watched them play whenever he could go to the ball park.

ragamuffin N. person wearing tattered clothes. He felt sorry for the *ragamuffin* who was begging for food and gave him money to buy a meal.

ramification N. branching out; subdivision. We must examine all the *ramifications* of this problem.

ramp N. slope; inclined plane. The house was built with *ramps* instead of stairs in order to enable the man in the wheel chair to move easily from room to room and floor to floor.

rampant ADJ. rearing up on hind legs; unrestrained. The *rampant* weeds in the garden killed all the plants which had been planted in the spring.

rancid ADJ. having the odor of stale fat. A *rancid* odor filled the ship's galley.

rancor N. bitterness; hatred. Let us forget our *rancor* and cooperate in this new endeavor.

rant V. rave; speak bombastically. As we heard him *rant* on the platform, we could not understand his strange popularity with many people.

rapacious ADJ. excessively grasping; plundering. Hawks and other *rapacious*

ā — ale; ă — add; ä — arm; á — ask; ē — eve; ĕ — end; ê — err, her; ə — event, allow,
ī — ice; ĭ — ill; ō — old; ŏ — odd; ô — orb; oo — food; ou — out; th — thin; ū — use;
ŭ — up; zh — pleasure

birds and animals may be killed at any time.

rapprochement (*ră-prŏsh'-*) N. reconciliation. Both sides were eager to affect a *rapprochement* but did not know how to undertake a program designed to bring about harmony.

rarefied ADJ. made less dense (of a gas). The mountain climbers had difficulty breathing in the *rarefied* atmosphere.

ratiocination N. reasoning; act of drawing conclusions from premises. Poe's "The Gold Bug" is a splendid example of the author's use of *ratiocination*.

rationalize V. reason; justify an improper act. Do not try to *rationalize* your behavior by blaming your companions.

raucous ADJ. harsh and shrill. His *raucous* laughter irritated me.

ravage (*răv'-*) V. plunder; despoil. The marauding army *ravaged* the countryside.

ravening (*răv'-*) ADJ. rapacious; seeking prey. We kept our fires burning all night to frighten the *ravening* wolves.

ravenous (*răv'-*) ADJ. extremely hungry. The *ravenous* dog upset several garbage pails in its search for food.

raze V. destroy completely. The owners intend to *raze* the hotel and erect an office building on the site.

realm N. kingdom; sphere. The *realm* of possibilities for the new invention was endless.

rebate N. discount. We offer a *rebate* of ten percent to those who pay cash.

recalcitrant ADJ. obstinately stubborn. Donkeys are reputed to be the most *recalcitrant* of animals.

recant V. repudiate; withdraw previous statement. Unless you *recant* your confession, you will be punished severely.

recapitulate V. summarize. Let us *recapitulate* what has been said thus far before going ahead.

recession N. withdrawal; retreat. The *recession* of the troops from the combat area was completed in an orderly manner.

recipient N. receiver. Although he had been the *recipient* of many favors, he was not grateful to his benefactor.

reciprocal ADJ. mutual; exchangeable; interacting. The two nations signed a *reciprocal* trade agreement.

reciprocate V. repay in kind. If they attack us, we shall be compelled to *reciprocate* and bomb their territory.

recluse (*-cloōs*) N. hermit. The *recluse* lived in a hut in the forest.

reconcile V. make friendly after quarrel; correct inconsistencies. Each month we *reconcile* our check book with the bank statement.

ā — ale; ă — add; ä — arm; â — ask; ē — eve; ĕ — end; ê — err, her; ə — event, allow, ī — ice; ĭ — ill; ō — old; ŏ — odd; ô — orb; ōō — food; ou — out; th — thin; ū — use; ŭ — up; zh — pleasure

recondite ADJ. abstruse; profound; secret. He read many *recondite* books in order to obtain the material for his scholarly thesis.

reconnaissance N. survey of enemy by soldiers; reconnoitering. If you encounter any enemy soldiers during your *reconnaissance*, capture them for questioning.

recourse N. resorting to help when in trouble. The boy's only *recourse* was to appeal to his father for aid.

recreant (rĕk'-) N. coward; betrayer of faith. The religious people ostracized the *recreant* who had abandoned their faith.

recrimination N. countercharges. Loud and angry *recriminations* were her answer to his accusations.

rectify V. correct. I want to *rectify* my error before it is too late.

rectitude N. uprightness. He was renowned for his *rectitude* and integrity.

recumbent ADJ. reclining; lying down completely or in part. The command "AT EASE" does not permit you to take a *recumbent* position.

recuperate (rĕ-kū'-) V. recover. The doctors were worried because the patient did not *recuperate* as rapidly as they had expected.

recurrent ADJ. occurring again and again. These *recurrent* attacks disturbed us and we consulted a physician.

redolent (rĕd'-) ADJ. fragrant; odorous; suggestive of an odor. Even though it is February, the air is *redolent* of spring.

redoubtable ADJ. formidable; causing fear. He was a *redoubtable* foe.

redress (-drĕs') N. remedy; compensation. Do you mean to tell me that I can get no *redress* for my injuries? also V.

redundant ADJ. superfluous; excessively wordy; repetitious. Your composition is *redundant;* you can easily reduce its length.

reek V. emit (odor). The room *reeked* with stale tobacco smoke.

refection N. slight refreshment. In our anxiety to reach our destination as rapidly as possible, we stopped on the road for only a slight *refection.*

refectory N. dining hall. In this huge *refectory*, we can feed the entire student body at one sitting.

refraction N. bending of a ray of light. When you look at a stick inserted in water, it looks bent because of the *refraction* of the light by the water.

refractory ADJ. stubborn; unmanageable. The *refractory* horse was eliminated from the race.

refulgent ADJ. radiant. We admired the *refulgent* moon and watched it for a while.

refutation N. disproof of opponents' arguments. I will wait until I hear the

ā — ale; ă — add; ä — arm; à — ask; ē — eve; ĕ — end; ê — err, her; ə — event, allow, i — ice; ĭ — ill; ō — old; ŏ — odd; ô — orb; ōō — food; ou — out; th — thin; ū — use; ŭ — up; zh — pleasure

refutation before deciding whom to favor.

regal ADJ. royal. He had a *regal* manner.

regale (-*gāl'*) V. entertain. John *regaled* us with tales of his adventures in Africa.

regatta (-*gat'*-) N. boat or yacht race. Many boating enthusiasts followed the *regatta* in their own yachts.

regeneration N. spiritual rebirth. Modern penologists strive for the *regeneration* of the prisoners.

regime (*re-zhēm'*) N. method or system of government. When a Frenchman mentions the Old *Regime*, he refers to the government existing before the revolution.

regimen (*rĕj'*-) N. prescribed diet and habits. I doubt whether the results warrant our living under such a strict and inflexible *regimen*.

rehabilitate V. restore to proper condition. We must *rehabilitate* those whom we send to prison.

reimburse V. repay. Let me know what you have spent and I will *reimburse* you.

reiterate V. repeat. I shall *reiterate* this message until all have understood it.

ETYMOLOGY 24.

PUT, PUTAT (to trim, to calculate)
   computation   a reckoning
   amputate   cut off
   putative   supposed (calculated)
QUAER, QUAESIT (to ask)
   inquiry   investigation
   inquisitive   questioning
   query   question

TEST — Word List 24 — Synonyms and Antonyms

Each of the following questions consists of a word printed in bold, followed by five words or phrases numbered 1 to 5. Choose the numbered word or phrase which is most nearly the same as or the opposite of the word in bold and write the number of your choice on your answer paper.

ā — ale; ă — add; ä — arm; à — ask; ē — eve; ĕ — end; ê — err, her; ə — event, allow, ī — ice; ĭ — ill; ō — old; ŏ — odd; ô — orb; ōō — food; ou — out; th — thin; ū — use; ŭ — up; zh — pleasure

461. regal 1. oppressive 2. common 3. major 4. basic 5. entertaining

462. rebate 1. relinquish 2. settle 3. discount 4. cancel 5. elicit

463. quandary 1. quagmire 2. dilemma 3. epigram 4. enemy 5. finish

464. refractory 1. articulate 2. sinkable 3. vaunted 4. useless 5. manageable

465. raze 1. shave 2. heckle 3. finish 4. tear down 5. write

466. putrid 1. sick 2. lovely 3. aromatic 4. arrogant 5. humid

467. recuperate 1. reenact 2. engage 3. recapitulate 4. recover 5. encounter

468. ravage 1. rank 2. revive 3. plunder 4. pillory 5. age

469. quaff 1. drug 2. imbibe 3. seal 4. scale 5. joke

470. rectify 1. remedy 2. avenge 3. create 4. assemble 5. attribute

471. raucous 1. mellifluous 2. uncooked 3. realistic 4. veracious 5. anticipating

472. pusillanimous 1. poverty-stricken 2. chained 3. posthumous 4. cowardly 5. strident

473. recreant 1. vacationing 2. faithful 3. indifferent 4. obliged 5. reviving

474. quixotic 1. rapid 2. exotic 3. longing 4. timid 5. idealistic

475. rehabilitate 1. clothe 2. destroy 3. avenge 4. vanish 5. embarrass

476. qui vive 1. alive 2. fast 3. gloomy 4. vivid 5. awake

477. reimburse 1. remunerate 2. constitute 3. dip 4. demolish 5. patronize

478. regatta 1. impertinence 2. boat race 3. satisfaction 4. saturation 5. quiz

479. reiterate 1. gainsay 2. revive 3. revenge 4. repeat 5. return

480. refulgent 1. overflowing 2. effortless 3. dim 4. noisy 5. snoring

---

Word List 25   rejuvenate-rostrum

rejuvenate v. make young again. The charlatan claimed that his elixir would *rejuvenate* the aged and weary.

relegate v. banish; consign to inferior position. If we *relegate* these experi-

ā — ale; ǎ — add; ä — arm; à — ask; ē — eve; ě — end; ê — err, her; ə — event, allow, ī — ice; ǐ — ill; ō — old; ǒ — odd; ô — orb; ōō — food; ou — out; th — thin; ū — use; ǔ — up; zh — pleasure

enced people to positions of unimportance because of their political persuasions, we shall lose the services of valuably trained personnel.

relevancy N. pertinence; reference to the case in hand. I was impressed by the *relevancy* of your remarks. relevant, ADJ.

relinquish V. abandon. I will *relinquish* my claims to this property if you promise to retain my employees.

relish V. savor; enjoy. I *relish* a good joke as much as anyone else. also N.

remediable (-mē'-) ADJ. reparable. Let us be grateful that the damage is *remediable*.

remedial ADJ. curative; corrective. Because he was a slow reader, he decided to take a course in *remedial* reading.

reminiscence N. recollection. Her *reminiscences* of her experiences are so fascinating that she ought to write a book.

remiss ADJ. negligent. He was accused of being *remiss* in his duty.

remnant N. remainder. I suggest that you wait until the store places the *remnants* of these goods on sale.

remonstrate (-mŏn'-) V. protest. I must *remonstrate* about the lack of police protection in this area.

remunerative ADJ. compensating; rewarding. I find my new work so *remunerative* that I may not return to my previous employment. remuneration, N.

rend V. split; tear apart. In his grief, he tried to *rend* his garments.

render V. deliver; provide; represent. He *rendered* aid to the needy and indigent.

rendezvous (ron'-dĭ-vōō) N. meeting place. The two fleets met at the *rendezvous* at the appointed time.

renegade N. deserter; apostate. Because he refused to support his fellow members in their drive, he was shunned as a *renegade*.

renounce V. abandon; discontinue; disown; repudiate. She refused to *renounce* her faith.

renovate V. restore to good condition; renew. They claim that they can *renovate* worn shoes so that they look like new ones.

renunciation N. giving up; renouncing. Do not sign this *renunciation* of your right to sue until you have consulted a lawyer.

reparable (rĕp'-) ADJ. capable of being repaired. Fortunately, the damages we suffered in the accident were *reparable*.

reparation N. amends; compensation. At the peace conference, the defeated country promised to pay *reparations* to the victors.

ā — ale; ă — add; ä — arm; â — ask; ē — eve; ĕ — end; ê — err, her; ə — event, allow; ī — ice; ĭ — ill; ō — old; ŏ — odd; ô — orb; ōō — food; ou — out; th — thin; ū — use; ŭ — up; zh — pleasure

repartee N. clever reply. He was famous for his witty *repartee* and his sarcasm.

repellent ADJ. driving away; unattractive. Mosquitoes find the odor so *repellent* that they leave any spot where this liquid has been sprayed.

repercussion N. rebound; reverberation; reaction. I am afraid that this event will have serious *repercussions*.

repertoire N. list of works of music, drama, etc., a performer is prepared to present. The opera company decided to include *Madame Butterfly* in its *repertoire* for the following season.

replenish V. fill up again. The end of rationing enabled us to *replenish* our supply of canned food.

replete (-plēt') ADJ. filled to capacity; abundantly supplied. This book is *replete* with humorous situations.

replica N. copy. Are you going to hang this *replica* of the Declaration of Independence in the classroom or in the auditorium?

repository N. storehouse. Libraries are *repositories* of the world's best thoughts.

reprehensible ADJ. deserving blame. I find your present attitude *reprehensible*.

reprieve N. temporary stay. During the twenty-four hour *reprieve*, the lawyers sought to make the stay of execution permanent.

reprimand V. reprove severely. I am afraid that my parents will *reprimand* me when I show them my report card.   also N.

reprisal N. retaliation. I am confident that we are ready for any *reprisals* the enemy may undertake.

reprobation N. severe disapproval. The students showed their *reprobation* of his act by refusing to talk with him.

repudiate V. disown; disavow. He announced that he would *repudiate* all debts incurred by his wife.

repugnance N. loathing. She looked at the snake with *repugnance*.

requiem N. mass for the dead; dirge. They played Mozart's *Requiem* at the funeral.

requisite N. necessary requirement. Many colleges state that a student must offer three years of a language as a *requisite* for admission.

requite V. repay; revenge. The wretch *requited* his benefactors by betraying them.

rescind V. cancel. Because of public resentment, the king had to *rescind* his order.

ā — ale; ă — add; ä — arm; â — ask; ē — eve; ĕ — end; ê — err, her; ə — event, allow,
ī — ice; ĭ — ill; ō — old; ŏ — odd; ô — orb; o͞o — food; ou — out; th — thin; ū — use;
ŭ — up; zh — pleasure

rescission N. abrogation; annulment. The *rescission* of the unpopular law was urged by all political parties.

resonant (rĕz'-) ADJ. echoing; resounding; possessing resonance. His *resonant* voice was particularly pleasing.

respite (rĕs'-pĭt) N. delay in punishment; interval of relief; rest. The judge granted the condemned man a *respite* to enable his attorneys to file an appeal.

resplendent ADJ. brilliant; lustrous. The toreador wore a *resplendent* costume.

restitution N. reparation; indemnification. He offered to make *restitution* for the window broken by his son.

restive ADJ. unmanageable; fretting under control. We must quiet the *restive* animals.

resuscitate V. revive. The lifeguard tried to *resuscitate* the drowned child by applying artificial respiration.

retaliate V. repay in kind (usually for bad treatment). Fear that we will *retaliate* immediately deters our foe from attacking us.

retentive ADJ. holding; having a good memory. The pupil did not need to spend much time in study as he had a *retentive* mind.

reticence N. reserve; uncommunicativeness; inclination to be silent. Because of the *reticence* of the key witness, the case against the defendant collapsed.

retinue N. following; attendants. The queen's *retinue* followed her down the aisle.

retraction N. withdrawal. He dropped his libel suit after the newspaper published a *retraction* of its statement.

retribution N. vengeance; compensation; punishment for offenses. The evangelist maintained that an angry God would exact *retribution* from the sinners.

retrieve V. recover; find and bring in. The dog was intelligent and quickly learned to *retrieve* the game killed by the hunter.

retroactive ADJ. of a law which dates back to a period before its enactment. Because the law was *retroactive* to the first of the year, we found he was eligible for the pension.

retrograde V. going backward; degenerating. Instead of advancing, our civilization seems to have *retrograded* in ethics and culture. retrogression, N.

retrospective ADJ. looking back on the past. It is only when we become *retrospective* that we can appreciate the tremendous advances

---

ā — ale; ă — add; ä — arm; å — ask; ē — eve; ĕ — end; ê — err, her; ə — event, allow, ĭ — ice; ĭ — ill; ō — old; ŏ — odd; ô — orb; ōō — food; ou — out; th — thin; ū — use; ŭ — up; zh — pleasure

made during this century.

revelry N. boisterous merrymaking. New Year's Eve is a night of *revelry*.

reverberate V. echo; resound. The entire valley *reverberated* with the sound of the church bells.

reverie N. day-dream; musing. He was awakened from his *reverie* by the teacher's question.

revile V. slander; vilify. He was avoided by all who feared that he would *revile* and abuse them if they displeased him.

revulsion N. sudden violent change of feeling; reaction. Many people in this country who admired dictatorships underwent a *revulsion* when they realized what Hitler and Mussolini were trying to do.

rhetoric N. art of effective communication; insincere language. All writers, by necessity, must be skilled in *rhetoric*.   rhetorical, ADJ.

rheumy (*rōō'-mĭ*) ADJ. pertaining to a discharge from nose and eyes. His *rheumy* eyes warned us that he was coming down with a cold.

ribald (*rĭb'-*) ADJ. wanton; profane. He sang a *ribald* song which offended many of us.

rife ADJ. abundant; current. In the face of the many rumors of scandal, which are *rife* at the moment, it is best to remain silent.

rift N. opening; break. The plane was lost in the stormy sky until the pilot saw the city through a *rift* in the clouds.

rigor N. severity. Many settlers could not stand the *rigors* of the New England winters.

rime N. white frost. The early morning dew had frozen and everything was covered with a thin coat of *rime*.

risible ADJ. inclined to laugh; ludicrous. His remarks were so *risible* that the audience howled with laughter.   risibility, N.

risqué (*ris-kā'*) ADJ. verging upon the improper; off-color. Please do not tell your *risqué* anecdotes at this party.

roan ADJ. brown mixed with gray or white. You can distinguish this horse in a race because it is *roan* while all the others are bay or chestnut.

robust (*-bŭst'*) ADJ. vigorous; strong. The candidate for the football team had a *robust* physique.

rococo (*rō-cōc'-ō*) ADJ. ornate; highly decorated. At the present time, architects avoid *rococo* designs.

roseate (*rō'-zĭ-ĕt*) ADJ. rosy; optimistic. I am afraid you will have to alter your *roseate* views in the light of the distressing news that has just arrived.

rostrum N. platform for speech-making; pulpit. The crowd murmured angrily

---

ā — ale; ă — add; ä — arm; â — ask; ē — eve; ĕ — end; ê — err, her; ə — event, allow, i — ice; ĭ — ill; ō — old; ŏ — odd; ô — orb; ōō — food; ou — out; th — thin; ū — use; ŭ — up; zh — pleasure

and indicated that they did not care to listen to the speaker who
was approaching the *rostrum*.

ETYMOLOGY 25.

RID, RIS (to laugh)
      derision scorn
      risibility inclination to laughter
      ridiculous deserving to be laughed at
ROG, ROGAT (to ask)
      interrogate to question
      prerogation privilege
      derogatory disparaging (asking a question to belittle)

TEST — Word List 25 — Synonyms

Each of the questions below consists of a word printed in bold,
followed by five words or phrases numbered 1 to 5. Choose the
numbered word or phrase which is most nearly similar in meaning
to the word in bold and write the number of your choice on your
answer paper.

481. **restive** 1. buoyant 2. restless 3. remorseful 4. resistant 5. retiring
482. **replenish** 1. polish 2. repeat 3. reinstate 4. refill 5. refuse
483. **remonstrate** 1. display 2. restate 3. protest 4. resign 5. reiterate
484. **repugnance** 1. belligerence 2. tenacity 3. renewal 4. pity 5. loathing
485. **repercussion** 1. reverberation 2. restitution 3. resistance 4. magnificence 5. acceptance
486. **remiss** 1. lax 2. lost 3. foolish 4. violating 5. ambitious
487. **repudiate** 1. besmirch 2. appropriate 3. annoy 4. reject 5. avow
488. **repellent** 1. propulsive 2. unattractive 3. porous 4. stiff 5. elastic
489. **remedial** 1. therapeutic 2. corrective 3. traumatic 4. philandering 5. psychotic

ā — ale; ă — add; ä — arm; â — ask; ē — eve; ĕ — end; ê — err, her; a — event, allow,
i — ice; ĭ — ill; ō — old; ŏ — odd; ô — orb; ōō — food; ou — out; th — thin; ū — use;
ŭ — up; zh — pleasure

490. reprisal 1. reevaluation 2. assessment 3. loss 4. retaliation 5. nonsense
491. repartee 1. witty retort 2. willful departure 3. spectator 4. monologue 5. sacrifice
492. relish 1. desire 2. nibble 3. savor 4. vindicate 5. avail
493. replica 1. museum piece 2. famous site 3. battle emblem 4. facsimile 5. replacement
494. reparation 1. result 2. compensation 3. alteration 4. retaliation 5. resistance
495. robust 1. vigorous 2. violent 3. vicious 4. villanous 5. voracious
496. retinue 1. continuation 2. attendants 3. application 4. beleaguer 5. assessment
497. rife 1. direct 2. scant 3. abundant 4. grim 5. mature
498. reticence 1. reserve 2. fashion 3. treachery 4. loquaciousness 5. magnanimity
499. retrograde 1. receding 2. inclining 3. evaluating 4. concentrating 5. directing
500. retentive 1. grasping 2. accepting 3. repetitive 4. avoiding 5. fascinating

---

Word List 26   rote-silt

rote N. repetition. He recited the passage by *rote* and gave no indication he understood what he was saying.

rotundity N. roundness; sonorousness of speech. Washington Irving emphasized the *rotundity* of the governor by describing his height and circumference.

rubble N fragments. Ten years after World War II, some of the *rubble* left by enemy bombings could still be seen.

rubicund ($r\overline{oo}'$-) ADJ. having a healthy reddish color; ruddy; florid. His *rubicund* complexion was the result of an active outdoor life.

ruddy ADJ. reddish; healthy-looking. His *ruddy* complexion indicated that he had spent much time in the open.

rudimentary ADJ. not developed; elementary. His dancing was limited to a few *rudimentary* steps.

rueful ADJ. regretful; sorrowful; dejected. The artist has captured the sadness of childhood in his portrait of the boy with the *rueful* countenance.

ā — ale; ǎ — add; ä — arm; á — ask; ē — eve; ĕ — end; ê — err, her; ə — event, allow, ī — ice; ǐ — ill; ō — old; ŏ — odd; ô — orb; ōō — food; ou — out; th — thin; ū — use; ǔ — up; zh — pleasure

ruminate v. chew the cud; ponder. We cannot afford to wait while you *ruminate* upon these plans.

rummage v. ransack; thoroughly search. When we *rummaged* through the trunks in the attic, we found many souvenirs of our childhood days.

ruse N. trick; stratagem. You will not be able to fool your friends with such an obvious *ruse*.

rusticate v. banish to the country; dwell in the country. I like the city life so much that I can never understand how people can *rusticate* in the suburbs.

ruthless ADJ. pitiless. The escaped convict was a dangerous and *ruthless* murderer.

sacerdotal (-dō'-) ADJ. priestly. The priest decided to abandon his *sacerdotal* duties and enter the field of politics.

sacrilegious (-lē-) ADJ. desecrating; profane. His stealing of the altar cloth was a very *sacrilegious* act.

sacrosanct (săc'-) ADJ. most sacred; inviolable. The brash insurance salesman invaded the *sacrosanct* privacy of the office of the president of the company.

sadistic (-dĭs'-) ADJ. inclined to cruelty. If we are to improve conditions in this prison, we must first get rid of the *sadistic* warden.

saffron ADJ. orange-colored; colored like the autumn crocus. The Halloween cake was decorated with *saffron*-colored icing.

saga (sah'-) N. Scandinavian myth; any legend. This is a *saga* of the sea and of the men who risk their lives on it.

sagacious ADJ. keen; shrewd; having insight. He is much too *sagacious* to be fooled by a trick like that.

salient (sā'-lĭ-ĕnt) ADJ. prominent. One of the *salient* features of that newspaper is its excellent editorial page.

saline (sāl'-īn) ADJ. salty. The slightly *saline* taste of this mineral water is pleasant.

sallow ADJ. yellowish; sickly in color. We were disturbed by his *sallow* complexion.

salubrious (-lōō'-) ADJ. healthful. Many people with hay fever move to more *salubrious* sections of the country during the months of August and September.

salutary ADJ. tending to improve; beneficial; wholesome. The punishment had a *salutary* effect on the boy as he became a model student.

salvage v. rescue from loss. All attempts to *salvage* the wrecked ship failed.

sangfroid (sahn-frwa') N. coolness in a trying situation. The captain's

ā — ale; ă — add; ä — arm; à — ask; ē — eve; ĕ — end; ê — err, her; ə — event, allow, ī — ice; ĭ — ill; ō — old; ŏ — odd; ô — orb; ōō — food; ou — out; th — thin; ū — use; ŭ — up; zh — pleasure

sangfroid helped to allay the fears of the passengers.

sanguinary ADJ. bloody. The battle of Iwo Jima was unexpectedly *sanguinary*.

sanguine ADJ. cheerful; hopeful. Let us not be too *sanguine* about the outcome.

sapid (săp'-) ADJ. savory; tasty; relishable. This chef has the knack of making most foods more *sapid* and appealing.

sapient (sā'-pĭ-) ADJ. wise; shrewd. The students enjoyed the professor's *sapient* digressions more than his formal lectures.

sardonic ADJ. disdainful; sarcastic; cynical. I cannot stand his *sardonic* wit.

sate V. satisfy to the full; cloy. Its hunger *sated*, the lion dozed.

satiate V. surfeit; satisfy fully. The guests, having eaten until they were *satiated*, now listened inattentively to the speakers.

satiety (-tĭ'-e-tĭ) N. condition of being crammed full; glutted state; repletion. Shelley mentions "Love's sad *satiety*" in his "Ode to a Skylark."

saturate V. soak. Their clothes were *saturated* by the rain.

saturnine (săt'-ur-nīn) ADJ. gloomy. The *saturnine* professor had few pupils.

saunter V. stroll slowly. As we *sauntered* through the park, we stopped frequently to admire the spring flowers.

savant (să-von') N. scholar. Our faculty includes many world famous *savants*.

savoir faire (săv'-wah fər') N. tact; poise; sophistication. I envy his *savoir faire;* he always knows exactly what to do and say.

savor V. have a distinctive flavor, smell, or quality. I think your choice of a successor *savors* of favoritism.

scavenger N. collector and disposer of refuse; animal that devours refuse and carrion. The coyote is a *scavenger*.

schism (sĭzm) N. division; split. Let us not widen the *schism* by further bickering.

scintilla N. shred; least bit. You have not produced a *scintilla* of evidence to support your argument.

scintillate V. sparkle; flash. I enjoy her dinner parties because the food is excellent and the conversation *scintillates*.

scion (sī'-ən) N. offspring. The farm boy felt out of place in the school attended by the *scions* of the wealthy and noble families.

scourge N. lash; whip; severe punishment. They feared the plague and regarded it as a deadly *scourge*.

scrupulous ADJ. conscientious; extremely thorough. I can recommend him for a position of responsibility for I have found him a very *scrupulous* young man.

scullion N. menial kitchen worker. Lynette was angry because she thought she had been given a *scullion* to act as her defender.

ā — ale; ă — add; ä — arm; à — ask; ē — eve; ĕ — end; ê — err, her; ə — event, allow, i — ice; ĭ — ill; ō — old; ŏ — odd; ô — orb; ōo — food; ou — out; th — thin; ū — use; ŭ — up; zh — pleasure

scurrilous ADJ. obscene; indecent. I should horsewhip you for your *scurrilous* remarks about my daughter.

scuttle V. sink. The sailors decided to *scuttle* their vessel rather than surrender it to the enemy.

sebaceous (-bā'-) ADJ. oily; fatty. The *sebaceous* glands secrete oil to the hair follicles.

secession N. withdrawal. The *secession* of the Southern states provided Lincoln with his first major problem after his inauguration.

secular ADJ. worldly; not pertaining to church matters; temporal. The church leaders decided not to interfere in *secular* matters.

sedate ADJ. composed; grave. The parents were worried because they felt their son was too quiet and *sedate*.

sedentary (sed'-) ADJ. requiring sitting. Because he had a *sedentary* occupation, he decided to visit a gymnasium weekly.

sedulous ADJ. diligent. Stevenson said that he played the "*sedulous* ape" and diligently imitated the great writers of the past.

seethe V. be disturbed; boil. The nation was *seething* with discontent as the noblemen continued their arrogant ways.

seine (sān) N. net for catching fish. When the shad run during the spring, you may see fishermen with *seines* along the banks of our coastal rivers.

semblance N. outward appearance; guise. Although this book has a *semblance* of wisdom and scholarship, a careful examination will reveal many errors and omissions.

senility N. old age; feeble-mindedness of old age. Most of the decisions are being made by the junior members of the company because of the *senility* of the president.

sensual ADJ. devoted to the pleasures of the senses; carnal; voluptuous. I cannot understand what caused him to drop his *sensual* way of life and become so ascetic.

sententious ADJ. terse; concise; aphoristic. After reading so many wordy and redundant speeches, I find his *sententious* style particularly pleasing.

sepulcher N. tomb. Annabel Lee was buried in the *sepulcher* by the sea.

sequester V. retire from public life; segregate; seclude. Although he had hoped for a long time to *sequester* himself in a small community, he never was able to drop his busy round of activities in the city.

serendipity N. gift for finding vaulable things not searched for. Many scientific discoveries are a matter of *serendipity*.

serenity N. calmness; placidity. The *serenity* of the sleepy town was shattered

ā — ale; ă — add; ä — arm; à — ask; ē — eve; ĕ — end; ê — err, her; ə — event, allow,
ī — ice; ĭ — ill; ō — old; ŏ — odd; ô — orb; ōō — food; ou — out; th — thin; ū — use;
ŭ — up; zh — pleasure

by a tremendous explosion.

serrated (sĕ'-rā-tĕd) ADJ. having a sawtoothed edge. The beech tree is one of many plants that has *serrated* leaves.

servile (sêr'-vĭl) ADJ. slavish; cringing. Uriah Heep was a very *servile* individual.

severance N. division; partition; separation. The *severance* of church and state is a basic principle of our government.

shackle V. chain; fetter. The criminal's ankles were *shackled* to prevent his escape.

shambles N. slaughter house; scene of carnage. By the time the police arrived, the room was a *shambles*.

sheaf N. bundle of stalks of grain; any bundle of things tied together. The lawyer picked up a *sheaf* of papers as he rose to question the witness.

sheathe V. place into a case. As soon as he recognized the approaching men, he *sheathed* his dagger and hailed them as friends.

sherbet N. water-ice. I prefer raspberry *sherbet* to ice cream since it is less fattening.

shibboleth N. watchword; slogan. We are often misled by *shibboleths*.

shimmer V. glimmer intermittently. The moonlight *shimmered* on the water as the moon broke through the clouds for a moment.

shoal N. shallow place. The ship was stranded on a *shoal* and had to be pulled off by tugs.

shoddy ADJ. sham; not genuine; inferior. You will never get the public to buy such *shoddy* material.

sidereal (sī-dē'-rē-) ADJ. relating to the stars. The study of *sidereal* bodies has been greatly advanced by the new telescope.

silt N. sediment deposited by running water. The harbor channel must be dredged annually to remove the *silt*.

ETYMOLOGY 26.

RUPT (to break)
> **interrupt** to break into
> **bankrupt** insolvent
> **rupture** a break

SCRIB, SCRIPT (to write)
> **transcribe** copy
> **script** writing

ā — ale; ă — add; ä — arm; á — ask; ē — eve; ĕ — end; ê — err, her; a — event, allow,
ī — ice; ĭ — ill; ō — old; ŏ — odd; ô — orb; ōō — food; ou — out; th — thin; ū — use;
ŭ — up; zh — pleasure

circumscribe enclose, limit (write around)

SCI (to know)

science knowledge

omniscient knowing all

conscious aware

SED, SESS, SID (to sit)

sedentary inactive (sitting)

session meeting

residence place where one dwells

SENT, SENS (to think, to feel)

resent show indignation

sensitive showing feeling

consent agree

SEQUE, SECUT (to follow)

consecutive following in order

sequence arrangement

sequel that which follows

TEST — Word List 26 — Antonyms

Each of the questions below consists of a word printed in bold, followed by five words or phrases numbered 1 to 5. Choose the numbered word or phrase which is most nearly opposite in meaning to the word in bold and write the number of your choice on your answer paper.

501. scurrilous 1. savage 2. scabby 3. decent 4. volatile 5. major

502. sagacious 1. foolish 2. bitter 3. voracious 4. veracious 5. fallacious

503. rudimentary 1. pale 2. fundamental 3. asinine 4. developed 5. quiescent

504. sanguine 1. choloric 2. sickening 3. warranted 4. irritated 5. pessimistic

505. sadistic 1. happy 2. quaint 3. kind-hearted 4. vacant 5. fortunate

506. ruddy 1. robust 2. witty 3. wan 4. exotic 5. creative

507. salvage 1. remove 2. outfit 3. burn 4. lose 5. confuse

508. sacerdotal 1. religious 2. frank 3. authoritative 4. violent 5. lay

ā — ale; ă — add; ä — arm; å — ask; ē — eve; ĕ — end; ê — err, her; ə — event, allow, ī — ice; ĭ — ill; ō — old; ŏ — odd; ô — orb; ōō — food; ou — out; th — thin; ū — use; ŭ — up; zh — pleasure

509. rubicund 1. dangerous 2. pallid 3. remote 4. indicative 5. nonsensical

510. salubrious 1. salty 2. bloody 3. miasmic 4. maudlin 5. wanted

511. ruthless 1. merciful 2. majestic 3. mighty 4. militant 5. maximum

512. rotundity 1. promenade 2. nave 3. grotesqueness 4. slimness 5. impropriety

513. sallow 1. salacious 2. ruddy 3. colorless 4. permitted 5. minimum

514. rueful 1. sad 2. content 3. capable 4. capital 5. zealous

515. secular 1. vivid 2. clerical 3. punitive 4. positive 5. varying

516. shoddy 1. superior 2. incomplete 3. inadequate 4. querulous 5. garrulous

517. sedentary 1. vicarious 2. loyal 3. accidental 4. active 5. afraid

518. servile 1. menial 2. puerile 3. futile 4. lowly 5. haughty

519. sententious 1. paragraphed 2. positive 3. posthumous 4. pacific 5. wordy

520. senility 1. virility 2. loquaciousness 3. forgetfulness 4. youth 5. majority

---

Word List 27   simian-sundry

simian ADJ. monkeylike. This strange animal has *simian* characteristics.

simile (sǐm'-ǐ-lē) N. comparison of one thing with another, using the word *like* or *as*. We are constantly using *similes* and metaphors to convey our thoughts to others.

simulate V. feign. He *simulated* insanity in order to avoid punishment for his crime.

sinecure (sī'-ne-cūr) N. well paid position with little responsibility. My job is no *sinecure;* I work long hours and have much responsibility.

sinister ADJ. evil. We must defeat the *sinister* forces that seek our downfall.

sinuous ADJ. winding; bending in and out; not morally honest. The snake moved in a *sinuous* manner.

skimp V. provide scantily; live very economically. They were forced to *skimp* on necessities in order to make their limited supplies last the winter.

ā — ale; ǎ — ǎdd; ä — ärm; å — åsk; ē — ēve; ě — ěnd; ê — êrr, hêr; ə — ęvent, ạllow.
ī — īce; ǐ — ǐll; ō — ōld; ǒ — ǒdd; ô — ôrb; ōō — fōōd; ou — out; th — thin; ū — ūse;
ǔ — ǔp; zh — plęasure

skittish ADJ. lively; frisky. He is as *skittish* as a kitten playing with a piece of string.

skulk V. move furtively and secretly. He *skulked* through the less fashionable sections of the city in order to avoid meeting any of his former friends.

slake V. quench; sate. When we reached the oasis, we were able to *slake* our thirst.

sleazy ADJ. flimsy; unsubstantial. This is a *sleazy* material; it will not wear well.

sloth (*slŏth*) N. laziness. Such *sloth* in a young person is deplorable.

slough (*slŭf*) V. cast off. Each spring, the snake *sloughs* off its skin.

slovenly ADJ. untidy; careless in work habits. Such *slovenly* work habits will never produce good products.

sluggard N. lazy person. "You are a *sluggard*, a drone, a parasite," the angry father shouted at his lazy son.

sobriety N. soberness. The solemnity of the occasion filled us with *sobriety*.

sojourn N. temporary stay. After his *sojourn* in Florida, he began to long for the colder climate of his native New England.

solecism N. construction that is flagrantly incorrect grammatically. I must give this paper a failing mark because it contains many *solecisms*.

solicitous ADJ. worried; concerned. The employer was very *solicitous* about the health of his employees as replacements were difficult to get.

soliloquy N. talking to oneself. The *soliloquy* is a device used by the dramatist to reveal a character's innermost thoughts and emotions.

solstice N. point at which the sun is farthest from the equator. The winter *solstice* usually occurs on December 21.

solvent ADJ. able to pay all debts. By dint of very frugal living, he was finally able to become *solvent* and avoid bankruptcy proceedings.

somnambulist N. sleepwalker. Lady Macbeth became a *somnambulist*.

somnolent ADJ. half asleep. The heavy meal and the overheated room made us all *somnolent* and indifferent to the speaker.

sonorous (*-nō'-*) ADJ. resonant. His *sonorous* voice resounded through the hall.

soupcon (*sōōp'-sawn*) N. suggestion; hint; taste. A *soupcon* of garlic will improve this dish.

spangle N. small metallic piece sewn to clothing for ornamentation. The thousands of *spangles* on her dress sparkled in the glare of the stage lights.

spasmodic ADJ. fitful; periodic. The *spasmodic* coughing in the auditorium annoyed the performers.

spatial ADJ. relating to space. It is difficult to visualize the *spatial* extent of our

ā — ale; ă — add; ä — arm; à — ask; ē — eve; ĕ — end; ê — err, her; ə — event, allow;
ī — ice; ĭ — ill; ō — old; ŏ — odd; ô — orb; ōō — food; ou — out; th — thin; ū — use;
ŭ — up; zh — pleasure

universe.

spawn V. lay eggs. Fish ladders had to be built in the dams to assit the salmon returning to *spawn* in their native streams.

specious (*spē'*-) ADJ. seemingly reasonable but incorrect. Let us not be misled by such *specious* arguments.

spectral ADJ. ghostly. We were frightened by the *spectral* glow that filled the room.

splenetic (*splĕ-nĕt'*-) ADJ. spiteful; irritable; peevish. People shunned him because of his *splenetic* temper.

sporadic (*-răd'*-) ADJ. occurring irregularly. Although there are *sporadic* outbursts of shoorting, we may report that the major rebellion has been defeated.

sportive ADJ. playful. Such a *sportive* attitude is surprising in a person as serious as you usually are.

spurious ADJ. false; counterfeit. He tried to pay the bill with a *spurious* dollar bill.

squalid (*skwŏl'*-) ADJ. dirty; neglected; poor. It is easy to see how crime can breed in such a *squalid* neighborhood.

squander V. waste. The prodigal son *squandered* the family estate.

stagnant ADJ. motionless; stale; dull. The *stagnant* water was a breeding ground for disease.

staid ADJ. sober; sedate. His conduct during the funeral ceremony was *staid* and solemn.

stamina N. strength; staying power. I doubt that he has the *stamina* to run the full distance of the marathon race.

stanch (*stähnch*) V. check flow of blood. It is imperative that we *stanch* the gushing wound before we attend to the other injuries.

statute N. law. We have many *statutes* in our law books which should be repealed.

stein N. beer mug. He thought of college as a place where one drank beer from *steins* and sang songs of lost lambs.

stellar ADJ. pertaining to the stars. He was the *stellar* attraction of the entire performance.

stentorian ADJ. extremely loud. The town crier had a *stentorian* voice.

stigmatize V. brand; mark as wicked. I do not want to *stigmatize* this young offender for life by sending him to prison.

stint N. supply; allotted amount; assigned portion of work. He performed his daily *stint* cheerfully and willingly.

stipend (*stī'*-) N. pay for services. There is a nominal *stipend* attached to this position.

ā — ale; ă — add; ä — arm; à — ask; ē — eve; ĕ — end; ê — err, her; ə — event, allow.
i — ice; ĭ — ill; ō — old; ŏ — odd; ô — orb; ōō — food; ou — out; th — thin; ū — use;
ŭ — up; zh — pleasure

stoic (*stō'-ĭk*) N. person who is indifferent to pleasure or pain. He bore the pain like a *stoic*.

stolid ADJ. dull; impassive. I am afraid that this imaginative poetry will not appeal to such a *stolid* person.

stratagem (*străt'-*) N. deceptive scheme. We saw through his clever *stratagem*.

striated (*strī'-āt-*) ADJ. marked with parallel bands. The glacier left many *striated* rocks.

stricture N. critical comments; severe and adverse criticism. His *strictures* on the author's style are prejudiced and unwarranted.

strident (*strī'-*) ADJ. loud and harsh. She scolded him in a *strident* voice.

stringent (*strĭn'-jent*) ADJ. binding; rigid. I think these regulations are too *stringent*.

stupor N. state of apathy; daze; lack of awareness. In his *stupor*, the addict was unaware of the events taking place around him.

stymie V. present an obstacle; stump. The detective was *stymied* by the contradictory evidence in the robbery investigation.   also N.

suavity (*swähv'-*) N. urbanity; polish. He is particularly good in roles that require *suavity* and sophistication.

subaltern (*sŭb'-*) N. subordinate. The captain treated his *subalterns* as though they were children rather than commissioned officers.

subjugate V. conquer; bring under control. It is not our aim to *subjugate* our foe; we are interested only in establishing peaceful relations.

sublimate V. refine; purify. We must strive to *sublimate* these desires and emotions into worthwhile activities.

sublime ADJ. exalted; noble; uplifting. We must learn to recognize *sublime* truths.

sub rosa ADV. in strict confidence; privately. I heard of this *sub rosa* and I cannot tell you about it.

subsequent ADJ. following; later. In *subsequent* lessons, we shall take up more difficult problems.

subservient ADJ. behaving like a slave; servile; obsequious. He was proud and dignified; he refused to be *subservient* to anyone.

subsidiary ADJ. subordinate; secondary. This information may be used as *subsidiary* evidence but is not sufficient by itself to prove your argument.

subsistence N. existence; means of support; livelihood. In these days of inflated prices, my salary provides a mere *subsistence*.

substantiate V. verify; support. I intend to *substantiate* my statement by producing witnesses.

ā — ale; ă — add; ä — arm; à — ask; ē — eve; ĕ — end; ê — err, her; ə — event, allow.
ī — ice; ĭ — ill; ō — old; ŏ — odd; ô — orb; ōō — food; ou — out; th — thin; ū — use;
ŭ — up; zh — pleasure

subterfuge N. pretense; evasion. As soon as we realized that you had won our support by a *subterfuge*, we withdrew our endorsement of your candidacy.

subtlety (sŭt'-l-tē) N. nicety; cunning; guile; delicacy. The *subtlety* of his remarks was unnoticed by most of his audience.

subversive ADJ. tending to overthrow or ruin. We must destroy such *subversive* publications.

succinct (sŭk-sĭnkt') ADJ. brief; terse; compact. His remarks are always *succinct* and pointed.

succor N. aid; assistance; relief. We shall be ever grateful for the *succor* your country gave us when we were in need.

succulent ADJ. juicy; full of richness. He developed the *succulent* theme fully.

suffuse V. spread over. A blush *suffused* her cheeks when we teased her about her love affair.

sully V. tarnish; soil. He felt that it was beneath his dignity to *sully* his hands in such menial labor.

sultry ADJ. sweltering. He could not adjust himself to the *sultry* climate of the tropics.

summation N. act of finding the total; summary. In his *summation*, the lawyer emphasized the testimony given by the two witnesses.

sumptuous ADJ. lavish; rich. I cannot recall when I have had such a *sumptuous* feast.

sunder V. separate; part. Northern and southern Ireland are politically and religiously *sundered*.

sundry ADJ. various; several. My suspicions were aroused when I read *sundry* items in the newspapers about your behavior.

ETYMOLOGY 27.

SOLV, SOLUT (to loosen)
       absolve free from blame
       dissolute morally lax
       absolute complete (not loosened)
SPEC, SPECT (to look at)
       spectator observer
       aspect appearance
       circumspect cautious (looking around)

ā — ale; ă — add; ä — arm; à — ask; ē — eve; ĕ — end; ê — err, her; ə — event, allow,
ī — ice; ĭ — ill; ō — old; ŏ — odd; ô — orb; oo — food; ou — out; th — thin; ū — use;
ŭ — up; zh — pleasure

TEST — Word List 27 — Synonyms and Antonyms

Each of the questions below consists of a word printed in bold, followed by five words or phrases numbered 1 to 5. Choose the numbered word or phrase which is most nearly the same as or the opposite of the word in bold and write the number of your choice on your answer paper.

521. squander 1. fortify 2. depart 3. roam 4. preserve 5. forfeit

522. somnolent 1. stentorian 2. settled 3. half-awake 4. soothed 5. ambulatory

523. skittish 1. tractable 2. inquiring 3. dramatic 4. vain 5. frisky

524. sportive 1. competing 2. playful 3. indignant 4. foppish 5. fundamental

525. solvent 1. enigmatic 2. bankrupt 3. fiducial 4. puzzling 5. gilded

526. sloth 1. penitence 2. filth 3. futility 4. poverty 5. industry

527. spasmodic 1. intermittent 2. fit 3. inaccurate 4. violent 5. physical

528. sobriety 1. inebriety 2. aptitude 3. scholasticism 4. monotony 5. aversion

529. sleazy 1. fanciful 2. creeping 3. substantial 4. uneasy 5. warranted

530. solstice 1. equinox 2. sunrise 3. pigsty 4. interstices 5. iniquity

531. slovenly 1. half-baked 2. loved 3. inappropriate 4. tidy 5. rapidly

532. sinister 1. unwed 2. ministerial 3. good 4. returned 5. splintered

533. sonorous 1. resonant 2. reassuring 3. repetitive 4. resinous 5. sisterly

534. slough 1. toughen 2. trap 3. violate 4. cast off 5. depart

535. spurious 1. genuine 2. angry 3. mitigated 4. interrogated 5. glorious

536. stringent 1. binding 2. reserved 3. utilized 4. lambent 5. indigent

537. sublime 1. unconscious 2. respected 3. exalted 4. sneaky 5. replaced

---

ā — ale; ă — add; ä — arm; à — ask; ē — eve; ĕ — end; ê — err, her; ə — event, allow,
ī — ice; ĭ — ill; ō — old; ŏ — odd; ô — orb; ōō — food; ou — out; th — thin; ū — use;
ŭ — up; zh — pleasure

538. stamina   1. patience   2. pistils   3. weakness   4. fascination   5. patina
539. sporadic   1. seedy   2. latent   3. vivid   4. inconsequential   5. often
540. suavity   1. ingeniousness   2. indifference   3. urbanity   4. constancy   5. paucity

---

Word List 28   superannuated-transcribe

superannuated ADJ. retired on pension because of age. The *superannuated* man was indignant because he felt that he could still perform a good day's work.

supercilious ADJ. contemptuous; haughty. I resent your *supercilious* and arrogant attitude.

superficial ADJ. trivial; shallow. Since your report gave only a *superficial* analysis of the problem, I cannot give you more than a passing grade.

superfluity (*-flū'-*) N. excess; overabundance. We have a definite lack of sincere workers and a *superfluity* of leaders.

supersede V. cause to be set aside; replace. This regulation will *supersede* all previous rules.

supine (*-pīn'*) ADV. lying on back. The defeated pugilist lay *supine* on the canvas.

suppliant ADJ. entreating; beseeching. He could not resist the dog's *suppliant* whimpering, and he gave it some food.   also N.

supplicate V. petition humbly; pray to grant a favor. We *supplicate* your majesty to grant him amnesty.

supposititious ADJ. assumed; counterfeit; hypothetical. I find no similarity between your *supposititious* illustration and the problem we are facing.

surcease (*-sēs'*) N. cessation. He begged the doctors to grant him *surcease* from his suffering.

surfeit (*sûr'-fĭt*) V. cloy; overfeed. I am *surfeited* with the sentimentality of the average motion picture film.

surly (*sûr'-lē*) ADJ. rude; cross. Because of his *surly* attitude, many people avoided his company.

surmise (*-mīz'*) V. guess. I *surmise* that he will be late for this meeting.

ā — ale; ă — add; ä — arm; á — ask; ē — eve; ĕ — end; ê — err, her; ə — event, allow,
ī — ice; ĭ — ill; ō — old; ŏ — odd; ô — orb; ōō — food; ou — out; th — thin; ū — use;
ŭ — up; zh — pleasure

surreptitious ADJ. secret. News of their *surreptitious* meeting gradually leaked out.

surveillance (-vāl′-) N. watching; guarding. The FBI kept the house under constant *surveillance* in the hope of capturing all the criminals at one time.

sustenance N. means of support, food, nourishment. In the tropics, the natives find *sustenance* easy to obtain.

swathe (swāth) v. wrap around; bandage. When I visited him in the hospital, I found him *swathed* in bandages.

swelter v. be oppressed by heat. I am going to buy an air conditioning unit for my apartment as I do not intend to *swelter* through another hot and humid summer.

sycophantic (sĭk′-) ADJ. servilely flattering. The king enjoyed the *sycophantic* attentions of his followers.

sylvan ADJ. pertaining to the woods; rustic. His paintings of nymphs in *sylvan* backgrounds were criticized as overly sentimental.

synchronous (sĭng′-) ADJ. similarly timed; simultaneous with. We have many examples of scientists in different parts of the world who have made *synchronous* discoveries.

synthesis N. combining parts into a whole. Now that we have succeeded in isolating this drug, our next problem is to plan its *synthesis* in the laboratory.

synthetic ADJ. artificial; resulting from synthesis. During the twentieth century, many *synthetic* products have replaced natural ones.

tacit ADJ. understood; not put into words. We have a *tacit* agreement.

taciturn ADJ. habitually silent; talking little. New England landers are reputedly *taciturn* people.

tactile ADJ. pertaining to the organs or sense of touch. His calloused hands had lost their *tactile* sensitivity.

tainted ADJ. contaminated; corrupt. Health authorities are always trying to prevent the sale and use of *tainted* food.

talisman N. charm. She wore the *talisman* to ward off evil.

tantalize v. tease; torture with disappointment. Tom loved to *tantalize* his younger brother.

tantrum N. fit of petulance; caprice. The child learned that he could have almost anything if he went into *tantrums*.

tautological ADJ. needlessly repetitious. In the sentence "It was visible to the eye," the phrase "to the eye" is *tautological*.

tawdry ADJ. cheap and gaudy. He won a few *tawdry* trinkets at Coney Island.

tedium N. boredom; weariness. We hope this radio will help overcome the

ā — ale; ă — add; ä — arm; å — ask; ē — eve; ĕ — end; ê — err, her; ə — event, allow, ī — ice; ĭ — ill; ō — old; ŏ — odd; ô — orb; oo — food; ou — out; th — thin; ū — use; ŭ — up; zh — pleasure

tedium of your stay in the hospital.

temerity (-*mĕr'*-) N. boldness; rashness. Do you have the *temerity* to argue with me?

tempo N. speed of music. I find the conductor's *tempo* too slow for such a brilliant piece of music.

temporal ADJ. not lasting for ever; limited by time; secular. At one time in our history, *temporal* rulers assumed that they had been given their thrones by divine right.

temporize V. avoid committing oneself; gain time. I cannot permit you to *temporize* any longer; I must have a definite answer today.

tenacious ADJ. holding fast. I had to struggle to break his *tenacious* hold on my arm.   tenacity, N.

tenet N. doctrine; dogma. I cannot accept the *tenets* of your faith.

tentative ADJ. provisional; experimental. Your *tentative* plans sound plausible.

tenuous ADJ. thin; rare; slim. The allegiance of our allies is held by rather *tenuous* ties.

tenure N. holding of an office; time during which such an office is held. He has permanent *tenure* in this position.

tepid (*tĕp'*-) ADJ. lukewarm. During the summer, I like to take a *tepid* bath.

terminus N. last stop of railroad. After we reached the railroad *terminus*, we continued our journey into the wilderness on saddle horses.

terrestrial ADJ. on the earth. We have been able to explore the *terrestrial* regions much more thoroughly than the aquatic or celestial regions.

terse ADJ. concise; abrupt; pithy. I admire his *terse* style of writing.

tertiary ADJ. third. He is so thorough that he analyzes *tertiary* causes where other writers are content with primary and secondary reasons.

testy ADJ. irritable; short-tempered. My advice is to avoid discussing this problem with him today as he is rather *testy*.

tether V. tie with a rope. Before we went to sleep, we *tethered* the horses to prevent their wandering off during the night.

theocracy N. government of a community by religious leaders. Some Pilgrims favored the establishment of a *theocracy* in New England.

therapeutic ADJ. curative. These springs are famous for their *therapeutic* qualities.

thermal ADJ. pertaining to heat. The natives discovered that the hot springs gave excellent *thermal* baths and began to develop their community as a health resort.

thrall N. slave; bondage. The captured soldier was held in *thrall* by the conquering army.

ā — ale; ă — add; ä — arm; à — ask; ē — eve; ĕ — end; ê — err, her; ə — event, allow,
ī — ice; ĭ — ill; ō — old; ŏ — odd; ô — orb; o͞o — food; ou — out; th — thin; ū — use;
ŭ — up; zh — pleasure

threnody N. song of lamentation; dirge. When he died, many poets wrote *threnodies* about his passing.

throes N. violent anguish. She was in the *throes* of despair.

throttle V. strangle. The criminal tried to *throttle* the old man.

thwart V. baffle; frustrate. He felt that everyone was trying to *thwart* his plans.

timidity N. lack of self-confidence or courage. If you are to succeed as a salesman, you must first lose your *timidity*.

tipple V. drink (alcoholic beverages) frequently. He found that his most enjoyable evenings occurred when he *tippled* with his friends at the local pub.

tirade N. extended scolding; denunciation. Long before he had finished his *tirade*, we were sufficiently aware of the seriousness of our misconduct.

titanic ADJ. gigantic. *Titanic* waves beat against the shore during the hurricane.

tithe (tīth) N. tax of one-tenth. Because he was an agnostic, he refused to pay his *tithes* to the clergy.

titular ADJ. nominal holding of title without obligations. Although he was the *titular* head of the company, the real decisions were made by his general manager.

toady V. flatter for favors. I hope you see through those who are *toadying* you for special favors.

toga N. Roman outer robe. Marc Antony pointed to the slashes in Caesar's *toga*.

tome N. large volume. He spent much time in the libraries poring over ancient *tomes*.

topography N. physical feature of a region. Before the generals gave the order to attack, they ordered a complete study of the *topography* of the region.

torpid ADJ. dormant; dull; lethargic. The *torpid* bear had just come out of his cave after his long hibernation.

torso N. trunk of statue with head and limbs missing; human trunk. This *torso*, found in the ruins of Pompeii, is now on exhibition in the museum in Naples.

tortuous ADJ. winding; full of curves. Because this road is so *tortuous*, it is unwise to go faster than twenty miles per hour on it.

touchy ADJ. sensitive; irascible. Do not discuss this phase of the problem as he is very *touchy* about it.

toxic ADJ. poisonous. We must seek an antidote for whatever *toxic* substance he has eaten.

ā — ale; ă — add; ä — arm; à — ask; ē — eve; ĕ — end; ê — err, her; ə — event, allow, ī — ice; ĭ — ill; ō — old; ŏ — odd; ô — orb; ōō — food; ou — out; th — thin; ū — use; ŭ — up; zh — pleasure

tract N. pamphlet; a region of indefinite size. The King granted William Penn a *tract* of land in the New World.

tractable ADJ. docile. You will find the children in this school very *tractable* and willing to learn.

traduce V. expose to slander. His opponents tried to *traduce* the candidate's reputation by spreading rumors about his past.

tranquillity N. calmness; peace. After the commotion and excitement of the city, I appreciate the *tranquillity* of these fields and forests.

transcend V. exceed; surpass. This accomplishment *transcends* all our previous efforts.   transcendental, ADJ.

transcribe V. copy. When you *transcribe* your notes, please send a copy to Mr. Smith and keep the original for our files.   transcription, N.

ETYMOLOGY 28.

TANG, TACT (to touch)
  tangent   touching
  contact   touching with, meeting
  contingent   depending upon
TEMPOR (time)
  contemporary   at same time
  extemporaneous   impromptu
  temporize   to delay
TEN, TENT (to hold)
  tenable   able to be held
  tenacity   retention
  tenure   holding of office
TERR (land)
  terrestrial   pertaining to earth
  subterranean   underground

TEST — Word List 28 — Synonyms

Each of the following questions consists of a word printed in bold, followed by five words or phrases numbered 1 to 5. Choose the numbered word or phrase which is most nearly the same as or the opposite of the word in bold and write the number of your choice on your answer paper.

ā — ale; ă — add; ä — arm; à — ask; ē — eve; ĕ — end; ê — err, her; ə — event, allow, ī — ice; ĭ — ill; ō — old; ŏ — odd; ô — orb; ōō — food; ou — out; th — thin; ū — use; ŭ — up; zh — pleasure

541. superannuated 1. senile 2. experienced 3. retired 4. attenuated 5. accepted

542. surfeit 1. belittle 2. cloy 3. drop 4. estimate 5. claim

543. tacit 1. spoken 2. allowed 3. neural 4. understood 5. unwanted

544. supercilious 1. haughty 2. highbrow 3. angry 4. subservient 5. philosophic

545. surreptitious 1. secret 2. snakelike 3. nightly 4. abstract 5. furnished

546. talisman 1. chief 2. juror 3. medicine man 4. amulet 5. gift

547. superficial 1. abnormal 2. portentous 3. shallow 4. angry 5. tiny

548. swathed 1. wrapped around 2. waved 3. gambled 4. rapt 5. mystified

549. tawdry 1. orderly 2. meretricious 3. reclaimed 4. filtered 5. proper

550. suppliant 1. intolerant 2. swallowing 3. beseeching 4. finishing 5. flexible

551. sycophantic 1. quiet 2. recording 3. servilely flattering 4. frolicsome 5. eagerly awaiting

552. tenacious 1. fast running 2. intentional 3. obnoxious 4. holding fast 5. collecting

553. supposititious 1. irreligious 2. experimental 3. subjunctive 4. hypothetical 5. grammatical

554. synthetic 1. simplified 2. doubled 3. tuneful 4. artificial 5. fiscal

555. tepid 1. boiling 2. lukewarm 3. freezing 4. gaseous 5. cold

556. tantalize 1. tease 2. wax 3. warrant 4. authorize 5. total

557. tenuous 1. vital 2. thin 3. careful 4. dangerous 5. necessary

558. temerity 1. timidity 2. resourcefulness 3. boldness 4. tremulousness 5. caution

559. tentative 1. prevalent 2. certain 3. mocking 4. wry 5. experimental

560. temporal 1. priestly 2. scholarly 3. secular 4. sleepy 5. sporadic

---

ā — ale; ă — add; ä — arm; å — ask; ē — eve; ĕ — end; ê — err, her; ə — event, allow, ī — ice; ĭ — ill; ō — old; ŏ — odd; ô — orb; o͞o — food; ou — out; th — thin; ū — use; ŭ — up; zh — pleasure

Word List 29   transgression-veer

transgression N. violation of a law; sin. Forgive us our *transgressions*.

transient ADJ. fleeting; quickly passing away; staying for a short time. This hotel caters to a *transient* trade.

transition N. going from one state of action to another. During the period of *transition* from oil heat to gas heat, the furnace will have to be shut off.

translucent ADJ. partly transparent: We could not recognize the people in the next room because of the *translucent* curtains which separated us.

transmute V. change; convert to something different. He was unable to *transmute* his dreams into actualities.

transparent ADJ. permitting light to pass through freely; easily detected. Your scheme is so *transparent* that it will fool no one.

transpire V. exhale; become known; happen. In spite of all our efforts to keep the meeting a secret, news of our conclusions *transpired*.

travail (*trǎ'-vāl*) N. painful labor. How long do you think a man can endure such *travail* and degradation without rebelling?

traverse V. go through or across. When you *traverse* this field, be careful of the bull.

travesty N. comical parody; treatment aimed at making something appear ridiculous. The decision the jury has arrived at is a *travesty* of justice.

treatise N. article treating a subject systematically and thoroughly. He is preparing a *treatise* on the Elizabethan playwrights for his graduate degree.

trek V. travel; migrate. The tribe *trekked* further north that summer in search of available game.

tremor N. trembling; slight quiver. She had a nervous *tremor* in her right hand.

tremulous ADJ. trembling; wavering. She was *tremulous* more from excitement than from fear.

trenchant ADJ. cutting; keen. I am afraid of his *trenchant* wit for it is so often sarcastic.

trepidation N. fear; trembling agitation. We must face the enemy without *trepidation* if we are to win this battle.

tribulation N. distress; suffering. After all the trials and *tribulations* we have gone through, we need this rest.

tribunal N. court of justice. The decision of the *tribunal* was final.

tribute N. tax levied by a ruler; mark of respect. The colonists refused to pay

ā — ale; ă — add; ä — arm; å — ask; ē — eve; ĕ — end; ê — err, her; ə — event, allow,
ī — ice; ĭ — ill; ō — old; ŏ — odd; ô — orb; ōō — food; ou — out; th — thin; ū — use;
ŭ — up; zh — pleasure

tribute to a foreign despot.

trident (trī′-) N. three-pronged spear. Neptune is usually depicted as rising from the sea, carrying his *trident* on his shoulder.

trilogy (tril′-) N. group of three works. Romain Rolland's novel "Jean Christophe" was first published as a *trilogy*.

trite ADJ. hackneyed; commonplace. The plot of this play is *trite*.

troth N. pledge of good faith especially in betrothal. He gave her his *troth* and vowed he would cherish her always.

truculent (trŭ′-kū-) ADJ. aggressive; savage. They are a *truculent* race, ready to fight at any moment.

truism N. self-evident truth. Many a *truism* is well expressed in a proverb.

trumpery N. objects that are showy, valueless, deceptive. All this finery is mere *trumpery*.

tryst (trĭst) N. meeting. The lovers kept their *tryst* even though they realized their danger.

tumbrel N. tip-cart. The *tumbrels* became the vehicles which transported the condemned people from the prisons to the guillotine.

tumid ADJ. swollen; pompous; bombastic. I especially dislike his *tumid* style.

turbid ADJ. muddy; having the sediment disturbed. The water was *turbid* after the children had waded through it.

turbulence N. state of violent agitation. We were frightened by the *turbulence* of the ocean during the storm.

turgid (tûr′-jĭd) ADJ. swollen; distended. The *turgid* river threatened to overflow the levees and flood the countryside.

turnkey N. jailer. By bribing the *turnkey*, the prisoner arranged to have better food brought to him in his cell.

turpitude N. depravity. A visitor may be denied admittance to this country if he has been guilty of moral *turpitude*.

tutelage N. guardianship; training. Under the *tutelage* of such masters of the instrument, he made rapid progress as a virtuoso.

tyro (tī′-rō) N. beginner; novice. For a mere *tyro*, you have produced some marvelous results.

ubiquitous ADJ. being everywhere; omnipresent. You must be *ubiquitous* for I meet you wherever I go.

ulterior ADJ. situated beyond; unstated. You must have an *ulterior* motive for your behavior.

ultimate ADJ. final; not susceptible to further analysis. Scientists are searching for the *ultimate* truths.

ultimatum (-mā′-) N. last demand; warning. Since they have ignored our *ultimatum*, our only recourse is to declare war.

ā — ale; ă — add; ä — arm; à — ask; ē — eve; ĕ — end; ê — err, her; ə — event, allow; ī — ice; ĭ — ill; ō — old; ŏ — odd; ô — orb; ōō — food; ou — out; th — thin; ū — use; ŭ — up; zh — pleasure

umbrage (ŭm'-brĭj) N. resentment; anger; sense of injury or insult. She took *umbrage* at his remarks.

unanimity N. complete agreement. We were surprised by the *unanimity* with which our proposals were accepted by the different groups.

unassuaged ADJ. unsatisfied; not soothed. His anger is *unassuaged* by your apology.

unassuming ADJ. modest. He is so *unassuming* that some people fail to realize how great a man he really is.

unbridled ADJ. violent. He had a sudden fit of *unbridled* rage.

uncanny ADJ. strange; mysterious. You have the *uncanny* knack of reading my innermost thoughts.

unconscionable ADJ. unscrupulous; excessive. He found the loan shark's demands *unconscionable* and impossible to meet.

uncouth ADJ. outlandish; clumsy; boorish. Most biographers portray Lincoln as an *uncouth* and ungainly young man.

unction N. the act of anointing with oil. The anointing of a person near death is called extreme *unction*.

unctuous ADJ. oily; bland; insincerely suave. I am suspicious of his *unctuous* manner.

undulate V. move with a wavelike motion. The waters *undulated* in the breeze.

unearth V. dig up. When they *unearthed* the city, the archeologists found many relics of an ancient civilization.

unearthly ADJ. not earthly; weird. There is an *unearthly* atmosphere in his work which amazes the casual observer.

unequivocal ADJ. plain; obvious. My answer to your proposal is an *unequivocal* and absolute "No."

unfaltering ADJ. steadfast. She approached the guillotine with *unfaltering* steps.

unfeigned ADJ. genuine; real. I am sure her surprise was *unfeigned*.

ungainly ADJ. awkward. He is an *ungainly* young man.

unguent (ŭng'-gwĕnt) N. ointment. Apply this *ungent* to the sore muscles before retiring.

unimpeachable ADJ. blameless and exemplary. His conduct in office was *unimpeachable*.

unique ADJ. without an equal; single in kind. You have the *unique* distinction of being the first student whom I have had to fail in this course.

unison N. unity of pitch; complete accord. The choir sang in *unison*.

unkempt ADJ. disheveled; with uncared-for appearance. The beggar was dirty and *unkempt*.

unmitigated ADJ. harsh; severe; not lightened. I sympathize with you in your

ā — ale; ă — add; ä — arm; à — ask; ē — eve; ĕ — end; ê — err, her; ə — event, allow, ĭ — ice; ĭ — ill; ō — old; ŏ — odd; ô — orb; ōō — food; ou — out; th — thin; ū — use; ŭ — up; zh — pleasure

unmitigated sorrow.

unruly ADJ. disobedient; lawless. The only way to curb this *unruly* mob is to use tear gas.

unseemly ADJ. unbecoming; indecent. Your levity is *unseemly* at this time.

unsullied ADJ. untarnished. I am happy that my reputation is *unsullied*.

untenable ADJ. unsupportable. I find your theory *untenable* and must reject it.

unwitting ADJ. unintentional; not knowing. He was the *unwitting* tool of the swindlers.

unwonted ADJ. unaccustomed. He hesitated to assume the *unwonted* role of master of ceremonies at the dinner.

unbraid v. scold; reproach. I must *upbraid* him for his misbehavior.

urbane (-*bān'*) ADJ. suave; refined; elegant. The courtier was *urbane* and sophisticated.   urbanity, N.

usury N. lending money at illegal rates of interest. The loan shark was found guilty of *usury*.

uxorious (*ŭks-ō'-*) ADJ. excessively devoted to one's wife. His friends laughed at him because he was so *uxorious* and permitted his wife to henpeck him.

vacillation N. fluctuation; wavering. His *vacillation* when confronted with a problem annoyed all of us who had to wait until he made his decision.

vacuous ADJ. empty; inane. He was annoyed by her *vacuous* remarks.

vagary (-*gā'-*) N. caprice; whim. She followed every *vagary* of fashion.

vainglorious ADJ. boastful; excessively conceited. He was a *vainglorious* and arrogant individual.

validate v. confirm; ratify. I will not publish my findings until I *validate* my results.

vanguard N. forerunners; advance forces. We are the *vanguard* of a tremendous army that is following us.

vantage N. position giving an advantage. They fired upon the enemy from behind trees, walls, and any other point of *vantage* they could find.

vapid (*văp'-*) ADJ. insipid; inane. He delivered an uninspired and *vapid* address.

variegated ADJ. many-colored. He will not like this blue necktie as he is addicted to *variegated* clothing.

vaunted ADJ. boasted; bragged; highly publicized. This much *vaunted* project proved a disappointment when it collapsed.

veer v. change in direction. After what seemed an eternity, the wind *veered* to the east and the storm abated.

ā — ale; ă — add; ä — arm; á — ask; ē — eve; ĕ — end; ê — err, her; ə — event, allow,
ī — ice; ĭ — ill; ō — old; ŏ — odd; ô — orb; ōo — food; ou — out; th — thin; ū — use;
ŭ — up; zh — pleasure

ETYMOLOGY 29.

URB (city)

> **urban**   pertaining to city
> **urbane**   polished, sophisticated (pertaining to city dweller)
> **suburban**   outside of city

TEST — Word List 29 — Antonyms

Each of the questions below consists of a word printed in bold, followed by five words or phrases numbered 1 to 5. Choose the numbered word or phrase which is most nearly opposite in meaning to the word in bold and write the number of your choice on your answer paper.

561. unimpeachable   1. fruitful   2. rampaging   3. faulty   4. pensive   5. thorough

562. ulterior   1. tipped   2. stated   3. sparkling   4. uncompromising   5. corrugated

563. transient   1. carried   2. close   3. permanent   4. removed   5. certain

564. ungainly   1. ignorant   2. graceful   3. detailed   4. dancing   5. pedantic

565. tyro   1. infant   2. rubber   3. personnel   4. idiot   5. expert

566. unfeigned   1. pretended   2. fashionable   3. wary   4. switched   5. colonial

567. turbulence   1. reaction   2. approach   3. impropriety   4. calm   5. hostility

568. unearth   1. conceal   2. gnaw   3. clean   4. fling   5. reach

569. turbid   1. clear   2. improbable   3. invariable   4. honest   5. turgid

570. ultimate   1. competing   2. throbbing   3. poisonous   4. incipient   5. powerful

571. trite   1. correct   2. original   3. distinguished   4. premature   5. certain

572. vaunted   1. unvanquished   2. fell   3. belittled   4. exacting   5. believed

573. unkempt   1. bombed   2. washed   3. neat   4. shabby   5. tawdry

---

ā — ale; ǎ — add; ä — arm; à — ask; ē — eve; ě — end; ê — err, her; ə — event, allow, ī — ice; ǐ — ill; ō — old; ǒ — odd; ô — orb; o͞o — food; ou — out; th — thin; ū — use; ǔ — up; zh — pleasure

574. **unsullied**   1. tarnished   2. countless   3. soggy   4. papered   5. homicidal

575. **vacillation**   1. remorse   2. relief   3. respect   4. steadfastness   5. inoculation

576. **unruly**   1. chatting   2. obedient   3. definite   4. lined   5. curious

577. **untenable**   1. supportable   2. tender   3. sheepish   4. tremulous   5. adequate

578. **vanguard**   1. regiment   2. rear   3. echelon   4. protection   5. loyalty

579. **unseemly**   1. effortless   2. proper   3. conductive   4. pointed   5. informative

580. **unwitting**   1. clever   2. intense   3. sensitive   4. freezing   5. intentional

---

Word List 30   vegetate-zephyr

vegetate V. live in a monotonous way. I do not understand how you can *vegetate* in this quiet village after the adventurous life you have led.

vehement ADJ. impetuous; with marked vigor. He spoke with *vehement* eloquence in defense of his client.

vellum N. parchment. Bound in *vellum* and embossed in gold, this book is a beautiful example of the binder's craft.

venal (vē'-) ADJ. capable of being bribed. The *venal* policeman accepted the bribe offered him by the speeding motorist whom he had stopped.

veneer N. thin layer; cover. Casual acquaintances were deceived by his *veneer* of sophistication and failed to recognize his fundamental shallowness.

venerable ADJ. deserving high respect. We do not mean to be disrespectful when we refuse to follow the advice of our *venerable* leader.

venerate V. revere. In China, the people *venerate* their ancestors.

venial (vē'-nĭ-) ADJ. forgivable; trivial. We may regard a hungry man's stealing as a *venial* crime.

vent N. a small opening; outlet. The wine did not flow because the air *vent* in the barrel was clogged.

vent V. express; utter. He *vented* his wrath on his class.

ventral V. abdominal. We shall now examine the *ventral* plates of this serpent.

venturous ADJ. daring. The five *venturous* young men decided to look for a

---

ā — ale; ă — add; ä — arm; â — ask; ē — eve; ĕ — end; ê — err, her; ə — event, allow.
ī — ice; ĭ — ill; ō — old; ŏ — odd; ô — orb; ōō — food; ou — out; th — thin; ū — use;
ŭ — up; zh — pleasure

new approach to the mountain top.

veracious ADJ. truthful. I can recommend him for this position because I have always found him *veracious* and reliable.

verbiage N. pompous array of words. After we had waded through all the *verbiage*, we discovered that the writer had said very little.

verbose (-bōs') ADJ. wordy. This article is too *verbose*; we must edit it.

verdant ADJ. green; fresh. The *verdant* meadows in the spring are always an inspiring sight.

verdigris N. a green coating on copper which has been exposed to the weather. Despite all attempts to protect the statue from the elements, it became coated with *verdigris*.

verity N. truth; reality. The four *verities* were revealed to Buddha during his long meditation.

vernal ADJ. pertaining to spring. We may expect *vernal* showers during the entire month of April.

versatile ADJ. having many talents; capable of working in many fields. Leonardo da Vinci was a very *versatile* man.

vertex N. summit. Let us drop a perpendicular line from the *vertex* of the triangle to the base.

vertigo (vêr'-) N. dizziness. We test potential plane pilots for susceptibility to spells of *vertigo*.

vestige N. trace; remains. We discovered *vestiges* of early Indian life in the cave.

viand (vī'-) N. food. There was a variety of *viands* at the feast.

vicarious ADJ. acting as a substitute; done by a deputy. Many people get a *vicarious* thrill at the movies by imagining they are the characters on the screen.

vicissitude N. change of fortune. We must accept life's *vicissitudes*.

victuals (vĭt'-lz) N. food. I am very happy to be able to provide you with these *victuals*.

vie V. contend; compete. When we *vie* with each other for his approval, we are merely weakening ourselves and strengthening him.

vigilance N. watchfulness. Eternal *vigilance* is the price of liberty.

vilify V. slander. Why is he always trying to *vilify* my reputation?

vindicate V. clear of charges. I hope to *vindicate* my client and return him to society as a free man.

vindictive ADJ. revengeful. He was very *vindictive* and never forgave an injury.

viper N. poisonous snake. The habitat of the horned *viper*, a particularly venomous snake, is sandy regions like the Sahara or the Sinai deserts.

ā — ale; ă — add; ä — arm; å — ask; ē — eve; ĕ — end; ê — err, her; ə — event, allow. ī — ice; ĭ — ill; ō — old; ŏ — odd; ô — orb; ōō — food; ou — out; th — thin; ū — use; ŭ — up; zh — pleasure

virago (-rā'-gō) N. shrew. Rip Van Winkle's wife was a veritable *virago*.

virile ADJ. manly. I admire his *virile* strength.

virtuoso N. highly skilled artist. Heifetz is a violin *virtuoso*.

virulent (vĭr'-) ADJ. extremely poisonous. The virus is highly *virulent* and has made many of us ill for days.

virus (vī'-) N. disease communicator. The doctors are looking for a specific medicine to control this *virus*.

visage (vĭz'-) N. face; appearance. The stern *visage* of the judge indicated that he had decided to impose a severe penalty.

viscid (vĭs'-ĭd) ADJ. sticky; adhesive. This is a *viscid* liquid.

viscous (vĭs'-kŭs) ADJ. sticky; gluey. Melted tar is a *viscous* substance.

visionary ADJ. produced by imagination; fanciful; mystical. He was given to *visionary* schemes which never materialized.

vitiate (vī'-shĭ-āt) V. spoil the effect of; make inoperative. Fraud will *vitiate* the contract.

vitriolic ADJ. corrosive; sarcastic. Such *vitriolic* criticism is uncalled for.

vituperative ADJ. abusive; scolding. He became more *vituperative* as he realized that we were not going to grant him his wish.

vivacious ADJ. animated; gay. She had always been *vivacious* and sparkling.

vociferous ADJ. clamorous; noisy. The crowd grew *vociferous* in its anger and threatened to take the law into its own hands.

vogue N. popular fashion. Slacks became the *vogue* on many college campuses.

volatile (vŏl'-) ADJ. evaporating rapidly; light-hearted; mercurial. Ethyl chloride is a very *volatile* liquid.

volition N. act of making a conscious choice. She selected this dress of her own *volition*.

voluble ADJ. fluent; glib. He was a *voluble* speaker, always ready to talk.

voluptuous ADJ. gratifying the senses. The nobility during the Renaissance led *voluptuous* lives.

voracious (-rā'-) ADJ. ravenous. The wolf is a *voracious* animal.

votary N. follower of cult. He was a *votary* of every new movement in literature and art.

vouchsafe V. grant condescendingly; guarantee. I can safely *vouchsafe* you a fair return on your investment.

vulnerable ADJ. susceptible to wounds. Achilles was *vulnerable* only in his heel.

vying V. contending. Why are we *vying* each other for his favors?

waggish ADJ. mischievous; humorous; tricky. He had a *waggish* wit.

waive V. give up temporarily; yield. I will *waive* my rights in this matter in order

ā — ale; ă — add; ä — arm; å — ask; ē — eve; ĕ — end; ê — err, her; a — event, allow, ī — ice; ĭ — ill; ō — old; ŏ — odd; ô — orb; ōō — food; ou — out; th — thin; ū — use; ŭ — up; zh — pleasure

to expedite our reaching a proper decision.

wan ADJ. having a pale or sickly color; pallid. Suckling asked, ''Why so pale and *wan*, fond lover?''

wane V. grow gradually smaller. The moon will *wane* for several days.

wanton ADJ. unruly; unchaste; excessive. His *wanton* pride cost him many friends.

wary ADJ. very cautious. The spies grew *wary* as they approached the sentry.

wheedle V. cajole; coax; deceive by flattery. She knows she can *wheedle* almost anything she wants from her father.

whet V. sharpen; stimulate. The odors from the kitchen are *whetting* my appetite; I will be ravenous by the time the meal is served.

whimsical ADJ. capricious; fanciful; quaint. *Peter Pan* is a *whimsical* play.

whit N. smallest speck. There is not a *whit* of intelligence or understanding in your observations.

wily ADJ. cunning; artful. He is as *wily* as a fox in avoiding trouble.

winsome ADJ. agreeable; gracious; engaging. By her *winsome* manner, she made herself liked by everyone who met her.

witless ADJ. foolish; idiotic. Such *witless* and fatuous statements will create the impression that you are an ignorant individual.

witticism N. witty saying; facetious remark. What you regard as *witticisms* are often offensive to sensitive people.

wizardry N. sorcery; magic. Merlin amazed the knights with his *wizardry*.

wizened (*wiz'-*) ADJ. withered; shriveled. The *wizened* old man in the home for the aged was still active and energetic.

wont (*wōnt*) N. custom; habitual procedure. As was his *wont*, he jogged two miles every morning before going to work.

worldly ADJ. engrossed in matters of this earth; not spiritual. You must leave your *worldly* goods behind you when you go to meet your Maker.

wraith (*rāth*) N. ghost; phantom of a living person. It must be a horrible experience to see a ghost; it is even more horrible to see the *wraith* of a person we know to be alive.

wreak V. inflict. I am afraid he will *wreak* his wrath on the innocent as well as the guilty.

wrest V. pull away; take by violence. With only ten seconds left to play, our team *wrested* victory from their grasp.

zealot N. fanatic; person who shows excessive zeal. It is good to have a few *zealots* in our group for their enthusiasm is contagious.

zenith N. point directly overhead in sky; summit. The sun was at its *zenith*.

zephyr N. soft gentle breeze; west wind. When these *zephyrs* blow; it is good to be in an open boat under a full sail.

ā — ale; ă — add; ä — arm; å — ask; ē — eve; ĕ — end; ê — err, her; ə — event, allow, ī — ice; ĭ — ill; ō — old; ŏ — odd; ô — orb; ōō — food; ou — out; th — thin; ū — use; ŭ — up; zh — pleasure

ETYMOLOGY 30.

VENE, VENT (to come)
> **intervene** come between
> **prevent** stop
> **convention** meeting

VIA (way)
> **deviation** departure from way
> **viaduct** roadway (arched)
> **trivial** trifling (small talk at crossroads)

VID, VIS (to see)
> **vision** sight
> **evidence** things seen
> **vista** view

VINC, VICT, VANQU (to conquer)
> **invincible** unconquerable
> **victory** winning
> **vanquish** to defeat

VOC, VOCAT (to call)
> **avocation** calling, minor occupation
> **provocation** calling or rousing the anger of
> **invocation** calling in prayer

VOLV, VOLUT (to roll)
> **revolve** roll around
> **evolve** roll out, develop
> **convolution** coiled state

TEST — Word List 30 — Synonyms and Antonyms

Each of questions below consists of a word printed in bold, followed by five words or phrases numbered 1 to 5. Choose the numbered word or phrase which is most nearly the same as or the opposite of the word in bold and write the number of your choice on your answer paper.

581. vestige 1. trek 2. trail 3. trace 4. trial 5. tract
582. venturous 1. timorous 2. confiscatory 3. lethal 4. tubercular 5. dorsal

ā — ale; ă — add; ä — arm; à — ask; ē — eve; ĕ — end; ê — err, her; ə — event, allow; ī — ice; ĭ — ill; ō — old; ŏ — odd; ô — orb; ōo — food; ou — out; th — thin; ū — use; ŭ — up; zh — pleasure

583. **vehement** 1. substantial 2. regular 3. calm 4. cautious 5. sad
584. **verdant** 1. poetic 2. green 3. red 4. autumnal 5. frequent
585. **venerate** 1. revere 2. age 3. reject 4. reverberate 5. degenerate
586. **verity** 1. sanctity 2. reverence 3. falsehood 4. rarity 5. household
587. **venial** 1. unforgivable 2. unforgettable 3. unmistaken 4. fearful 5. fragrant
588. **vicarious** 1. substitutional 2. aggressive 3. sporadic 4. reverent 5. internal
589. **venal** 1. springlike 2. honest 3. angry 4. indifferent 5. going
590. **veracious** 1. worried 2. slight 3. alert 4. truthful 5. instrumental
591. **vellum** 1. schedule 2. scenario 3. parchment 4. monastery 5. victim
592. **visage** 1. doubt 2. personality 3. hermitage 4. face 5. armor
593. **vertex** 1. whirlpool 2. drift 3. vehicle 4. base 5. context
594. **virulent** 1. sensuous 2. malignant 3. masculine 4. conforming 5. approaching
595. **viand** 1. wand 2. gown 3. food 4. orchestra 5. frock
596. **viscid** 1. talkative 2. affluent 3. sticky 4. sweet 5. embarrassed
597. **vigilance** 1. bivouac 2. guide 3. watchfulness 4. mob rule 5. posse
598. **vindictive** 1. revengeful 2. fearful 3. divided 4. literal 5. convincing
599. **vilify** 1. erect 2. eulogize 3. better 4. magnify 5. horrify
600. **vindicate** 1. point out 2. blame 3. declare 4. evict 5. menace

ā — ale; ǎ — add; ä — arm; â — ask; ē — eve; ĕ — end; ê — err, her; ə — event, allow.
ī — ice; ǐ — ill; ō — old; ŏ — odd; ô — orb; ōō — food; ou — out; th — thin; ū — use;
ŭ — up; zh — pleasure

Answers to Word Tests

Word Test 1 (page 26)

1. 5	8. 1	15. 1
2. 4	9. 3	16. 2
3. 2	10. 2	17. 3
4. 5	11. 1	18. 4
5. 1	12. 3	19. 1
6. 5	13. 5	20. 1
7. 3	14. 4	

Word Test 2 (page 32)

21. 2	28. 2	35. 4
22. 2	29. 2	36. 5
23. 4	30. 3	37. 5
24. 5	31. 4	38. 4
25. 5	32. 4	39. 3
26. 1	33. 3	40. 2
27. 1	34. 4	

Word Test 3 (page 38)

41. 2	48. 4	55. 3
42. 3	49. 4	56. 4
43. 1	50. 5	57. 2
44. 4	51. 4	58. 3
45. 5	52. 3	59. 3
46. 3	53. 1	60. 4
47. 3	54. 2	

Word Test 4 (page 45)

61. 4	68. 3	75. 2
62. 5	69. 4	76. 2
63. 2	70. 5	77. 1
64. 1	71. 4	78. 3
65. 3	72. 4	79. 2
66. 2	73. 2	80. 1
67. 2	74. 1	

Word Test 5 (page 51)

81. 2	88. 3	95. 4
82. 5	89. 5	96. 2
83. 2	90. 3	97. 3
84. 5	91. 3	98. 1
85. 4	92. 3	99. 5
86. 2	93. 1	100. 1
87. 4	94. 4	

Word Test 6 (page 56)

101. 2	108. 2	115. 3
102. 1	109. 1	116. 2
103. 1	110. 4	117. 4
104. 4	111. 1	118. 4
105. 5	112. 5	119. 5
106. 1	113. 5	120. 4
107. 1	114. 4	

Word Test 7 (page 62)

121. 5	128. 4	135. 2
122. 1	129. 3	136. 2
123. 5	130. 2	137. 3
124. 3	131. 3	138. 4
125. 1	132. 5	139. 4
126. 1	133. 1	140. 4
127. 1	134. 2	

Word Test 8 (page 68)

141. 4	148. 3	155. 1
142. 1	149. 1	156. 5
143. 3	150. 5	157. 5
144. 2	151. 4	158. 3
145. 2	152. 4	159. 2
146. 2	153. 1	160. 3
147. 1	154. 2	

Word Test 9 (page 74)

161. 3	168. 3	175. 4
162. 3	169. 2	176. 1
163. 2	170. 2	177. 3
164. 3	171. 3	178. 2
165. 4	172. 3	179. 4
166. 3	173. 1	180. 2
167. 4	174. 1	

Word Test 10 (page 80)

181. 3	188. 2	195. 5
182. 3	189. 2	196. 1
183. 3	190. 5	197. 4
184. 3	191. 1	198. 1
185. 4	192. 4	199. 3
186. 5	193. 5	200. 2
187. 4	194. 1	

Word Test 11 (page 86)

201. 3	208. 1	215. 2
202. 3	209. 3	216. 5
203. 4	210. 4	217. 1
204. 5	211. 2	218. 2
205. 1	212. 2	219. 3
206. 1	213. 1	220. 1
207. 5	214. 5	

Word Test 12 (page 92)

221. 1	228. 5	235. 1
222. 4	229. 3	236. 3
223. 3	230. 1	237. 2
224. 2	231. 3	238. 5
225. 1	232. 4	239. 5
226. 3	233. 1	240. 2
227. 1	234. 4	

Word List 13 (page 97)

241. 3	248. 1	255. 3
242. 5	249. 3	256. 2
243. 1	250. 2	257. 1
244. 2	251. 4	258. 3
245. 2	252. 4	259. 2
246. 4	253. 1	260. 2
247. 3	254. 5	

Word List 14 (page 103)

261. 4	268. 1	275. 2
262. 2	269. 3	276. 1
263. 1	270. 2	277. 2
264. 1	271. 1	278. 2
265. 3	272. 1	279. 4
266. 4	273. 3	280. 3
267. 5	274. 5	

Word Test 15 (page 108)

281. 2	288. 1	295. 1
282. 4	289. 4	296. 1
283. 2	290. 1	297. 4
284. 1	291. 2	298. 3
285. 1	292. 3	299. 2
286. 3	293. 3	300. 2
287. 3	294. 2	

Word Test 16 (page 114)

301. 2	308. 2	315. 1
302. 5	309. 2	316. 2
303. 2	310. 5	317. 1
304. 2	311. 2	318. 2
305. 5	312. 1	319. 4
306. 3	313. 3	320. 2
307. 1	314. 3	

Word Test 17 (page 120)

321. 3	328. 2	335. 3
322. 4	329. 5	336. 4
323. 5	330. 1	337. 5
324. 2	331. 2	338. 5
325. 1	332. 4	339. 2
326. 5	333. 5	340. 3
327. 2	334. 1	

Word Test 18 (page 126)

341. 3	348. 2	355. 5
342. 3	349. 5	356. 2
343. 1	350. 1	357. 2
344. 2	351. 1	358. 1
345. 4	352. 1	359. 1
346. 2	353. 2	360. 4
347. 1	354. 4	

Word Test 19 (page 131)

361. 2	368. 5	375. 3
362. 2	369. 2	376. 1
363. 5	370. 3	377. 4
364. 3	371. 3	378. 3
365. 1	372. 1	379. 1
366. 2	373. 3	380. 2
367. 5	374. 3	

Word Test 20 (page 137)

381. 1	388. 4	395. 3
382. 3	389. 2	396. 3
383. 1	390. 3	397. 1
384. 5	391. 2	398. 3
385. 4	392. 4	399. 3
386. 1	393. 2	400. 3
387. 1	394. 2	

Word Test 21 (page 143)

401. 2	408. 3	415. 5
402. 4	409. 4	416. 4
403. 1	410. 5	417. 3
404. 3	411. 4	418. 2
405. 3	412. 5	419. 5
406. 3	413. 1	420. 2
407. 2	414. 2	

Word Test 22 (page 149)

421. 2	428. 1	435. 1
422. 3	429. 4	436. 5
423. 3	430. 1	437. 3
424. 4	431. 1	438. 5
425. 5	432. 2	439. 3
426. 5	433. 5	440. 2
427. 1	434. 1	

Word Test 23 (page 155)

441. 3	448. 4	455. 5
442. 1	449. 5	456. 1
443. 2	450. 2	457. 5
444. 4	451. 1	458. 1
445. 3	452. 3	459. 1
446. 3	453. 4	460. 3
447. 2	454. 5	

Word Test 24 (page 160)

461. 2	468. 3	475. 2
462. 3	469. 2	476. 5
463. 2	470. 1	477. 1
464. 5	471. 1	478. 2
465. 4	472. 4	479. 4
466. 3	473. 2	480. 3
467. 4	474. 5	

Word Test 25 (page 166)

481. 2	488. 2	495. 1
482. 4	489. 2	496. 2
483. 3	490. 4	497. 3
484. 5	491. 1	498. 1
485. 1	492. 3	499. 1
486. 1	493. 4	500. 1
487. 4	494. 2	

Word Test 26 (page 172)

501. 3	508. 5	515. 2
502. 1	509. 2	516. 1
503. 4	510. 3	517. 4
504. 5	511. 1	518. 5
505. 3	512. 4	519. 5
506. 3	513. 2	520. 4
507. 4	514. .2	

Word Test 27 (page 178)

521. 4	528. 1	535. 1
522. 3	529. 3	536. 1
523. 5	530. 1	537. 3
524. 2	531. 4	538. 3
525. 2	532. 3	539. 5
526. 5	533. 1	540. 3
527. 1	534. 4	

Word Test 28 (page 183)

541. 3	548. 1	555. 2
542. 2	549. 2	556. 1
543. 4	550. 3	557. 2
544. 1	551. 3	558. 3
545. 1	552. 4	559. 5
546. 4	553. 4	560. 3
547. 3	554. 4	

Word Test 29 (page 189)

561. 3	568. 1	575. 4
562. 2	569. 1	576. 2
563. 3	570. 4	577. 1
564. 2	571. 2	578. 2
565. 5	572. 3	579. 2
566. 1	573. 3	580. 5
567. 4	574. 1	

Word Test 30 (page 194)

581. 3	588. 1	595. 3
582. 1	589. 2	596. 3
583. 3	590. 4	597. 3
584. 2	591. 3	598. 1
585. 1	592. 4	599. 2
586. 3	593. 4	600. 2
587. 1	594. 2	

3 Testing Your Knowledge of Vocabulary

College entrance and scholarship tests include many questions to determine the extent and power of a candidate's vocabulary. In addition to the questions which call for synonyms or antonyms (examples of which have appeared in connection with the word lists), these tests make use of the sentence completion and the word analogy types of questions.

The Synonym Question and the Antonym Question

These are similar in nature to the questions which have appeared previously. Allow 15 minutes for each test.

EVALUATION OF RESULTS

45— 50	excellent
38— 44	superior
32— 37	satisfactory
25— 31	average
19— 24	below average but passing
18— 0	unsatisfactory

Synonym Test A

Each of the questions below consists of a word printed in bold, followed by five words or phrases numbered 1 to 5. Choose the numbered word or phrase which is most nearly similar in meaning to the word in bold and write the number of your choice on your answer paper.

EXAMPLE

wily   1. willing   2. cunning   3. agile   4. sad   5. slow   **answer 2**

  1. **hirsute**   1. damp   2. bearded   3. humorous   4. formerly   5. sad
  2. **panacea**   1. pancake   2. praise   3. inactivity   4. cure-all   5. talk

3. **celibate** 1. single 2. double 3. married 4. bald 5. hypocritical

4. **chasten** 1. discipline 2. pursue 3. sanctify 4. stop 5. start

5. **meretricious** 1. conspicuous 2. blonde 3. tawdry 4. angry 5. aping

6. **requiem** 1. recess 2. assignment 3. profanity 4. dirge 5. musing

7. **effigy** 1. proxy 2. profundity 3. boldness 4. exit 5. dummy

8. **blissful** 1. maudlin 2. dour 3. beatific 4. moot 5. modish

9. **homogeneous** 1. heterogeneous 2. motley 3. scrambled 4. different 5. similar

10. **wraith** 1. apparition 2. garland 3. Christmas decoration 4. anger 5. excitement

11. **disparity** 1. argumentation 2. difference 3. belittlement 4. harmony 5. discord

12. **variegate** 1. set type 2. multi-color 3. differ 4. reject 5. reply in kind

13. **filch** 1. pretend 2. dirty 3. embarrass 4. steal 5. honor

14. **infinite** 1. verbal 2. indefinite 3. endless 4. strange 5. vague

15. **demise** 1. residence 2. dismissal 3. accident 4. act 5. death

16. **frugality** 1. extravagance 2. ripening 3. thrift 4. resentment 5. miserliness

17. **unequaled** 1. outstanding 2. different 3. praised 4. unique 5. strange

18. **adversity** 1. opponent 2. hardship 3. opening 4. public announcement 5. agency

19. **fastidious** 1. speedy 2. precise 3. squeamish 4. hungry 5. slow

20. **disconcert** 1. sing in harmony 2. pretend 3. cancel program 4. confuse 5. interrupt

21. **amenities** 1. prayers 2. ceremonies 3. pageantries 4. pleasantries 5. social functions

22. **mores** 1. morals 2. customs 3. taxes 4. fiscal year 5. swamp

23. **vestige** 1. clothing 2. trace 3. undergarment 4. hallway 5. hope

24. **perfunctory** 1. thorough 2. impossible 3. lively 4. listless 5. sly

25. **indigence** 1. nativity 2. tolerance 3. gossiping 4. poverty 5. eating

26. **virago** 1. bacillus 2. chastity 3. shrew 4. wanton 5. tirade

27. **persiflage** 1. banter 2. oppression 3. sarcasm 4. bigotry 5. simile

28. **loquacious** 1. situated 2. gregarious 3. taciturn 4. antisocial 5. garrulous

29. **phlegmatic** 1. stolid 2. respiratory 3. animated 4. pneumatic 5. aroused

30. **saturnine** 1. planetary 2. gloomy 3. astronomic 4. hopeful 5. temperate

31. **misanthropy** 1. badinage 2. generosity 3. vivacity 4. miserliness 5. hatred

32. **chicanery** 1. foulness 2. aroma 3. chastity 4. trickery 5. poultry

33. **penury** 1. custom 2. poverty 3. numismatics 4. affluence 5. criminology

34. **expiated** 1. vapid 2. assumed 3. disinclined 4. atoned 5. eroded

35. **vindictive** 1. revengeful 2. triumphant 3. strategic 4. demonstrative 5. bigoted

36. **frustration** 1. satiety 2. facility 3. thwarting 4. nostalgia 5. lethargy

37. **punctilious** 1. scrupulous 2. varied 3. ready 4. prompt 5. vicarious

38. **haggard** 1. gaunt 2. irascible 3. wise 4. sluggish 5. witty

39. **staid** 1. weary 2. remaining 3. sedate 4. afraid 5. unkempt

40. **pedagogue** 1. demagogue 2. peddler 3. bicyclist 4. teacher 5. pupil

41. **decorous** 1. adorned 2. ugly 3. insane 4. proper 5. childish

42. **onerous** 1. possessive 2. proud 3. droll 4. burdensome 5. sly

43. **expedient** 1. precise 2. expert 3. expendable 4. advisable 5. erratic

44. **succulent** 1. asking help 2. wicked 3. anxious 4. concise 5. juicy

45. **nepotism** 1. favoritism 2. pool 3. philosophy 4. rule of a despot 5. hedonism

46. **propensity** 1. inclination 2. intelligence 3. probity 4. dishonesty 5. act

47. **tawdry** 1. refined 2. yellow-orange 3. ancient 4. forward 5. gaudy

48. **inculcate** 1. corroborate 2. lack 3. teach 4. destroy 5. avenge

49. **tortuous** 1. winding 2. sadistic 3. cruel 4. like a turtle 5. carefree

50. **mollify** 1. sweeten 2. appease 3. applaud 4. worry 5. discourage

Synonym Test B

Each of the questions below consists of a word printed in bold, followed by five words or phrases numbered 1 to 5. Choose the numbered word or phrase which is most nearly similar in meaning to the word in bold and write the number of your choice on your answer paper.

51. **regime**   1. military group   2. summary   3. rule   4. estimate   5. manor
52. **rudimentary**   1. pale   2. fundamental   3. asinine   4. developed   5. quiescent
53. **professedly**   1. meekly   2. cruelly   3. bravely   4. pedantically   5. ostensibly
54. **retrospect**   1. special kind of telescope   2. microscope   3. prism   4. review of the past   5. forecast of future events
55. **impeccable**   1. poverty-stricken   2. faultless   3. dirty   4. criminal   5. impervious
56. **abettor**   1. gambler   2. slaughter-house   3. encourager   4. factor   5. author
57. **debilitate**   1. argue   2. engage   3. remove hair   4. soothe   5. enfeeble
58. **junta**   1. junction   2. jungle   3. small boat   4. secret faction   5. embrace
59. **harass**   1. annoy   2. harness   3. involve   4. injure   5. consider
60. **erudite**   1. rough   2. unpolished   3. scholarly   4. magnificent   5. ornate
61. **abrade**   1. rub off   2. bleed   3. embellish   4. erase   5. poison
62. **inane**   1. lifeless   2. senseless   3. hopeless   4. faithless   5. crazy
63. **culpable**   1. free   2. guilty   3. vindicable   4. wholesome   5. vindictive
64. **ingenuous**   1. sophisticated   2. clever   3. cunning   4. naive   5. artificial
65. **fealty**   1. sense of touch   2. loyalty   3. anger   4. anxiety   5. personality
66. **cogent**   1. geared   2. formidable   3. strong   4. weak   5. convincing
67. **expunge**   1. rationalize   2. purge   3. exhale   4. eradicate   5. assign
68. **indigenous**   1. wealthy   2. having stomach trouble   3. native   4. scholarly   5. bald
69. **condiment**   1. vegetable   2. salad   3. meat dish   4. relish   5. sugar

70. **fortuitous**   1. lucky   2. accidental   3. rich   4. prearranged   5. concerted
71. **adipose**   1. liquid   2. weighty   3. major   4. sharp   5. fatty
72. **duplicity**   1. two-pronged spear   2. mimeograph   3. hypocrisy   4. candor   5. two-story apartment
73. **cryptic**   1. obscure   2. written   3. copied   4. dead   5. puzzling
74. **homily**   1. cereal   2. household   3. suburb   4. sermon   5. pension
75. **dormant**   1. animated   2. hibernating   3. active   4. vigorous   5. birdlike
76. **asperity**   1. roughness   2. dream   3. ambition   4. smoothness   5. sarcastic remark
77. **altercation**   1. adjustment   2. repair   3. quarrel   4. split personality   5. echo
78. **captious**   1. prominent   2. carping   3. critical   4. caustic   5. epigrammatic
79. **accolade**   1. balcony   2. outer garment   3. drink   4. honor   5. fruit
80. **deprecate**   1. plead earnestly against   2. denounce   3. belittle   4. devaluate   5. dishonor
81. **bombastic**   1. inflated   2. explosive   3. retaliatory   4. meek   5. enraged
82. **inter**   1. carry   2. hint   3. bury   4. interfere   5. act as go-between
83. **acumen**   1. keenness   2. brilliance   3. swiftness   4. greediness   5. ferocity
84. **inundate**   1. overwhelm   2. surrender   3. flood   4. destroy   5. conquer
85. **cantata**   1. symphony   2. concerto   3. opera   4. choral work   5. military march
86. **sumptuous**   1. swampy   2. irritable   3. meagre   4. fancy   5. lavish
87. **tractable**   1. practicable   2. amenable   3. indisposed   4. critical   5. artistic
88. **querulous**   1. questioning   2. critical   3. complaining   4. curious   5. ambiguous
89. **morose**   1. calm   2. gloomy   3. misty   4. damp   5. diseased
90. **surmise**   1. dawn   2. plan   3. unexpected event   4. tragedy   5. guess
91. **ubiquitous**   1. affluent   2. resigning   3. omnipresent   4. omnipotent   5. omniscient
92. **attrition**   1. addition   2. regret   3. attitude   4. abrasion   5. concentration
93. **reticence**   1. reserve   2. retention   3. regret   4. brazenness   5. hostility

94. **chagrin**   1. chin   2. mortification   3. elation   4. intuition   5. chamber
95. **plaudit**   1. concentration   2. commendation   3. complaint   4. comparison   5. scholar
96. **viva voce**   1. lively   2. in writing   3. belligerently   4. thematically   5. orally
97. **malfeasance**   1. seasickness   2. criticism   3. cure   4. misconduct   5. poor performance
98. **hamlet**   1. actor   2. benefactor   3. small rodent   4. village   5. introvert
99. **pneumatic**   1. pertaining to air   2. automatic   3. sick   4. elastic   5. plotted
100. **tepid**   1. enraged   2. equatorial   3. transported   4. lukewarm   5. embarrassed

---

Antonym Test A

Each of the questions below consists of a word printed in bold, followed by five words or phrases numbered 1 to 5. Choose the numbered word or phrase which is most nearly opposite in meaning to the word in bold and write the number of your choice on your answer paper.

EXAMPLE

win   1. conquer   2. lose   3. forfeit   4. surrender   **answer 2**

1. **abominate**   1. love   2. loathe   3. abhor   4. despise   5. attach
2. **ravenous**   1. famished   2. nibbling   3. sated   4. starving   5. unsatisfied
3. **pithy**   1. central   2. federal   3. homogeneous   4. tautological   5. gregarious
4. **adamant**   1. yielding   2. primitive   3. elementary   4. primeval   5. inflexible
5. **ephemeral**   1. evergreen   2. deciduous   3. biennial   4. everlasting   5. tactile
6. **synthetic**   1. cosmetic   2. artificial   3. plastic   4. viscous   5. natural
7. **vivacious**   1. animated   2. dramatic   3. versatile   4. phlegmatic   5. vigilant
8. **audacity**   1. quivering   2. cowardice   3. conciseness   4. patricide   5. bravado
9. **irascible**   1. pictorial   2. piscatorial   3. bellicose   4. cranky   5. good-natured

10. **bucolic**   1. citified   2. rustic   3. intoxicated   4. sick   5. healthy
11. **infinitesimal**   1. everlasting   2. colossal   3. picayune   4. microscopic   5. telescopic
12. **gelid**   1. lurid   2. torpid   3. torrid   4. piebald   5. vapid
13. **circuitous**   1. entertaining   2. direct   3. round-about   4. labyrinthine   5. radial
14. **anathema**   1. national song   2. factual report   3. name   4. concept   5. benediction
15. **clandestine**   1. open   2. sunny   3. swampy   4. pugnacious   5. banal
16. **abhor**   1. detest   2. absolve   3. accuse   4. bedizen   5. adore
17. **flamboyant**   1. decorated   2. apparition   3. plain   4. female   5. terse
18. **redundant**   1. tautological   2. repeated   3. curt   4. voluble   5. opulent
19. **impoverished**   1. impecunious   2. affluent   3. rococo   4. iniquitous   5. pendent
20. **obsequious**   1. fawning   2. servile   3. supercilious   4. improper   5. first
21. **discrete**   1. wise   2. foolish   3. unkempt   4. separate   5. continuous
22. **fatuous**   1. inane   2. thin   3. witty   4. planned   5. stout
23. **amenable**   1. responsive   2. intractable   3. indifferent   4. agreeable   5. correct
24. **fallacious**   1. erroneous   2. faulty   3. accurate   4. afraid   5. plucky
25. **altruism**   1. honesty   2. tolerance   3. bigotry   4. thievery   5. selfishness
26. **indifferent**   1. curious   2. varied   3. uniform   4. alike   5. uninquisitive
27. **cohesive**   1. attached   2. detached   3. associated   4. affiliated   5. sticky
28. **insipid**   1. tasty   2. silly   3. angry   4. active   5. emaciated
29. **discord**   1. noise   2. amity   3. irritation   4. scrap   5. use
30. **priority**   1. anxiety   2. irregular   3. subsequence   4. piety   5. impishness
31. **crabbed**   1. crowded   2. saccharine   3. sour   4. condemned   5. salty
32. **corroboration**   1. proof   2. arrest   3. invalidation   4. alibi   5. alias
33. **decorum**   1. ribaldry   2. balladry   3. high collar   4. solo   5. freedom
34. **vivacious**   1. surgical   2. lively   3. girlish   4. inactive   5. boyish

35. **ingenuous**   1. clever   2. stupid   3. naive   4. young   5. sophisticated
36. **alleviate**   1. allow   2. aggravate   3. instigate   4. belittle   5. refuse
37. **obsolete**   1. mechanical   2. fancy   3. free   4. renovated   5. old
38. **jocund**   1. small   2. frantic   3. amazing   4. gay   5. intelligent
39. **sanguine**   1. bloody   2. gloomy   3. happy   4. thin   5. red-faced
40. **languid**   1. pusillanimous   2. indifferent   3. sad   4. vigorous   5. motley
41. **respite**   1. recess   2. intermission   3. exertion   4. dinner   5. anger
42. **obloquy**   1. shame   2. fame   3. name   4. colloquy   5. inquiry
43. **placate**   1. nettle   2. label   3. soothe   4. reply   5. retaliate
44. **complacent**   1. satisfied   2. agreeable   3. nasty   4. querulous   5. asking
45. **assent**   1. save   2. inquire   3. resent   4. introduce   5. disavow
46. **retrogression**   1. imagination   2. deterioration   3. violation   4. articulation   5. amazement
47. **noisome**   1. quiet   2. fragrant   3. eager   4. foul   5. riotous
48. **permanent**   1. indifferent   2. tardy   3. mutable   4. improper   5. disheveled
49. **covetous**   1. unfinished   2. uncovered   3. undesirous   4. birdlike   5. plying
50. **corporeal**   1. earthy   2. privileged   3. solid   4. spiritual   5. ethical

---

Antonym Test B

Each of the questions below consists of a word printed in bold, followed by five words or phrases numbered 1 to 5. Choose the numbered word or phrase which is most nearly opposite in meaning to the word in bold and write the number of your choice on your answer paper.

51. **zealot**   1. heretic   2. hypocrite   3. person who is careless   4. person who is rich   5. person who is indifferent
52. **abstemious**   1. fastidious   2. punctilious   3. pusillanimous   4. dissipated   5. prodigal
53. **satiety**   1. starvation   2. dissatisfaction   3. pretense   4. lowest class   5. grandeur
54. **deciduous**   1. undecided   2. hesitant   3. evergreen   4. annual   5. perennial

55. **innocuous** 1. large 2. toxic 3. spotless 4. impeccable 5. sober

56. **germane** 1. Teutonic 2. healthful 3. irrelevant 4. massive 5. puny

57. **egregious** 1. notorious 2. splendid 3. abortive 4. maturing 5. birdlike

58. **nepotism** 1. midnight 2. partiality 3. impartiality 4. dawn 5. noon

59. **autonomous** 1. magnanimous 2. ambiguous 3. exiguous 4. dependent 5. operated by hand

60. **exculpate** 1. pardon 2. destroy 3. create 4. convict 5. admonish

61. **earthy** 1. pithy 2. salty 3. watery 4. refined 5. moldy

62. **contentious** 1. pacific 2. bellicose 3. satisfied 4. dissatisfied 5. hungry

63. **gainsay** 1. deny 2. lose money 3. audit 4. applaud 5. affirm

64. **ameliorate** 1. harden 2. coarsen 3. aggravate 4. improve 5. scrape

65. **ignominious** 1. disgraceful 2. erudite 3. scholarly 4. incognito 5. laudatory

66. **evanescent** 1. permanent 2. incandescent 3. ephemeral 4. putrid 5. perfunctory

67. **corpulent** 1. sallow 2. cooperative 3. emaciated 4. enterprising 5. red-blooded

68. **jocund** 1. round 2. flat 3. jocular 4. jugular 5. melancholy

69. **hibernal** 1. Irish 2. estival 3. English 4. festival 5. wintry

70. **ebullient** 1. intoxicated 2. placid 3. effervescent 4. gregarious 5. jovial

71. **assuage** 1. solve 2. abate 3. isolate 4. irritate 5. demonstrate

72. **indigenous** 1. alien 2. pleasing 3. comestible 4. disgusting 5. irate

73. **dearth** 1. birth 2. scantiness 3. abundance 4. brilliance 5. morning

74. **deleterious** 1. sane 2. intoxicated 3. sober 4. wholesome 5. adding

75. **fell** 1. downed 2. risen 3. propitious 4. cruel 5. official

76. **exemplary** 1. deplorable 2. imitative 3. outstanding 4. particular 5. additional

77. **choleric** 1. red 2. serene 3. severe 4. stern 5. irritable

78. **baroque** 1. common 2. boatlike 3. rococo 4. simple 5. stupid

79. **dilettante** 1. amateur 2. professional 3. postponement 4. party 5. frenzy

80. **amorphous** 1. diaphonic 2. translucent 3. organized 4. opaque 5. chaotic

81. **capricious** 1. whimsical 2. consistent 3. goatlike 4. honest 5. hypocritical

82. **salubrious** 1. healthy 2. plagued 3. rustic 4. fashioned 5. miasmic

83. **disparity** 1. equality 2. aspersion 3. allusion 4. equanimity 5. suture

84. **apothegm** 1. perpendicular 2. pithy statement 3. prolix statement 4. terse statement 5. letter

85. **chary** 1. lavish 2. malevolent 3. insinuating 4. sparing 5. irritable

86. **candor** 1. hypocrisy 2. ingenuousness 3. sweetmeat 4. pleasure 5. velocity

87. **equivocate** 1. lie 2. whisper 3. balance 4. be truthful 5. be unequal

88. **estranged** 1. reconciled 2. separated 3. foreign 4. traded 5. embarrassed

89. **pretentious** 1. real 2. excusing 3. modest 4. unpardonable 5. typical

90. **sub rosa** 1. under the rose 2. clandestinely 3. fashionably 4. openly 5. simply

91. **subservient** 1. obsequious 2. omnipresent 3. fawning 4. haughty 5. miserly

92. **untenable** 1. rented 2. maintainable 3. occupied 4. permanent 5. picayune

93. **herbivorous** 1. ravenous 2. omnivorous 3. carnivorous 4. voracious 5. veracious

94. **opulence** 1. glamor 2. sobriety 3. badinage 4. penury 5. petulance

95. **threnody** 1. elegy 2. eulogy 3. ballade 4. paean 5. epic

96. **vaunted** 1. lauded 2. belittled 3. berated 4. worried 5. wicked

97. **cede** 1. yield 2. harvest 3. annex 4. examine 5. mimic

98. **obfuscate** 1. clarify 2. magnify 3. intensify 4. belittle 5. becloud

99. **concave** 1. hollow 2. solid 3. convex 4. complex 5. broken

100. **precipitate** 1. wary 2. steep 3. audacious 4. masterly 5. conquered

---

Vocabulary Test A

In each line following you will find one bold word followed by five words or phrases numbered 1 to 5. In each case choose the word or phrase that has most nearly the same meaning as the bold word.

1. **filch** 1. hide 2. swindle 3. drop 4. steal 5. covet
2. **urbane** 1. well-dressed 2. polished 3. rural 4. friendly 5. prominent
3. **decant** 1. bisect 2. speak wildly 3. bequeath 4. pour off 5. abuse verbally
4. **antithesis** 1. contrast 2. conclusion 3. resemblance 4. examination 5. dislike
5. **heretical** 1. heathenish 2. impractical 3. quaint 4. rash 5. unorthodox
6. **coalesce** 1. associate 2. combine 3. contact 4. conspire 5. cover
7. **charlatan** 1. clown 2. philanthropist 3. jester 4. dressmaker 5. quack
8. **gauche** 1. clumsy 2. stupid 3. feeble-minded 4. impudent 5. foreign
9. **redundant** 1. necessary 2. plentiful 3. sufficient 4. diminishing 5. superfluous
10. **atrophy** 1. lose leaves 2. soften 3. waste away 4. grow 5. spread
11. **resilience** 1. submission 2. elasticity 3. vigor 4. determination 5. recovery
12. **analogy** 1. similarity 2. transposition 3. variety 4. distinction 5. appropriateness
13. **facetious** 1. obscene 2. shrewd 3. impolite 4. complimentary 5. witty
14. **diatribe** 1. debate 2. monologue 3. oration 4. tirade 5. conversation
15. **malediction** 1. curse 2. mispronunciation 3. grammatical error 4. tactless remark 5. epitaph
16. **aggregate** 1. result 2. difference 3. quotient 4. product 5. sum
17. **aplomb** 1. caution 2. timidity 3. self-assurance 4. short-sightedness 5. self-restraint
18. **therapeutic** 1. curative 2. restful 3. warm 4. stimulating 5. professional
19. **transmute** 1. remove 2. change 3. duplicate 4. carry 5. explain
20. **attrition** 1. annihilation 2. encirclement 3. counter attack 4. appeasement 5. wearing down
21. **truncate** 1. divide equally 2. end swiftly 3. cut off 4. act cruelly 5. cancel
22. **oscillate** 1. confuse 2. kiss 3. turn 4. vibrate 5. whirl
23. **inoculate** 1. make harmless 2. infect 3. cure 4. overcome 5. darken

24. **perusal** 1. approval 2. estimate 3. reading 4. translation 5. computation
25. **querulous** 1. peculiar 2. fretful 3. inquisitive 4. shivering 5. annoying
26. **autonomy** 1. tyranny 2. independence 3. plebiscite 4. minority 5. dictatorship
27. **machinations** 1. inventions 2. ideas 3. mysteries 4. plots 5. alliances
28. **schism** 1. government 2. religion 3. division 4. combination 5. coalition
29. **pusillanimous** 1. cowardly 2. extraordinary 3. ailing 4. evil-intentioned 5. excitable
30. **terminology** 1. technicality 2. finality 3. formality 4. explanation 5. nomenclature
31. **stipend** 1. increment 2. bonus 3. commission 4. gift 5. salary
32. **litigation** 1. publication 2. argument 3. endeavor 4. law suit 5. ceremony
33. **fiasco** 1. disappointment 2. turning point 3. loss 4. celebration 5. complete failure
34. **vagary** 1. caprice 2. confusion 3. extravagance 4. loss of memory 5. shiftlessness
35. **graphic** 1. serious 2. concise 3. short 4. detailed 5. vivid
36. **connotation** 1. implication 2. footnote 3. derivation 4. comment 5. definition
37. **tortuous** 1. crooked 2. difficult 3. painful 4. impassable 5. slow
38. **fulminating** 1. throbbing 2. pointed 3. wavelike 4. thundering 5. bubbling
39. **circumvent** 1. freshen 2. change 3. control 4. harass 5. frustrate
40. **cartel** 1. rationing plan 2. world government 3. industrial pool 4. skilled craft 5. instrument of credit
41. **prevaricate** 1. hesitate 2. lie 3. protest 4. ramble 5. remain silent
42. **incredulous** 1. argumentative 2. imaginative 3. indifferent 4. irreligious 5. skeptical
43. **placate** 1. amuse 2. appease 3. embroil 4. pity 5. reject
44. **cognizant** 1. afraid 2. aware 3. capable 4. ignorant 5. optimistic
45. **dissonance** 1. disapproval 2. disaster 3. discord 4. disparity 5. dissimilarity
46. **imminent** 1. declining 2. distinguished 3. impending 4. terrifying 5. unlikely

47. **torsion** 1. bending 2. compressing 3. sliding 4. stretching 5. twisting
48. **accrued** 1. added 2. incidental 3. miscellaneous 4. special 5. unearned
49. **effrontery** 1. bad taste 2. conceit 3. dishonesty 4. impudence 5. snobbishness
50. **acquiescence** 1. advice 2. advocacy 3. compliance 4. friendliness 5. opposition

---

Vocabulary Test B

In each line below you will find one bold word followed by five words or phrases numbered 1 to 5. In each case choose the word or phrase that has most nearly the same meaning as the bold word.

1. **prolific** 1. meager 2. obedient 3. fertile 4. hardy 5. scanty
2. **assuage** 1. create 2. ease 3. enlarge 4. prohibit 5. rub out
3. **decorum** 1. wit 2. charm 3. adornment 4. seemliness 5. charity
4. **phlegmatic** 1. tolerant 2. careless 3. sensitive 4. stolid 5. sick
5. **intrepid** 1. quick-witted 2. brutal 3. fearless 4. torrid 5. hearty
6. **actuate** 1. frighten 2. direct 3. isolate 4. dismay 5. impel
7. **mountebank** 1. trickster 2. courier 3. scholar 4. cashier 5. pawnbroker
8. **laconic** 1. terse 2. informal 3. convincing 4. interesting 5. tedious
9. **boorish** 1. sporting 2. tiresome 3. argumentative 4. monotonous 5. rude
10. **erudite** 1. modest 2. egotistical 3. learned 4. needless 5. experienced
11. **acrimonious** 1. repulsive 2. enchanting 3. stinging 4. snobbish 5. disgusting
12. **embryonic** 1. hereditary 2. arrested 3. developed 4. functioning 5. rudimentary
13. **inexorable** 1. unfavorable 2. permanent 3. crude 4. relentless 5. incomplete
14. **protracted** 1. boring 2. condensed 3. prolonged 4. comprehensive 5. measured
15. **obsequious** 1. courteous 2. fawning 3. respectful 4. overbearing 5. inexperienced
16. **loquacious** 1. queer 2. logical 3. gracious 4. rural 5. voluble

17. **pugnacious** 1. bold 2. combative 3. brawny 4. pug-nosed 5. valiant
18. **astringent** 1. bossy 2. musty 3. flexible . 4. corrosive 5. contracting
19. **escarpment** 1. threat 2. limbo 3. cliff 4. behemoth 5. blight
20. **amenities** 1. prayers 2. ceremonies 3. pageantries 4. pleasantries 5. social functions
21. **deplore** 1. condone 2. forget 3. forgive 4. deny 5. regret
22. **banal** 1. commonplace 2. flippant 3. pathetic 4. new 5. unexpected
23. **abacus** 1. casserole 2. blackboard 3. slide rule 4. adding device 5. long spear
24. **seismism** 1. inundation 2. tide 3. volcano 4. earthquake 5. tornado
25. **ameliorate** 1. favor 2. improve 3. interfere 4. learn 5. straddle
26. **chary** 1. burned 2. careful 3. comfortable 4. fascinating 5. gay
27. **corpulent** 1. dead 2. fat 3. full 4. organized 5. similar
28. **enigma** 1. foreigner 2. ambition 3. instrument 4. officer 5. riddle
29. **inept** 1. awkward 2. intelligent 3. ticklish 4. tawdry 5. uninteresting
30. **inveterate** 1. evil 2. habitual 3. inconsiderate 4. reformed 5. unintentional
31. **obeisance** 1. salary 2. justification 3. conduct 4. deference 5. afterthought
32. **pedantic** 1. stilted 2. odd 3. footworn 4. selfish 5. sincere
33. **petulant** 1. lazy 2. loving 3. patient 4. peevish 5. wary
34. **proclivity** 1. backwardness 2. edict 3. rainfall 4. slope 5. tendency
35. **trenchant** 1. keen 2. good 3. edible 4. light 5. subterranean
36. **vapid** 1. carefree 2. crazy 3. insipid 4. spotty 5. speedy
37. **prognosticate** 1. forecast 2. ravish 3. salute 4. scoff 5. succeed
38. **propriety** 1. advancement 2. atonement 3. fitness 4. sobriety 5. use
39. **pulchritude** 1. beauty 2. character 3. generosity 4. intelligence 5. wickedness
40. **scrupulous** 1. drunken 2. ill 3. masterful 4. exact 5. stony
41. **reticent** 1. fidgety 2. repetitious 3. reserved 4. restful 5. truthful
42. **stipulate** 1. bargain 2. instigate 3. prefer 4. request 5. specify
43. **pseudo** 1. deep 2. obvious 3. pretended 4. provoking 5. spiritual

44. flotsam   1. dark sand   2. fleet   3. life preserver   4. shoreline   5. wreckage
45. awry   1. askew   2. deplorable   3. odd   4. simple   5. striking
46. nefarious   1. clever   2. necessary   3. negligent   4. short-sighted   5. wicked
47. glib   1. cheerful   2. delightful   3. dull   4. fluent   5. gloomy
48. paucity   1. abundance   2. ease   3. hardship   4. lack   5. stoppage
49. lucrative   1. debasing   2. fortunate   3. influential   4. monetary   5. profitable
50. indubitable   1. doubtful   2. fraudulent   3. honorable   4. safe   5. undeniable

---

Answers to Synonym and Antonym Tests

Synonym Test A (page 201)

1. 2	18. 2	35. 1
2. 4	19. 3	36. 3
3. 1	20. 4	37. 1
4. 1	21. 4	38. 1
5. 3	22. 2	39. 3
6. 4	23. 2	40. 4
7. 5	24. 4	41. 4
8. 3	25. 4	42. 4
9. 5	26. 3	43. 4
10. 1	27. 1	44. 5
11. 2	28. 5	45. 1
12. 2	29. 1	46. 1
13. 4	30. 2	47. 5
14. 3	31. 5	48. 3
15. 5	32. 4	49. 1
16. 3	33. 2	50. 2
17. 4	34. 4	

Synonym Test B (page 204)

51. 3	68. 3	85. 4
52. 2	69. 4	86. 5
53. 5	70. 2	87. 2
54. 4	71. 5	88. 3
55. 2	72. 3	89. 2
56. 3	73. 1	90. 5
57. 5	74. 4	91. 3
58. 4	75. 2	92. 4
59. 1	76. 1	93. 1
60. 3	77. 3	94. 2
61. 1	78. 2	95. 2
62. 2	79. 4	96. 5
63. 2	80. 1	97. 4
64. 4	81. 1	98. 4
65. 2	82. 3	99. 1
66. 5	83. 1	100. 4
67. 4	84. 3	

Antonym Test A (page 206)

1. 1	18. 3	35. 5
2. 3	19. 2	36. 2
3. 4	20. 3	37. 4
4. 1	21. 5	38. 4
5. 4	22. 3	39. 2
6. 5	23. 2	40. 4
7. 4	24. 3	41. 3
8. 2	25. 5	42. 2
9. 5	26. 1	43. 1
10. 1	27. 2	44. 4
11. 2	28. 1	45. 5
12. 3	29. 2	46. 2
13. 2	30. 3	47. 2
14. 5	31. 2	48. 3
15. 1	32. 3	49. 3
16. 5	33. 1	50. 4
17. 3	34. 4	

Antonym Test B (page 208)

51. 5	68. 5	85. 1
52. 4	69. 2	86. 1
53. 1	70. 2	87. 4
54. 3	71. 4	88. 1
55. 2	72. 1	89. 3
56. 3	73. 3	90. 4
57. 2	74. 4	91. 4
58. 3	75. 3	92. 2
59. 4	76. 1	93. 3
60. 4	77. 2	94. 4
61. 4	78. 4	95. 4
62. 1	79. 2	96. 2
63. 5	80. 3	97. 3
64. 3	81. 2	98. 1
65. 5	82. 5	99. 3
66. 1	83. 1	100. 1
67. 3	84. 3	

Vocabulary Test A (page 210)

1. 4	18. 1	35. 5
2. 2	19. 2	36. 1
3. 4	20. 5	37. 1
4. 1	21. 3	38. 4
5. 5	22. 4	39. 5
6. 2	23. 2	40. 3
7. 5	24. 3	41. 2
8. 1	25. 2	42. 5
9. 5	26. 2	43. 2
10. 3	27. 4	44. 2
11. 2	28. 3	45. 3
12. 1	29. 1	46. 3
13. 5	30. 5	47. 5
14. 4	31. 5	48. 1
15. 1	32. 4	49. 4
16. 5	33. 5	50. 3
17. 3	34. 1	

Vocabulary Test B (page 213)

1. 3	18. 5	35. 1
2. 2	19. 3	36. 3
3. 4	20. 4	37. 1
4. 4	21. 5	38. 3
5. 3	22. 1	39. 1
6. 5	23. 4	40. 4
7. 1	24. 4	41. 3
8. 1	25. 2	42. 5
9. 5	26. 2	43. 3
10. 3	27. 2	44. 5
11. 3	28. 5	45. 1
12. 5	29. 1	46. 5
13. 4	30. 2	47. 4
14. 3	31. 4	48. 4
15. 2	32. 1	49. 5
16. 5	33. 4	50. 5
17. 2	34. 5	

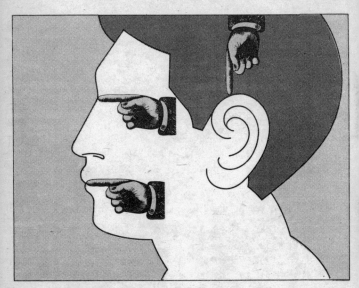

GRAMMAR
In Plain English

By Harriet Diamond and Phyllis Dutwin

Includes chapters on:

The Simple Sentence
Agreement in Time and Number
Addition and Correct Use of
 Descriptive Words and Phrases
Correct Use of Pronouns
Correct Sentence Structure
Punctuation and Capitalization
Style and Clarity of Expression
Commonly Misspelled Words and
 Hints and Rules for Correct Spelling
Homonyms and Correct Word Usage

A unique approach to grammar
stressing function and usage, with
no memorization of technical grammatical terms necessary. Students
use their own previously acquired
skills and abilities to learn the basic
concepts of grammar in an easy-to-
understand, cumulative manner.

304 pgs.
$5.50

At your local bookseller or order direct adding 10% postage plus applicable sales tax.
Barron's Educational Series, Inc.   Woodbury, New York 11797